THE KINGIS QUAIR

JAMES I OF SCOTLAND (artist unknown)
(*Scottish National Portrait Gallery*)

THE KINGIS QUAIR

OF

JAMES STEWART

Edited by

MATTHEW P. McDIARMID

Reader in English in the
University of Aberdeen

ROWMAN AND LITTLEFIELD

Totowa, New Jersey

ISBN 0-87471-156-8
Introduction and Notes © Matthew P. McDiarmid 1973

First published in the United States 1973
by Rowman and Littlefield, Totowa, New Jersey
Printed in Great Britain

Contents

List of Abbreviations

accus.	accusative	num.	numerical
adj.	adjective	OE	Old English
adv.	adverb	*OED*	*Oxford English Dictionary*
AN	Anglo-Norman	OF	Old French
art.	article	om.	omitted
aux.	auxiliary	ON	Old Norse
ch.	chapter	para.	paragraph
compar.	comparative	part.	participle
conj.	conjunction	ppl.	past participle
demon.	demonstrative	pl.	plural
DOST	*Dictionary of the Older Scottish Tongue*	possess.	possessive
		prep.	preposition
EETS	Early English Text Society	pres.	present
		pret.	preterit
EME	Early Middle English	pron.	pronoun
fem.	feminine	STS	Scottish Text Society
gen.	genitive	st.	stanza
imperat.	imperative	sb.	substantive
indef.	indefinite	superl.	superlative
infin.	infinitive	syll.	syllable
interj.	interjection	vb.	verb
interrog.	interrogative	vbl.	verbal
lit.	literally	W. Gmc.	West Germanic
ME	Middle English		

Introduction

GENERAL NOTE

In this century there have been several editions of *The Kingis Quair*: by W. W. Skeat 1911, A. Lawson 1910, W. M. Mackenzie 1939, J. Norton-Smith 1971.[1] The admirable study of J. R. Simon, *Le Livre Du Roi* 1967, is not an edition but a commentary on the text as reproduced from the single MS. The best of these texts is that of Skeat, for its more consistently sceptical and constructive criticism. His successors, faced by the many problems that demand a judgment, too often preferred a bad text to their own, and the poet's, good sense and sensibility. It is the hope of the present writer that he has pressed Skeat's critical approach yet more strictly and restored for inspection more of the poet than was hitherto available.

A phonological description of the *Quair* had not been attempted since Walter Wischmann's desultory study of 1887, and was forced on the editor by his growing awareness that an informed decision upon the basic nature of the poet's language, how truly it was reflected by the forms, orthographical and morphological, of the scribes, had to be taken, if the text was to be soundly criticized and the evidence bearing on the important issues of authorship, date, interpretation, fully adduced. It was a labour that involved a comprehensive review of what was supposed to be known about the characteristic sound-changes of the early Scots language as evidenced in its literature. Its performance was facilitated by many German studies, and among English ones

---

[1] *The Kingis Quair Together With A Ballad Of Good Counsel: By King James I Of Scotland.* Second And Revised Edition (first edition 1884), W. W. Skeat, The Scottish Text Society, 1911; *The Kingis Quair And The Quare of Jelusy*, ed. Alexander Lawson 1910; *The Kingis Quair*, ed. W. M. Mackenzie, 1939; *James I Of Scotland The Kingis Quair*, ed. J. Norton-Smith, 1971. The last of these studies appeared when all but the glossary of the present edition was ready for the press and, beyond its mention here and in some footnotes, gave the editor no cause to alter or add to what he had prepared.

particularly by the invaluable work of Francis Curtis, Ritchie Girvan and, of course, the editors of *The Dictionary of the Older Scottish Tongue*. If the treatment is imperfect in many respects—it could not be fully developed here—the necessary topics of such a discussion and the reasons for much of the editor's procedure will at least have been indicated. The analysis was helpful in another and indirect kind; even where it did not itself provide answers to the problems of interpretation and emendation it pointed to where answers had to be given. Similarly, in the complementary tasks of reconstructing and explaining the text the editor became increasingly aware how much his predecessors, including Skeat, had assumed an understanding that they and their readers did not possess.

In presenting the text of MS normal procedure has been followed, except for the use of 'j' to represent that sound. Syllabic *e* is marked.

The length of this Introduction does not require an excuse but its readers deserve an explanation. John Donne observed in his day that 'the new philosophy puts all in doubt'. If it did so it was because of old ignorance. In 1896 J. T. T. Brown, in *The Authorship of The Kingis Quair: A New Criticism*, was able to question received opinions about date as well as authorship only because the argument for the tradition was not known. Succeeding replies to his book merely confirmed this fact. The relevant knowledge is indeed still not easy to obtain; it is complex and difficult to order intelligibly, and it is the latter difficulty that largely accounts for the variety and extent of discussion that has had to be inflicted on readers whose primary concern is rightly with the understanding and appreciation of a great poem. Context, however, is always instructive and it is hoped that it has been convincingly supplied in this case.

THE MS.

Any discussion of *The Kingis Quair* that pretends to thoroughness must give a preliminary statement about the manuscript that contains it, particularly the date of the scribes' labours, their relative responsibilities, and the evidence that it offers of the extent of their interference with their copies. MS. Seld. Arch. B 24 in the Bodleian Library is a collection of poems that contains Chaucer's *Troilus, The*

Parlement of Foules (from a defective copy so that *ll.* 607–79 have been supplied), *The Legend of Good Women*, which is followed immediately by the *Quair*, also a number of minor English and Scots poems by such writers as John Walton (an excerpt from his 'Boethius'), Lydgate, Hoccleve, probably Dunbar, the unknown author of *The Quare of Jelusy*. The MS. has been notably described by Brown in the abovementioned study, by R. K. Root in *The Manuscripts Of Chaucer's Troilus* 1914, and by Sir William Craigie in *Essays And Studies* XXV, 1939.[1]

An upper date is given by the main scribe's note on fol. 120 of the birthdate of his king, James IV: 'Natiuitas principis nostri Jacobi quarti anno domini millesimo iiiic lxxii xvii die mensis marcii viz. In festo sancti patricii confessoris In monasterio sancte crucis prope Edenburgh.' It is then no earlier than the king's accession in 1488 and no later than his death at Flodden in 1513. The same limits are supplied by the name of the personage for whom the collection was made and more precise ones by what can be learned about the scribe and some of the poems that he copied.

The Sinclair coat of arms, rudely illuminated, appears on fol. 118 at the close of *Troilus*, and on fol. 230 has been written in a hand other than the scribe's, 'liber Henricii Domini Sinclair'. This can only be Henry Lord Sinclair, who enjoyed that title from 1488/9 to 1513. It was he who proposed to Gavin Douglas his translation of the *Aeneid* and from its dedication to him, *ll.* 79–104, we learn of his book-collecting—'Bukis to recollect, to reid and se,/Has gret delyte as euer had Ptoleme'. His marriage to Margaret Hepburn, the second daughter of Lord Hailes, probably had something to do with his choice of scribe, James Gray, mentioned as vicar of Hailes in 1490 (*Registrum Magni Sigilli*, no. 2210). The latter is doubtless the person of the same name who was briefly provided to the chancellorship of St Andrews in 1460 (*Fasti Ecclesiæ Scoticanæ Medii Aevi*, Second Draft, by D. E. R. Watt, St Andrews, 1969, p. 303); he was the illuminator of the Panmure MS. of *Scotichronicon* that was completed in 1481 and compiler of the 'Graye MS.', a commonplace book containing legal and historical memoranda along with some vernacular poems (cf. *The Makculloch and the Gray MSS.*, ed. G. Stevenson, Scottish Text Society,

---

[1] To the above can now be added the careful description given by J. Norton-Smith in his edition, 1971. It agrees with my division of scribal responsibilities.

1918), which is now in the National Library of Scotland.[1] It was in this notebook that George Neilson (*The Athenæum*, vol. 2, 1899, p. 836) correctly identified the hand of Lord Henry's scribe and observed on fol. 20 *verso*, in slightly abbreviated form, the same note of King James's birth. On fol. 22 *verso* of the same MS., recording the death of Archbishop Stewart, the king's brother, in January 1504, Gray describes himself as the archbishop's secretary and chancellor. He must then have been approaching his seventieth year and it does not seem likely that he would have undertaken a scribe's commission at a much later date. It may have been this factor that suggested the help of a colleague in completing the Selden MS. His age and the indication of two poems in the collection make it reasonable, therefore, that we should not look much beyond 1505 for his part in the copying of the *Quair*.

One of these poems, on fol. 137 *verso*, a prayer to the Virgin that begins, 'O hie Emperice and quene celestial', is very much in Dunbar's manner and has been generally attributed to him. The other is *The Quare of Jelusy*, written down by the second scribe before the brief reappearance of Gray's hand. Its author was also responsible for *Lancelot of the Laik* and an approximate date for both works can be given with some confidence. *Lancelot*, I find, makes large borrowings from Sir Gilbert Hay's *Buke of Knychthede* 1456 and both it and the *Quare* make frequent use of Hary's *Wallace*, c. 1478, particularly the descriptive prologues to its Books and the rhetorical ten-line stanzas of Books II and VI; it is only the *Lancelot*, of course, that reflects Hary's vigorous battle-scenes. Both poems again seem to show knowledge of work by Dunbar (who was writing at least by 1490[2]): line 62 in the romance, 'As crystall terys wich [wrongly 'with' in the STS edition] hong vpon the flouris', recalls *The Goldyn Terge* l. 17, 'Hir cristall teris I saw hyng on the flouris', and the lady of the *Quare*, who laments with 'cristall teris fallyng from hir eyne clere', l. 50, and 'colour . . . pale and grene', ll. 97-8, seems to owe her green complexion to 'Aurora with hir cristall ene' and 'visage paill and grene' in *The Thrissil and the Rois*, st. 2, written in May 1503.

[1] I concur with Norton-Smith's statement, *op. cit.*, p. xxx f, that Gray is also the scribe of the late fifteenth-century Hay MSS.

[2] Dunbar wrote his part of the 'Flyting' with Walter Kennedy c. 1490. See my review of J. W. Baxter's *William Dunbar* in *The Scottish Historical Review*, vol. XXXIII, no. 115, pp. 46-52.

Since other and later Sinclair names are scribbled into the MS.—
'Maurius Synclar' fol. 79, 'Villam (?) Lord' (probably Henry's suc-
cessor to the title) fol. 230, 'Elizabeth Synclar' fol. 231—it must have
remained for some time with the family; so that it was almost cer-
tainly a Sinclair, certainly not one of the scribes, who penned both the
marginal comments on the *Troilus* and this introductory note to our
poem: 'Heireftir followis the quair Maid be/King James of scotland
the first/ Callit the kingis quair and/ Maid quhen his Maiestie wes In/
Ingland'. The title that is today given to the poem is probably that by
which it was known to the owners of the MS., who would have a
special interest in it since it was their ancestor, the Earl of Orkney,
who had 'the cure' of Prince James when he made his fateful voyage.
Then as now it would be a convenient reference; it could hardly have
been the poet's description, as Craigie oddly supposed it to be, and if
there had been a known title the scribe would have supplied it. Nor
need the statement of the sixteenth-century note-maker on the place
of composition imply special knowledge in that respect, even if it
reflects a family tradition, for on that point at least the tradition could
easily have been affected by the poem itself and must in any case be
weighed alongside other kinds of evidence.

A cardinal source of error in arguments about the *Quair* has been
mis-representation of the work of the scribes. Brown, who seems to
have relied upon information from a friend, asserts that three hands
are evident: a second scribe begins his task where the *Quair* starts, on
fol. 192; a third takes over on fol. 209 *verso*, adding the twenty stanzas
that conclude the poem on fol. 211, and continues with Hoccleve's
Letter of Cupid, the anonymous *lufaris complaynt* and *Quare of Jelusy*,
which three poems occupy folios 211 *verso* to 228 *verso* inclusively;
the second scribe returns on fol. 229, the third on folios 230, 231,
where the manuscript ends. Craigie fails to mention the 'second'
scribe's reappearance but rightly observes that he is responsible for the
substituted first leaf of the MS. which had been damaged.

This division of work, as Root briefly observed, is plainly mistaken
in one very important respect, that the difference between the 'first'
and 'second' hand is solely that of the ink's colour and the size of the
lettering; the so-called first scribe wrote larger, thicker letters that
now show as a faded brown, contrasting with the black, thinner letters
of the so-called second scribe. But in all essential features, style, spelling

and punctuation, both sections reveal the same peculiarities. Their marginal illumination is from the same hand that was at work on fol. 192 where the *Quair* commences, particularly the illuminated capital *H* in *Heigh* l. 1 has occurred before, and the other flourished capitals of the poem are very much like the earlier ones; also the red line which borders previous folios of the MS. stops precisely where the 'third' scribe begins. There are, indeed, two scribes, and it is possible to compare their procedure in the *Quair* with a considerable quantity of work elsewhere, copies of poems whose texts have been established, thus enabling us to determine, at least approximately, the degree of interference that is to be expected from them. This possibility becomes important in view of Craigie's reference to the few Scotticisms of fol. 1 (supposed by him to be the only other specimen of work by the main scribe of the *Quair*) as evidence for his opinion that *The Kingis Quair* as we have it is the scribes' heavily scotticized and corrupted version of a purely English original.

In fact, not only is the above-mentioned leaf an absurdly slight basis —it tells us only that some scotticizing took place—for such a conclusion, but the much larger means of forming a judgment that we have seen to be available give no indication of such radical changes as Sir William's theory demands. What Root says of the main scribe's text of *Troilus* (collated from two English MSS.), that it is 'remarkably free from gross blunders' and has 'only superficially a Scottish cast' (*The Textual Tradition Of Troilus* 1914, pp. 27–8) is equally true of the copy of *The Legend Of Good Women*, which precedes the *Quair* in the MS.; and the same may be said of the second scribe's version of Hoccleve's *Litera* and of *The Quare of Jelusy*, where he has obviously been content to repeat the many Anglicisms of its Scots author.

The Chaucerian texts share with the *Quair* the consistent spellings, *quh* for *wh*, *suich* for *swich*, *-ant* for *-aunt*, the regular northern forms *maid*, *sum*, *nouthir*, *seildyn*, *airly*. They also share with it the false insertion *y* before the infinitive (in the *Legend ysee* 238, 825, *yset* 1637, *ywrite* 2357; in the *Quair ybete* st. 116) because of Scots failure to sound preceding final *e*, substitution of *-en* for *-e* in the same position and for the same reason, the use of *-ith* along with *-eth* in the third singular present, though the *Quair* also has *-(i)s*. They differ strikingly from it, however, in normally preferring *-ed* to *-it/-yt* for the preterit and past participle, and they have *schall*, *shal*, *scholde* for its unvarying

forms *sal, suld; wole, wold*, for its regular *will* and prevailing *wald*;
syn, 'since', where it always has *sen*; more often *thise* pl. than its
consistent *thir; any* and *many* in place of all but regular *ony, mony*;
with few exceptions *saugh* where it only has *saw*. A very significant
point is that they keep the Midland spelling *o* in the groups *-old, -ond,
-ong, -ow*, where the *Quair* has Northern *a* sometimes in the first case
and predominantly in the others; also *o* for close *ō* is very seldom re-
placed, as it mostly is in the *Quair*, by Northern *u*.

This marked difference of practice would be explained, of course, if
the scribes were copying from just such a heavily scotticized text as
Craigie would have their own to be, or if a considerable amount of
authorial Scotticisms were present to encourage it—which we will see
to be the case. The first of these suppositions cannot be tested (any
more than the equally considerable one that in some spellings they
have repeated the results of still earlier English scribal interference);
the second must be allowed more probability since the linguistic
account now to be given affirms other and more radical Northern
traits.

LANGUAGE

As this analysis of the phonology and accidence of *The Kingis Quair*
will demonstrate, the language of the poem is Northern or Scots
English with an irregular but pervasive mixture of Midland sounds
and forms. Its natural use shows that for the most part it is not an
'artificial dialect' (Skeat), a merely literary medium, the product of
studious but imperfect imitation of English texts; elements of such
imitation do not prevent an overall impression of customary speech.
The author has retained most of the characteristic Scots values, and
with them acquired others that have almost, but never wholly, re-
placed their Scots equivalents. Thus in certain positions and not others
Midland open *ō* for Northern *ā* has become habitual and *ī* from the
final spirant groups has all but regularly replaced Scots close *ē* (para.
14), while close *ō*, the diphthongs *ai, ei, oi, ui*, and short *i, u* in open
syllables, show their Scots developments. Also, distinctively Northern
consonantal changes have established themselves along with Midland
ones, and a basically Scots grammatical practice has assimilated English

forms. The most patent dialectal elements of vocabulary are words in mainly or peculiarly Northern use; the characteristic Midland ones are chiefly parts of speech. These conclusions are independent of those workings of scribal interference to which Sir William Craigie speciously referred all Scottish appearances in the poem.

The early linguistic work of Wischmann has already been mentioned. Skeat's chief service of the kind was his commentary on the author's use and disuse of syllabic *e*, and the recent work of Jean Robert Simon limits itself to a graphemic and formal examination of the Selden text.[1] Craigie's discussion offered one (unargued) statement that would have been important if true, the assertion that there are only two forms attested by rhyme for which a Scottish origin can reasonably be claimed.[2] He specifies *begouth* in st. 16, *regne* in rhyme with *benigne*, *digne* in st. 39 (presumably these words have the same Scots quality as rhymes in st. 125), but with them must be counted other Northern rhyme-words—*toforowe* (:*morowe*:*borowe*) 23, *sawe* pret. (:*drawe*) 82, *pleye*, 'lodge pleas' (:*weye*:*deye*) 86 on which see para. 11, *hyng* pres. pl. (:*repenting*) 89, *humily* (:*so will I*) 105, *junyt* (:*fortunyt*) 133, *remufe* (:*lufe*:*abufe*) 188 (see para. 16), *remyt* sb. (:*admytt*) 195, and the Northern imperfect rhymes in stanzas 15, 71, 111, that are here noted under para. 15. Also, it will not do to account for James's merely intermittent and entirely metrical use of final and medial *e* (see para. 20) by a reference to the very different degrees of licence practised by Hoccleve and Lydgate, or by the supposition of extensive scribal omissions. It is to be hoped that the reader of the following paragraphs will share the editor's view, that to 'restore' the *Quair* to 'its genuine Southern form' would be a wholly mistaken endeavour.

[1] Norton-Smith's brief linguistic comments (*op. cit.*, pp. xxvii–xxx) reflect Craigie's argument. He considers the language as 'primarily a literary vehicle . . . modified by the inclusion of some minor accompanying features . . . which we may loosely call "northern" and in some cases "Scottish" '. His comparison with occasional Northern elements in Lydgate is, of course, misleading.

[2] Such counts can be unduly impressive. Distinctively dialectal rhymes can only be a small proportion of those used.

Phonology[1]

VOWELS

1. OE ON *ā*. *1.1.* The use of Northern unrounded *ā* has to be considered in the combinations *-ald*, *-and*, *-ang*, *-aw*, *-aʒ*, also for early signs of its Scots development towards an *e*-type sound and coalescence with *ai*, *ei* of whatever origin. For discussion of these cases see paragraphs 2, 3, 11, 12. Outside the above groups the spelling does not appear in rhyme and internally is irregular, except for the convincing *hale* adv. (*hāllice*) 58, 101, 122, 126, 188, 189. *1.2.* Midland rounding of *ā* to open *ō* shows in alternate spellings within lines and is consistently intended in the rhymes. Even so, these require a comment. All are among the ordinary borrowings from the south as listed by Morsbach, pp. 187-9, and Luick, pp. 359-62. All but a few are supplied from a heavily worked nucleus, the commonest of such borrowings—*more*, *sore*, *stone*, *gone*, *allone*, *wo*, *mo*, *so*, *fro*. Rhymes with long close *o* (*ō*), or *o* lengthened in open syllables (e.g.—*fore* from *foran*), or short *o*, occur with the frequency that Morsbach associates with the adoption of speech-habits not originally the writer's own. Chaucer avoids these practices (the fact of his exceptional use of them, particularly his distinguishing of lengthened *o*, is noted by Luick, chs. 369, Anm. 4, 391, Anm. 4), and though all are to be found in Lydgate and his contemporaries it is not with the same density. James

---

1 The studies referred to in this section, usually by the author's surname, are the following: A. Ackermann, *Die Sprache der ältesten schottischen Urkunden*, 1897; K. Brunner, *Die Englische Sprache*, vol. 1, 1960; W. A. Craigie, 'The Language Of The Kingis Quair', *Essays and Studies* XXV, 1939; F. J. Curtis, 'An Investigation of the Rimes and Phonology of the Middle-Scotch Romance Clariodus', *Anglia* XVI, XVII; H. Gerken, *Die Sprache Des Bischofs Douglas Von Dunkeld*, 1898; R. Girvan, Introduction to *Ratis Raving*, Scottish Text Society, 1939; E. Glaive, *Der Sprachgebrauch in den altschottischen Gesetzen*, 1908; Ulf Jacobsson, *Philological Dialect Constituents In The Vocabulary Of Standard English*, 1962; R. Jordan, *Handbuch der mittelenglischen Grammatik*, 1934; K. Luick, *Historische Grammatik der Englischen Sprache*, 1921-40 (it is this work that is here normally intended by his name), *Untersuchungen Zur Englischen Lautgeschichte*, 1896, *Studien Zur Englischen Lautgeschichte*, 1903; L. Morsbach, *Mittelenglische Grammatik*, 1896; A. H. Sander, *Die Reimsprache in William Stewart's Chronicle of Scotland und der mittel-schottische Dialekt*, 1906; J. P. Oakden, *Alliterative Poetry in Middle English*, 1930; G. Smith, *Specimens of Middle Scots*, 1902; W. Wischmann, *Untersuchungen Uber Das Kingis Quair Jakobs I von Schottland*, 1887. The more important authorities are Curtis, Girvan, Jordan, Luick.

would appear to make no more distinction between these sounds than does the Scots author of *The Buke of the Howlat* (1446), who uses all the kinds of rhyme noted below. For full illustration of the *ǭ*-rhymes I have included those that coincide with *-old* (*-ald*). (a) *moon* sb. (*māne*): *doon* (*dōn*) 45 alongside *stone* (*stān*): *mone* (*māne*) 72, *gold* (*gōld*): *behold* (*-hāldan*) 47, *gold*: *mony-fold* (*manig fāld*) 95, *behold*: *gold*: *cold* (*cald*) 152, *hold*: *gold* 178; *mo* (*mā*): *ro* (*rā*): *ho* (*hōn*) 157, possibly *two* (Midland *twǭ* < *twǭ*, cf. Luick, ch. 370): *wo* (*wā*) 145. (b) *wote* (*wāt*): *dote* (OF *redoter*) 47, *throte* (*þrotu*): *wote* 48, *tofore* (*toforan*): *bore* past part. (*boren*): *lore* (*lār*) 181, and the many rhymes with *therefore*, *tofore*, *before*, 2, 141, 146, 149, 150, 151, 171, 172, 174, 176, 187. (c) *vpone*: *anone* (*on ān*) 151, *hold*: *wold* (*wālde*): *rold* past part. (OF *roller*). In fine, omitting from my count the *gold*-rhymes and two self-rhymes, of the thirty relevant rhyme-sets only half represent normal Chaucerian practice (30, 39, 44, 64, 72, 80, 99, 103, 107, 111, 131, 164, 182) and of these half again have words differently rhymed elsewhere. It should be noted that the suffix *-hede*, in rhyme and internally, is always preferred to *-hode* (*hād*).

2. *-ald*, *-and*, *-ang*. As noted in 1.2 *ǫld* (or an approximate sound more probably) is proved in the *gold*-rhymes; however, these are to be expected in other Scots poets and do not rule out alternative *āld* elsewhere, e.g. in recurrent *wald*. In the other two groups *a*-forms are almost certainly original along with *o*-spellings, a varying pronunciation being indicated especially in *ang*-words. 2.1. The *and*-rhymes are— *band* sb. (ON *band*): *hand*: *stand* 43, *fand* pret. sing.: *hand*: *stand* 79, *vnderstand* infin.: *hand* 84, *vnderstand* past part.: *hand* 84, *vnderstond* past part.: *fond* infin. (*fandian*): *hond* 127. Here *a* prevails and in the whole poem (omitting the two or three words where *u* is intended) there are 35 *a*- and 4 *o*-spellings, a proportion entirely strange to the scribe's habits in copying English poems. The Northern pres. part. in *-and* occurs only thrice, in *byndand* 107, *Afferand* 145, *lyvand* 197 but is convincing in the first two cases (see notes). Original *and* is also indicated in *wandis* 31, a mainly Northern word (Jacobsson, p. 169), and *standar* adj. 156.3. The poet's use of *and* would be encouraged not only by his Northern origin and companions but also by the increasing frequency of such forms in London and its neighbourhood (Morsbach, ch. 188; Jacobsson, ch. 17). Chaucer, who otherwise avoids them, has *stant*, twice used by James. 2.2. *ang*-spellings predominate though

not so decidedly. There are 27 of them, 35 including regular *thank* (*þancian*), to 23 with *ong*, again a proportion without precedent elsewhere in MS. The rhymes are these—*song* pret. sing.: *among* adv. (*ongemang*): *rong* pret. pl. 33, *sang* sb.: *amang* prep. 61, *langer: stranger* 68, *ʒong* (*ʒung*): *song* pret. sing. 80, *lang: hang* pret. pl. (ON *hengja*): *amang* adv. 81, *belangith: hangith* (*hangian*) 111, *hong* pret. sing. (ON *hengja*): *long* 160. In *song* 80 Wischmann finds the retraction of *ong* to *ung* that appears in West Midland areas and some parts about London (Jacobsson, ch. 18) and therefore in 33; more probably it is a rhyme of convenience suggested by the past part. which appears variously in Scots texts as *sung, song, songin*. In 33 *rong* can borrow its vowel-sound from Midland *rungen* but this would be against James's Northern practice in preterits; it is more likely to conceal correct Northern *rang* or represent its Midland pronunciation. In 81, 160 *hang, hong*, replacing the prevailing Midland form *hēng*, are clearly intended as the pret. of *hing* (*hengja*), the present tense of which is peculiar to the North (*OED*) and is proved in rhyme at 89. In 111 *hangith* intrans. is not peculiarly Northern, having established itself in London, e.g. in Chaucer's writing (Jacobsson, p. 170).

3. OE ON *āw, āg*. These are represented by 25 Northern *aw-* and only 4 Midland *ow*-spellings. *3.1*. Beside the rhyme-sequences in *aw* in 35, 67, 90, 154 occurs the exceptional *rowe* (*rōwan*): *throwe* (*þrawan*): *blowe* (*blāwan*), where the two last Midland rhymes are explicable by initial non-dialectal *rowe*. The spellings *knaw-* (*cnāwan*) 45, 101, 105, 128, 148, 149, and *saulis* (*sāwol*) 123, 186, 197 (monosyllabic) are regular here and very sparsely distributed in the scribe's other work. The imperfect rhymes in the half-lines that close 60 (*blawe, schake: wag, wake*) point to original *blawe*. *3.2. āg* appears only once as *ow*, in *owin* (*āʒen*) 43, but this spelling shows early in Scots records (Ackermann, p. 36).

4. *ah*(*t*) > *auh*(*t*), *oht* > *ought*. *4.1*. The illustrations in the first case are—*fauht* pret. pl. (*fæht*) 85, *aught* pret. pl. (*ahte*) 120; *straught* (*stræht*) 126, 151, 164 (past part.), *straucht* 158, with *streight* 23, 112; *lauch* imperat. (*hlæhhan*) 179. In middle Scots *strecht* is occasional, e.g. in Holland and Douglas, perhaps encouraged as Luick suggests (ch. 403, Anm. 4) by association with ME *streit*, which appears in 25 as *strayte* (OF *estreit*). The Northern preterits are notable—*faucht* monosyllabic with the vowel of the sing. instead of Midland *foghten*; *aught* after the

pron. *ȝe* (see para. 35.2), *flawe* (*flæh*) 61 for Midland *fleigh*, *sawe* sing. and plur. (*sæh* affected by *sāwon* perhaps) in rhyme with *drawe* (*dragan*) 82 and regular for Midland *seigh*. *4.2.* It has been said that the *u*-glide after *o* is peculiar to England (Luick, ch. 403; Jordan, chs. 122, 129; Curtis, chs. 58–71, though the latter is puzzled that the development should differ from that in *auht* and accepts the statement only on spelling evidence). This mistaken opinion seems to be due to simple failure to distinguish between periods and between contracted and uncontracted spellings in edited texts. My examination of the uncontracted ones, which are alone relevant, finds *oucht* regular in the Royal (c. 1440) and Cotton MSS. of Wyntoun, all but regular in *Ratis Raving* (*c.* 1440), predominant in the Scots Legends of the Saints (c. 1390). It is at least occasional beside prevailing *ocht* in Holland, Hary, Henryson, Dunbar. The many place-names in records with initial *Ouchter* as well as *Ochter* (Gaelic *uachdar* with *a* in unstressed positions approximating to short *o*) show how well established the form was. (Concerning the spelling *gh* see para. 26.) In this edition spellings have been regularized from the dozen uncontracted words (*nought* adv. is always contracted), the rhymes being these—*nought* pron. (*noht*): *rought* pret. pl. (*rohte*) 27, *thought* pret. (*þohte*): *ought* pron. (*oht*): *ybought* past part. (*-boht*) 36, *wrought* past part. (*wroht*): *thought* sb.: *brought* past part. (*broht*) 77. Non-dialectal *though* (ON *þoh*) is always preferred to Midland *theigh* (*þeh*). Of course, (*n*)*ought* pron. (*ōht* > *oht*) is common to Scots and English texts.

5. *-an, -ant, -ance, -ange.* The *an*-spelling is regular in such words as *man, began* (:*than*:*quhan*) 5, 63, 147. Characteristic Northern *mony* (*manig*) is frequent and normal; *ony* (*ænig*) appears five times—8, 31, 67, 140, 152—*any* once, 72. With the exception of *graunt* (AN *graunter*) 185, which is common enough in Scots verse, French loan-words here avoid the diphthong *au* before *n* that is usual in Midland texts, perhaps because of Central French influence and the correspondence of the Scots pres. part. in *-and* to the French part. in *-ant* and its derivatives (Curtis, chs. 28–35; Sander, ch. 9)—hence reverse *d* for *t* in *seruand* 86, 113, 184, *plesandly* 178. It may be, as Curtis suggests, that words like *remanant* sb.: *variant* adj. 137 were felt as participles. This, along with Latin models, may also explain regular *-ance*, as in *plesance*: *variance* 139, *circumstance*: *chance* 187, etc. However, it cannot be decided whether it is James who has such spellings or the scribe who

favours them throughout the Selden MS. The rhyming of *hant* (OF *haunter*), misread by Skeat as *haunt*, with *oliphant* (L. *elephantus*, OF *olifant*) seems significant.

6. OE *ǣ* (W. Gmc. *ā*) > *ē*. Open *ē* from this *ǣ* is generally characteristic of the south-middle and south-east districts of England (excluding Kent); close *ē* from the same source is to the same extent characteristic of the Anglian areas. This test, however, is of little value, especially where the number of indicative rhymes is small; Chaucer's London was open to Anglian influences and Northern rhymers conveniently use southern sounds. (Luick, chs. 117, 361; Jordan, chs. 47-9; Oakden, pp. 23-4.) The mixed usage of the *Quair* reflects its author's experience. Non-Anglian open *ē* shows in *were* (*wǣron*): *jenipere*: *there* (*þǣr*) 32 instead of usual Northern *war*, *thar*, but *were*, *there* are also found early in Scots writing (Curtis, ch. 204); *grete* (*grēat*): *wete* (*wǣt*) 51, which is paralleled by such rhymes as *wet*:*set* in Wyntoun and Hay's *Alexander* (1438); *bare* (*bera*): *hare* (*hǣr*) 157 (see close of para. 12), where rhyming of open *ē* with *e* lengthened in open syllables is not a Chaucerian practice (Luick, ch. 391, Anm. 4, Horn/Lehnert, ch. 123). Anglian close *ē* shows in *pepe* (EME *pẹpe*, cf. OED): *slepe* (*slǣpan*) 57, *wede* (*gewǣde*): *hede* sb. (*hēdan*) 81, *suete* (*swēte*): *mete* adj. (*mǣte*) 97, but of these *ǣ*-words only *wede* does not have rhyme-words with close *ē* in Chaucer.

7. *ā* for open *ē*(*ǣ*). Occasional examples in the North probably reflect Norse influence or native variants; they are usually accompanied by *e*-forms (Luick, ch. 383, Anm. 1): *quhare* (OE *hwār* beside *hwǣr*) all but regularly; *lat* (ON *lāta*, OE *lǣtan*) 7, 41, 78, 99, 187; *airly* (ON *ār-*, OE *ǣr-*) 23, 29, *maist* (OE *māst* beside *mǣst*) 182.

8. OE *æ* > *a*. This development is somewhat more extensive in Northern texts (Curtis, ch. 81; Luick, ch. 363, Anmm. 3-6). The *Quair* differs from these mainly in omitting the characteristic exception *wes* (*wæs*) while retaining its Scots un-voiced *s* (see para. 31), yet *was* is also common in Barbour and other early Scots poets. Examples of *a* are—*man*: *than* (*þænne*) 63: *quhan* (*hwænne*) 147, *ware* adj. (*wær*) 164, *gave* (*ʒæf*, affected by ON *gāvo*) 177; *sat* pret. sing.: *consecrat* 33, *satt* pret. plur.: *laureate* 197, where as in Northern use *a* is from the sing. *sæt*. There is no sign of Kentish *e* or the southern and south-midland pret. with *ẹ* (e.g. *seet*, 'sat', *ʒeef*, 'gave'); but alongside the usual Northern form *spred* pret. and past part. (*sprǣdan*) 21, 32, 179

is *sprad* (:*glad*) pret. pl. which, if not an eye-rhyme, is Southern *spradde* with Northern loss of the ending. A Norse rather than a Southern origin explains such spellings as regular *efter* (3, 81, 86, 89, 104, 181, 182), *sek-cloth* (ON *sekkr-*) 109, *ouerthwert* (ON *þvertt*) 82, 167 (Zachrisson, p. 61); *kest* pret. (ON *kasta*) is frequent and is from *kesten* by analogy with *lesten* (*læstan*), cf. Luick, ch. 382, Anm. 2.

9. *a* < *a*, *e* before *r* in a closed syllable. Coalescence under *a* occurs everywhere in the late fourteenth century (the earliest rhymed proofs are Scottish), though *a*-spellings only become common after 1450. In Scotland the *a* is lengthened and duly comes to share the native movement of *ā* to open *ē* (Luick, ch. 430; Jordan, chs. 59, 67; Jacobsson, ch. 22; Curtis, chs. 302-25, prefers for Scotland a simpler change of *ar*-words to *er*-). The rhymes are—*clerk*:*awerk* (*on weorc*) 4, *aduert*: *smert* (*smeortan*) 25, *charge*:*large*:*corage* 38, *astert* (ON *sterta*): *hert* (*heorte*): *smert* 44, *preserue*:*Mynerue*:*conserue* 112, *hart*:*art* 2 sing. (*eart*) 114, *heart*:*smert*:*ouerthwert* (ON *þvertt*) 167, *aspert* (OF *aspert*): *dert* (OF *dart*) 170. Coalescence is clear in 114, 170. Scots lengthening, particularly accepted for such words as *charge*, *large*, *dart* (Luick, ch. 413.5; Jordan, ch. 224), helps to explain *corage* 38 as a rhyme. Whether in most cases we have an *a*- or *e*-sound cannot be decided, but by *w*-influence *a* was early settled in Scots *werk* (Curtis, ch. 318) 4 and is represented in the frequent Northern spelling *warld* (*werld* < *weorold*) 3, 15, 26, 44, 51, 82, 122 (Curtis ch. 318; Jordan, ch. 270 Anm.); *world* occurs once, 47, and is the scribe's spelling when copying English poems.

10. *ai*, *ei*, *oi*, *ui*: are monophthongized in fourteenth-century Scotland with consequent lengthening of the first vowel (Luick, ch. 434; Jordan, ch. 238), but *au* before labials, elsewhere generally reduced to *ā*, is sometimes retained in the North (Luick, ch. 427; Glawe, p. 61). *10.1. ai*, *ei*—on this much argued case see paras. 11, 12. *10.2. oi* > *ọ*: *voce* (OF *vois*) 64, 74, 83, *chose* (OF *chois*) 92, 147; the name *Proigne* 55 is monosyllabic and may be pronounced with *ung* from *ọ̄ng* (see para. 16.1). *10.3. ui* > *u*: *fortunyt* past part.: *junyt* (OF *juint*) 133—the rhyme is not to be discounted simply because *u*, for metrical reasons, is unstressed in both words (see para. 16.1). *10.4 au*: *sauf* prep. 143, 165; *sauen* 102 may be a scribal shortening of *sauuen* (*sauven*); but before *mb*, *mp* we find *a* in *chamber* 30, 74, 97, *lampis* 72, *ensample* (the regular form in Hay) 148, 172.

11. OE *æg, eg*, OF *ai, ei*: coincide in *ai* in England (Luick, ch. 408) but, contrary to Luick's opinion, in *ei* in Scotland (Curtis, chs. 148–50), and certainly there show signs of development towards open *ē* early in the fifteenth century (see para. 12): *day* (*dæg*): *say* (*secgan*): *away* (*onweg*) 24, *aire* (OF *air*): *faire* (*fæger*) 75, *counsailis* (OF *cunseil*): *batailis* (OF *bataille*) 85, *pleye* vb. (OF *plai*): *weye* sb (*weg*): *deye* (*dēȝan*) 86, *assay* (OF *assai*): *nay* (ON *nei*) 89, *pleyne* (OF *plaindre*): *ageyne* (*ongegn*) 91, *weye* vb. (*weȝan*): *seye* (*secgan*): *conueye* (OF *cunvier*) 120, *faire*: *contraire* 144. In 86 the very rare Scots verb *pleye* (mistaken by Skeat for 'play' from *plegian*) can have either its English value as a noun, *plę̄* (Luick, ch. 416; Jordan, ch. 262), or its Scots sound *plę̄* both in noun and verb. (See *DOST* under its rhyme-words *fley* vb., 'put to flight', *key, wey* vb., *obey*; also Gerken, p. 32.) In either event *deye* must have *ē*, presumably its Scots pronunciation *dę̄* and not Chaucerian *dai* or rarer *dī*. That *weye*, which should have an open sound, is thus an incorrect rhyme, is no reason for rejecting the evidence of the rhyme-sequence for an *e*-quality of some kind in the *ai/ei* spellings; rhymes of close and open vowels are particularly common in the North and wherever both Midland and Northern influences are at work, as is the case with James's speech. The verb *weye* 120 belongs to the same special group of rhyme-words as does *pleye*. In *contraire* 144 *e* might be expected, and regular unstressed *e* in *counsele* points to a similar value in stressed *ai* of *counsailis* (:*batailis*) 85.

12. ME *ai, ei* and *ā*. According to Luick, chs. 408, 434, these diphthongs unite under *ai*, which in mid-fourteenth-century Scotland undergoes reduction with lengthening and so coalesces with *ā* from other sources, this sound being very gradually fronted towards open *ē*, which it fully attains only in the sixteenth century. This dating and account of the coalescence have been convincingly questioned by Curtis, chs. 148–50, Girvan, pp. lviii–lxiii, by the former on the ground of excessive complexity, by the latter on the evidence of the texts. They argue that coincidence occurred not under *ā* but by common development to an *e*-sound. Certainly rhymes of *ai/ei* with original *ā* and *ē* appear about the same time and not so early as they should if Luick's hypothesis were correct. Illustrations of the coalescence (one of Luick's two main proofs for Barbour is a misreading, the other doubtful) are disputed in *Bruce*, 1375, and the Scots Saints' Legends, c. 1390, admitted absent in Wyntoun, 1420–4, except in unstressed

syllables, found only once or twice in Hay's long *Alexander*, 1438, accepted by the editor of *Ratis Raving*, c. 1440—a decade or two later than Girvan dates it, since *ll.* 1242–8 appear to use Lydgate's *Pilgrimage*, 1426–28—in only two or three cases. Even in the late fifteenth-century MSS. of Hay's prose works (1456) the *i* sign of length that belongs with coalescence is not very frequent. The first poem to show that care has not normally been taken to separate diphthong and vowel is Holland's *Buke of the Howlat*, 1446, in which I find, for example, *fair* (*fæger*) in rhyme with both *lair* (*lār*) and *mistar* (OF *mestier*), the latter word also coinciding with *deir* (*dēore*), *heir* (*hēr*).

Doubtless the new pronunciation was current in James's boyhood, but poets tend to respect the rhymes of their predecessors, and in view of previous Scots practice there is no reason to impute to English habits the separation that is maintained in the *Quair*. Of course, awareness of the English sound *ǫ* would make it easy to avoid the Scots rhymes but, contrary to Wischmann's assumption, their avoidance does not need to imply English influence. In fact, proof of Scots *e* in *ai, ei* has been given in para. 11, and the reverse spelling *a*, alternating indifferently with the diphthong, is not likely to be merely scribal in all these words—*agane* (*ongegn*) 29, 162, 165, alongside *agayne*: *souirane* (OF *soverain*) 181, the last word also as *souereyne* 183, *plane* (OF *plain*) 36, 178 with *pleyne* 116, *pane* (OF *peine*) frequently but *payne* 14 *pace* (? OF *peise*) 131, *desate* (OF *deceite*) 135, regular *tham* (ON *þeim*) and *ressaue* (OF *receivre*) 52, 55, 84, 123, 145 (on which see Jordan, ch. 233 Anm. 3, ch. 259 Anm.). With these should probably go the Latin spelling *sanct*, 23, 62, 191, almost certainly sounded the same as French-derived *saint*. Such *a*-spellings are very rare occurrences in the scribe's English copying (though the pret. *maid* is the scribe's regular spelling, it may well be the author's also). Specially interesting is *bare* (*bera*): *hare* (*hēr*, ON *hār*) 157 since rhyme spellings are more reliable in the poem than internal ones (see note).

13. *e > i*. ME short close *e* becomes open and is raised to *i* (*y*) in areas of Anglian influence, most extensively in Northern and Scottish speech (Luick, chs. 379, 382 Anm. 3, *Studien*, p. 190). *13.1.* Before *ng*: peculiar to the North and regular in Scotland are *regne* (ON *hringja*, OF *regner*) pronounced 'ring' (:*benigne*: *digne*) 39—on this sound see also para. 25.5—and the present-tense forms *hingen* (ON *hengja*) 88, *hyng* (:*repenting*) 89 (see *OED*). *13.2.* Between *g, ʒ* and

a dental: regularly *ʒit* 63, 83, 193, *togider* 64, 68, 124. *13.3.* Before *l*: *befill* pret. (:*gude will*) beside *befell* (:*bell*) 11. *13.4.* In unstressed syllables: verbal inflections mostly have *i*, as in -*id*, -*it(yt)*, -*is* (where the northerly ending *s* is clearly demanded in some cases). At 6 *quitis* (:*appetitis*), misread by Skeat as the past part. with *is* does not prove *i* and at 111 MS. *goddes* (:*seknesse*) should be *goddesse*, but *junyt* (:*fortunyt*) 133 as a Northern pronunciation points to -*yt* (see para. 16.1). Significant also is the strong parasitic *i* between labial and *l* as in *humily* (:*so will I*) 105. *13.5.* Initial and final *in*:*inemye* (OF *enemi*) 24, 156, *inmytee* 87, *evin* (*efen*): *hevin* (*heofon*) 21, *enbroudin* past part. 152. Words differently derived but agreeing with the above tendency as preferring *i* to Chaucerian *e* are *birn* (*birnan*) 168, *birnyng* 48 in place of *brenn(yng)*, *wirken* (*wyrcan*) 68, *wirking* 146, 188, *dyrknesse* (*deorc* influenced by *dyrcan*) 71, *rynnis* (*irnan*) 74, *blissit* past part. (*bletsian*) 189 with Northern transference from *bliss* sb.

14. OE *ēg*, *ēh*, *īg* coincide in the poem in *ī*: *pyne* (*pīn*): *ruyne*: *nyne* (*nigon*) 28, *remedye*: *hye* (*hīgian*): *forby* (*forbī*) 30, *nye* (*nēh*): *hye* (*hīgian*) 77, *eye* (*ēge*): *deye* (*dēʒan*) 103, *cremesye* (OF *cremeisi*): *dayesye* (*dæges ēge*) 109, *eye*: *heye* (*hēh*) 110, *sye* pret. sing. (*sēh*): *eye* 157, *hye* (*hēh*): *to-wrye* (*wrīgian*): *hye* (*hīgian*) 164. (On the relevant sound-changes see particularly Luick chs. 401, 403, 407; *Untersuchungen*, ch. 154.) The exception to the above is Northern close *ē* in *deye* (:*pleye*:*weye*) 86 (on which see para. 11), *deis* (dissyllabic) 52, *dee* 57. In *eye* the second element of the Midland diphthong *īe* is not retained because of Northern loss and doubtless also the author's familiarity with Scots *ę̄*. *nyne*, *nye* adj. and *hye* adj. (influenced by *nigh*, *high*) are found in the North both as *ī* and *ę̄* forms, though in the last two cases predominantly with *ę̄* (Luick, *Studien*, pp. 151, 164; Jordan, ch. 100 Anm.), but in *sye*(:*eye*) the *ī* is peculiarly Midland; note, however, that this is the sole appearance of *sye*, evidently required for rhyme, the otherwise regular preterit being Northern *sawe*, also attested in rhyme at 87. Of the three forms with the spirant, *heigh* 1, 20, 146, *hich* 196, *hicht* sb. 172, only the last (probably scribal) is dialectal, for the generally Northern change *eht* > *iht* (Jordan, ch. 96 Anm.).

15. *i* > *ę̄*, u > *ǭ*. In the North short *i*, *u* are lengthened respectively to *ę̄*, *ǭ* in the open syllables of dissyllabic words, whence extended by analogy (Luick, chs. 380, 393; fully argued in *Studien*). Because of a further development of *ǭ* the treatment of *u* will be noticed under 16.2

but it should be observed here that proof of the change in one vowel is proof of it in the other. The change to $\bar{e}$ is clear: *vnsekir* (*-sicor*) 6, the vowel-rhymes *vnsekernesse: stereles* (*stēor-*) 15: *febilnesse* (AN *fēble-*) 71: *seknesse* (*sēoc-*) 111; *cleuerith* (ON *klifra*) 9, *cleuering* 159; *besy* (*bisig*) 64, 97, 121, 132; *geue* (*giefan*) 108, 113, 128, 172 but (*dryue* past part.:) *gyve* 92 for the sake of rhyme, *gevis* 115, *gevin* 92, 188; *clepe* (*clipian*) 18, 19, *clepen* 149, *cleping* 147, *clepit* 3, 111, 166; *wedowis* gen. sing. (*widuwe*) 156, *werdes* (*wirid* < *wyrd*) 9.

16. $\bar{o}$ > $\ddot{u}$; $\bar{o}h$, $\bar{o}g$ (with the same change as in $\bar{o}$) > *iuh, iu* (*euch, ew*). For these Northern and particularly Scottish developments see Luick, chs. 406, 407; Jordan, chs. 54, 119, 128; Girvan, pp. lxiii-lxvi. *16.1.* OE $\bar{o}$ > $\ddot{u}$. Proofs of this change are naturally rare but the proportion of *u*-spellings, 45 with *u* and 14 with *o*, has no parallel in the scribe's copying of known English poems, e.g. in the lengthy *Legend Of Good Women* he introduces *u* only once, *eu/ew* for *ow* not at all. Also it seems likely to be the poet's marked habit of alliterating vowels rather than the scribe's extension of it that accounts for such cases as the following—*begouth my buke* (*bōc*) 13, *all bludy* (*blōdig*) *ronne* 55, *doune thaire hudis* (*hōd*) 88, *Fortune hufing* (*hōven*) *on the ground* 159, *rude and crukit* (*crōked*) 195. In the rhymes *lufe:abufe:remufe* (OF *remouvoir*) 188 the *uf*-spelling is chiefly Northern and the verb indicates that the change has occurred in ME *remōven*. The coincidence of French $\ddot{u}$ with the same sound from $\bar{o}$ is reflected in the Northern *oy*-spellings, *proyne* (OF *proigner*) and *soyte* (OF *suite*) 64, *foynʒee* (OF *foine, fuine*) 157 (see Jordan, ch. 230). *16.2.* The change *u* > $\bar{o}$ (connected with the proved change i > $\bar{e}$, para. 15) > $\ddot{u}$ is indicated by *u*-spellings where, for example, Chaucer has *o: dure* (*duru*) 75, 97, *pure* (OF *povre*) 99, 101, regular *cum*- in its inflected forms and regular *lufe, abufe* (Luick, chs. 393, 406). *16.3.* OE $\bar{o}h$, $\bar{o}g$ > *iuh, iu*. Confirmatory rhymes with *iu* from OE *ēow* or French final *u* can only be chance occurrences in a poem of this size at this period (*e.g.* they are not in the later *Quare of Jelusy*) and are not found. Only one such rhyme is used in *Bruce, withdrew:knew*, ix. 256-7, a mere handful in Wyntoun's long chronicle and none in the more comparable *Ratis Raving* (c. 1440). Only with the *Howlat*, 1446, is there a notable number. That the diphthongizing of French final *u* has taken place in the *Quair* and that the spelling *ew* always represents *iu* is plain—*hewe* (*hēow*):*blewe* (OF *bleu*) 46, *hewe: renew* (*nēowe*): *dewe* (OF *deu*) 119, *hewis:glewis* (*glēow*):

anewis (AN *anius*) 160, *vertew* several times and *vertu* (OF *vertu*) once, *argewe* (*arguer*) 27, *tissew* (*tissu*) 49, *contynew* (*continuer*) 105. There is no reason in the scribe's practice elsewhere to attribute all such spellings to him. For *ōh*, *ōg* there are the distinguishing forms of the North, *-eugh* sing., *-ew* pl.: *beugh to beugh* (*bōh*) 35, *eneuch* sing. (*genōh*) 47, *bewis* (*bōgas*) 32, 191; *drewe* sing. 42 represents *drōh* affected by plur. *drōgon*. Midland *ow* is strictly reserved for the non-dialectal *ou* < *og*: *lowe* (ON *logi*) 48, *bow* (*boga*) 94, *enbroudin* (*-brogden*) 152, *wyndow* (ON *vindauga*) 177, and due to *w*-influence *suoun* past part. (*geswogen*) 73 (see Luick, chs. 402, 406).

17. *ü*:*ū*. In Scots verse of this early period French *ü* only occasionally rhymes on *ū* (Jordan, ch. 230, Anm. 3). In the poem rhymes like *cure*:*sure*:*auenture* 100 do not mix with such as *tour*:*floure*:*houre* 40 but there is the instance *fortunyt*: *junyt* 133 (see para. 10.3).

18. *-ynd*, *-ind*, *-und*. *ī*, *ū* before the normally lengthening group *nd* are often shortened in the North (though southern practice intrudes) but *ī* is there retained in *mynd* (*gemynde*), *kynd* (*gecynde*), as also *u* in *-ound* from French *-und* (Curtis, chs. 395–401; Luick, ch. 429. 2). With the *ynd* class of words, however, often goes *fynd* (*findan*) and with the *und* class regularly *sound* (*gesund*), *stound* (*stund*), irregularly *ground* (*grund*), *hound* (*hund*). James's practice is much like that of other Scots poets of his time (see Curtis's list of *und*-rhymes, ch. 517), with the same rhyming tendencies and exceptions—(1) *kynd*:*fynd*: *mynd* 27, *kynde*: *fynde*: *vnbynd* (*bindan*) 37, *mynd*:*kynd* 45, *mynd*: *mynd* 73, *mind*:*kynd* 154, *mynd*:*mynd*:*fynd* 158; (2) *stound*:*hound*:*ground* 53, *ground*:*stound*:*round* (OF *rund*) 118, *ground*:*sound*:*abound* (OF *abundir*) 165.

19. OE *ȳ* is unrounded to *ī* in the North and North Midlands particularly (Luick, ch. 287; Jordan, chs. 39–43). In the poem *ī* is regular in rhyme, there are no proofs of Kentish *e* but Midland *u* before *ch* appears. *19.1. fery*, 'ever-active' (see note), 156 is not a Kentish form and does not derive from OE *fȳrig* (cf. *fyre* sb. = *fīr* 1, 76) as Craigie suggests but from ON *fōerig*. Other *e*-spellings are explicable by Northern lengthening of *i* to *ę̄* in open syllables (para. 15), or by the non-dialectal approximation of a very open *i* to *e* (Curtis, chs. 389–90) as in *knet* (*cnyttan*) 31, especially frequent before *-st*:*lest* sb. (*lyst*) 5, 57, *lest* pret. sing. (*lystan*) 147 alongside recurring *list*, *lesty*, 'cunning' (see note), 157 from *lystig*, *lestnyt* pret. sing. (*hlystan*) 11. *19.2.* In place of

the Northern forms *mekil* (ON *mikill*), *swik* (*slīk*), *sic, sich,* appear Midland *mich* (*micel*), *moch* (*mycel*), *suich* (*swylc*), this last being regular for the scribe throughout the Selden MS. The spelling *trust*(*en*) (*trystan*) 130, 137 occurs with Northern *traist* (ON *treysta*) 130, *hortis* sb. pl. (OF *hurter*) in rhyme with *wortis* (*wyrt*); in these cases *u* and *o* for *u* are Midland (specially West Midland) features but do occur sporadically in Northern and Scots writings (Luick, ch. 286; Jacobsson, p. 204; *OED*).

20. Loss of *e* (*i*) in final and medial positions. This is much more evident in Northern verse, even in the fifteenth century (Luick, chs. 472–6; Jordan, chs. 290–1). In the *Quair* metrical function seems wholly to determine the sounding or unsounding of *e* (in some instances it is needlessly assumed by Skeat, cf. pp. xxvi–xxxi of his edition). There are many proofs of its loss, none of its retention in rhyme. For further details concerning the cases listed below see under 'Accidence'.

20.1. Final *e*. (a) Nouns: here *e* is mostly lost (apparently always in rhyme), e.g. in *hert* with the exceptions 48, 28, *chere* 81 but *cherë* 161, trisyllabic *jelousye* 87, *wise* 104 but not 120, trisyllabic *pacience* 117, *Mynerue* 126 (cp. *Bruce* MS. *Mynerff*), *ere* 172 but (?) not 152. (b) Adjectives. There is about equal loss and retention, the latter chiefly after *the*, the demon. and possess. prons., e.g. *quhite* 46, *hir quhytë* 48. The only likely exception to loss in words like *hye* adj. and vb., *nye* adj., *deye, eye* (see para. 14) is *hyë* adj. 130, less certainly *eye* 51. (c) Verbs: see below. (d) Adverbs: here too sounding is for metrical needs only, e.g. *fairë* 76 but not 80.

20.2. Medial and inflectional *e*. (a) Nouns. The penultimate syllable keeps *e* in *rypënesse* 16, *vnkyndënes* 87, 116, *chapëllet* 97 but not *chaplet* 46, 95, *erëmyn* 161 but not *ermyn* 157. Loss in the pl. ending shows in monosyllabic *wayes* 24, *eyne* 35, 89, *hertis* 122, *saulis* 197, and in dissyllabic *hevynnis* 34, *kalendis* 34, *aspectis* 107, *carolis* 121, *seruandis* 184. The gen. sing. loses *e*(*i*) in *hevynnis* 1, 196, *goldsmythis* 110, *wedowis* 156, *hertis* 168. (b) Pronouns: the inflection is sounded in *quhois* 56, *The quhois* 79, *Quhilkis* 62, lost in *quhois* 70 etc. (c) Present pl. and infinitive. In rhyme there are several proofs of loss (cf. 117, 119, 129, 134, 136), none of retention, but internally along with loss there is convenient use of Midland -*en* and -*e* (the scribe has -*en* elsewhere in MS where other MSS. have -*e*, and I have assumed that in cases where a final syllable is needed and none indicated he has found -*e* and has omitted it). (d) Preterit and past participle:vowel loss occurs in the endings of *forwalowit* 11, *ymaginit* 13, *puruait* and *pullit* 23, *comprisit* 28, *stellifyit:magnifyit* 52, *sighit* 71, *clippit* 75, *playit* 80, *vnreconsilit*: *begilit* 90, *lyvit* 91, *salute* (*salued*) 98, *glitterit* 153, *astonate* 98, 162 (see para. 35.6), *semyt* 163 but not 160, *abaist* 166 but *abaisit* 41, *hapint* 187. There are no Weak preterits in -*de*(*n*), -*te*(*n*) or Strong preterits plural in -*en*. (e) Adverbs: *e* is unetymologically inserted in *sterëles* (*stēor-*) 15, 16, *onëly* (*ān-*) 148, perhaps sounded in *benignëly* 104 (pronounced *beningëli*), but is silent in *namly* 9, *nycely* 12, *trewly* 141, *hertly* 144, 187, *onys* 182.

CONSONANTS

21. *c.* *21.1.* OE palatal *c* is sometimes replaced by *k*: *quhilk* (*hwilc*, ON *hvilīkr*) 180, *quhilkis* (dissyllabic) 62 beside usual *quhiche* (monosyllabic), *ilkë* 'same' (*ilca*) 154, *ilk* 163, *thilkë* 5, 119, *ylike* (ON -*līkr*) 70, 154 for *yliche*, *beseke* 176 with *beseche* 113, *beseching* 184; but there is preference of the Midland forms *eche* (*ǣlc*), *euerich* 27, *mich* (*mycel*), *moch, suich* (*swylc*). The invariable suffix -*ly* (ON *līgr*) is not dialectal. More common in the North than the Midlands are the *k*-forms *wirken* 68, *wyrking* 148, 188, *busk* (ON *buskr*) 135. *21.2.* Latin influence shows in *sanct* (with unpronounced *c*) 23, 191, *facture* 50, 66, the former a mainly Scots form.

22. *d* final and unstressed becomes *t* in Northern English (though it is still a spelling in Wyntoun and *Ratis Raving*). With a few exceptions in -*id*, -*d*, pret. and past part. have Scots -*it* (-*yt*), -*t*; similarly *nakitnesse* 109, *nakit* 194. The change seems clear in monosyllabic *sighit* 71, *clippit* 75, dissyllabic *salute* 98. Other cases are *touert* (-*weard*) 46, 174, *thidderwart* 185 but *furthward* 17, *vpward* 20, *outward* 136; *emeraut* (OF *esmeraude*) 46, *sluggart* (*slugge* with OF-*ard*) 58. Complete loss of final *d* appears only in Scots *sen*, 'grant' (*OED*) 57. Conversely French -*ant* appears as -*and* (see para. 5).

23. OE *ð*, *þ*. *23.1.* In Scottish texts voiced *d* before syllabic *r* is commonly found along with -*ðer* (Luick, chs. 725, 752. la): *fader* 122, *togider* 64, 68, 124, *hider* 166, *thidderwart* 185 with *quhethir* 24, *forthir* 99, 190, *brethir* 184. *23.2.* Exchange of medial *þ* with *d* is seen in *coud*(*e*) (*cuþe*) 2, 84, 92 beside *couth* rhyming with Northern *begouth* 16 (Jordan, ch. 185, Anm. 2). *23.3.* Final *ð* becomes *d* in unstressed *quod* (*cwæð*) 116, 142 but *deth* (*dēað*) 188 appears for Northern *deid*; *hundreth* (ON *hundrað*) 180 is Northern. *23.4.* Loss of *ð*, *þ* shows in the

Scots forms *toforowe* (*-forouth* < *forwith*, cf. *OED*), *ʒoure alleris* (*alðer* with superfluous pl. and genitival *-is*) 113, *syne* adv. (ON *siððan*) 192, 196, *sen* conj. (*siþþan*) regularly for Midland *sith*. **24. ME *v*, *f*.** *24.1.* Northern unvoicing of medial *v* after loss of final *e* (Jordan, ch. 217; Jacobsson, ch. 31) is indicated by such spellings as *hufing* (*hōven*) 159, *lufe* (*lufu*): *abufe* (*onbufan*): *remufe* (OF *remouvoir*) 188; at 121 (*in thy*) *lyue*: *stryue* (OF *estriver*) the noun is an eye-rhyme or is influenced by the adverbial phrase *on lyue*, since otherwise it has *f*, e.g. *lyf*:*ryf* (*rīf*) 121. Compare the parallel development of medial *s*, para. 31. *24.2.* Loss of *v* before *l*, *r* is said to be particularly Northern (Luick, ch. 428.3; Jacobsson, p. 236); *deuil* (*dēofol*) for the monophthong *dẹl* 56, monosyllabic *oure* prep. (*ofer*) 143, *ourehayle* 10, 158, *ouercome* 41, *ourset* 73, *ouerwent* 74. **25. OE *g*.** *25.1.* Initial palatal *g* (*ʒ*) shows in *ʒelde*, *ʒeris*, etc., and sometimes as *i*/*y* for the OE participial prefix *-ge*, brought in to supply the metre. *25.2.* Guttural *g* regular in the following words is due to Norse influence: *geue* (ON *gefa*), *forgeue*, *gif* conj., *agane* (*ongegn*). Northern *ʒate* (:*vnquestionate*) 125 has its vowel from OE *gatu*, its consonant from ME *ʒet* (Curtis, ch. 259); *forget* (ON *geta*) past part. 120 represents the shortened part. *forʒet* (*OED*). *25.3.* For the vocalization of medial and final *g* see paras. 3.2, 11, 14, 16.3. Guttural *ʒ* after *r* becomes *u* (*ow*): *morowe* (:*toforowe*):*borowe* vb. :*sorowe* 23, 49, 105 but is simply lost in *mornis* 29. *25.4.* In Northern speech the velar nasal in unstressed final *-ing* becomes dental *n* (Jordan, ch. 175), but this shows only in *Vnknawin* pres. part. 45 and reverse spellings like *twynklyng* 1 MS, *gardyng* sb. 33, *fallyng* past part. 45, 164, *cumyng* past part. 185. *25.5.* French liquid *n* after *ī* becomes guttural with shortening of the vowel in Scots, a change which, along with that noticed in para. 13.1, explains the rhymes *regne* ON (*hringja*, OF *regner*):*benigne*:*digne* 39; see also *signis* 76. **26. OE *h*.** For final *h* see paras. 14, 16.3. The spirant remains in regular *though* conj. (*þoh*) but is lost in *throu* (*þurh*) (:*ʒow*:*thou*) 63, etc. For the main scribe of the *Quair* *gh* is the normal spelling throughout the Selden MS., *ch* being only a random alternative.[1] OE *hw* is always represented by Scots *quh*. Silent *h* in *hable* adj. and vb. (OF *habiller*) 14, 39, 99 appears to be a particularly Scots spelling (*OED*), but the scribe introduces it elsewhere in MS.

[1] *gh* is also his spelling in the Hay MS.

27. OE *l*. *27.1*. This is retained in Northern *quhilk* (*hwilc*), non-dialectal *ilke* (*ilca*). *27.2*. As a Scots sign of vowel length it occurs in MS *walking* pres. part. (*wācian*) 173 but elsewhere *wak-*. Vocalization, which would have preceded such a spelling, is a fourteenth-century change though not proved in Scots verse till after 1450 (Girvan, p. xlvii); it can only be suspected in monosyllabic *pullit* pret. pl. 23. *27.3*. Final syllabic *l* is most frequently indicated in the North (Luick, ch. 474.3; Sander, chs. 40, 41) and shows in these distinctly dissyllabic or trisyllabic words—*noble* 3, 5, 37, 125; *feble* 13, 17, 149, 169, *febily* 98; *hable* 14, 39, 99, *doubilnesse* 18; *humble* 62, 124, *humily* (*:so will I*) 105, *humylnesse* 126; *sable* 157, *ensample* 148, 172.

28. *m*. *28.1*. Northern assimilation of *b* to preceding *m* in internal as well as final positions (Jordan, ch. 211) occurs: *clymbe*: *tyme*: *prime* 171, *nowmer* (OF *nombre*) 19, 22, 81; *humil-* (see para. 27.3). *28.2*. *m* becomes *n* before a labial with *r* in *enprise* 20, *enbroudin* 152. *28.3*. *p* is intruded between *m* and *n* (probably not sounded; Luick, ch. 743): *ympnis* 33, 197, *solempt* 79 where *n* is lost and silent Scots *t* has been intruded.

29. *n*. ME *-en* of the infin., pres. pl., pret. pl. is lost in Northern writing and shows here—in the last case not at all—as a metrical convenience. The loss or retention of final *n* in the possess. pron. and indef. art. follows the usual Midland and early Scots practice: *myn*, *thyn*, *ane/one*, *nan/none* are the rule before vowels and *h*. The Scots spelling of French liquid *n* is introduced in *foynȝee* (OF *foine*) 157 but is otherwise avoided, e.g. *feyn-*, *pleyne* (OF *plaindre*), *cheyne*.

30. Metathesis in certain words is characteristic of Northern English: *throu* (*þurh*) 51, 63; *bird* (*bridd*) 57, 178, *birdis* 35, 36, 64, 65, but for the sake of rhyme *brid* (*:hid*) 135, *bridis* (*:bydis*) 65, *thrist* sb. (*ðyrstan*) 69; *thrid* (*þridda*) 95 as in Chaucer but *birn* (ON *brinna*) 168, *birnyng* 48 as against his forms with *brenn-*.

31. *s*. *31.1*. OE *s* unstressed or made final by loss of the inflection with *e* becomes voiced in Midland English towards the end of the fourteenth century but not so in Northern English (Jordan, ch. 208; Brunner, I, pp. 375–6). In the *Quair* it is unvoiced: *wise* sb. (*wise*): *ryse* vb.: *excercise* 29, *wise*: *sacrifise*: *seruice* 52, 192: *prise* sb. (OF *pris*) 188, *fantise* sb.: *vprise* 142, *face*: *was*: *cas* 94. *31.2*. OE *sc* unstressed is simplified in the North to *s* (Jordan, ch. 183), hence usual *sall* (*sceal*), *suld* (*sceolde*); the Scots spelling *sch* represents the same unvoiced *s* in

schall 12, 27, *relesche* (OF *reles*) 25, 150, 176, 184, perhaps *blamischere* (OF *blesmir*) 140, and always replaces Midland *sh* (*sche, schip,* etc.).

Accidence

32. *Nouns.* For the basically Northern treatment of final and inflectional *e* see under para. *20.1*. Syllabic *-ce. -ge,* common to Midland and Northern verse where useful, show in *pryncë* 9, *chancë* 146, *chargë* 120. The pl. and gen. sing. have normally *-is, -s;* without *-s* are *eyne, eyen, deuil* 56, the favoured Northern form *brethir* 184. Names unless they end in *-s* have the gen. in *-is, Cupidis* 43, *Mineruis* 124 but *Venus* 5, 126. The weak gen. remains in the phrase *in Marye name* 17.

33. *Adjectives.* *33.1* In the sing. and pl. the sounding of *-e* is entirely at the poet's will and follows no rule. Skeat's specification of correct and incorrect imitation of Chaucer's practice—correct in the vocative case, *suetë* 57, in the pl. *fourë* 21, *freschë* 80, after *the, this, that* or the possess. pron., as in *the planë* 36, *this fairë* 178, *that freschë* 49, *hir suetë* 41; incorrect in the sing. and indef. adj., e.g. *fairë* 178, *l*.3, where *-e* is neither Chaucerian nor Scots (some of his other instances are metrically needless)—misleads by obscuring the fact that silent *-e* greatly predominates. *33.2.* The more commonly Northern and Scottish uses of the substantival adj. and following adj. appear in *that verray womanly* 42, *that faire* 66, *the certeyne* 138, *figure circulere* 1, *brestis wete* 55, *circle clere* 76, *doken foule* 109, *court riall* 125, *court dyvine* 151, *goddesse fortunate* 168, *sanctis marciall* 191, *menys fauorable* 192, etc. *33.3* The superl. and compar. have *-est, -er,* except for Northern *gudeliar* 49, *hyare* 131 and the verbal adjectives *druggare* and *lufare* 155, *standar* and *clymbare* 156, *draware* 157 (cp. Chaucer's *-er* in such words, *The Parlement of Foules* 176–80). For the indef. art. see para. 29.

34. *Pronouns.* *34.1.* The 3rd fem. sing. is *sche,* only once (67) the more common Scots form *scho;* its accus. and possess. form is always *hir.* *34.2.* The 2nd sing. after some monosyllabic verbs sometimes assimilates *th* to *t,* a Midland feature: *hastow* 57, *artow* 58, 173, *wostow* 59, *maistow* 170. *34.3* The 3rd pl. has the usual Northern forms, *thai, thame, thaire.* *34.4.* The dem. pl. is chiefly Northern *thir* but *thise* 86 and Midland *tho* (for *thā*) 39, 144 occur. *34.5.* The interrog. -indef. pron. *quho* has relative functions in *quhois, the quhois* (both sometimes dissyllabic), *quhom, quham.* *34.6.* Beside the common relative *that*

appear *quhiche, the quhiche,* Northern *quhilk* 180, dissyllabic *quhilkis* pl. 62; the early Scots form *at* does not appear. *34.7 ʒoure alleris* is the old compound gen. with addition of Scots *-is; otheris, mynes* 107.5 as examples of the absolute form are somewhat more common in Northern use than Midland.

35. *Verbs.* Para. 20 should be compared. *35.1.* The infin. is normally uninflected but sometimes has metrical *-en* and *-ë. 35.2.* The Present. The Northern rule of omitting endings before and after pronouns other than *thou, he/sche* but keeping them when at a remove from the pronoun or after other words, e.g. noun or relative, is observed in the first case and with some exceptions (for convenience of metre or rhyme) in the second. A Midland inflection, however, is often substituted for invariable Scots *-is, -s.* Examples are—(i) *I lufe* 139, *thou gynnis* 57, *he quitis* 6, *we thank* 196, *ʒe knaw* 101, *think thay* 115; (ii) *ʒe aught and mosten* 120, *mony . . . That feynis . . . And setten* 134, *mony . . . Quhich thinkis* 183, *flouris springis* 119, *effectis . . . Has* 107, *effectis . . . is* 120, but *I clepe and call* (:*all*) 19, *We proyne and play* 64. For the Northern pl. *has* see also 186, 188 (where *goddis* is the real subject). The Northern habit may also explain *I a man and lakkith* 27, *I wepe and stynten* 117, where *-th* and *-en* have no precedent in this position in the scribe's other work and are probably the poet's mistaken equivalents for correct Scots *-is* (compare similar procedures in the pl. below). The 2nd sing. has always *-is, -s* as in the North, e.g. *has* 54, 169, *seis* 83, 88 (dissyllabic), *wantis* 15, 169, etc., exceptions being confined to the contracted forms in *-ow* (see para. 34.2 and section 7 below; Selden is among the few Chaucer MSS. to have these forms). In the 3rd sing. both Northern *-is, -s*—certified by metre in *lufis* 44, *thinkis* 183 and by rhyme in *quitis* (:*appetitis*), *bydis* (:*bridis*) 65—and Midland *-th* are used; the contractions *stant* 15, 167, *abit* 163, *sitt* 196 are Chaucerian. The plural without inflection prevails but *-is* and *-en* are also used. As a pl. ending *-th* in *doith* 96, *dooth* 96, 116, *Styntith . . . murnyth* 118, *hath* 191, is unexampled in the scribe's copying outside the *Quair* and should therefore be presumed the author's false substitute for Northern *-s, -is,* according to the rule explained above; he would find only very rare cases of *-th* in his known English models, certainly too few to influence him, and the Southern dialect does not, as James does, have *doth* for sing. as well as pl. For common Midland *han* there is always *haue. 35.3* The imperat. pl., as commonly in Scots alongside

the special form in -*is*, is the same as the uninflected sing., e.g. *gye* and *conuoye* 19, *sing* and *Thank* 34; *Worschippe* 34 like *Worschip* 123 (also pl.) has stress on the first syll. and need not be trisyllabic. At 102 *schapith* for the imperat. sing. is a rare but known usage. Chaucer has it for formal effect (Craigie cites *The Nonne Preestes Tale* 435) and Douglas uses pl. -*is* in his addresses to a goddess. *35.4.* The pres. part. has Midland -*ing* except for *Vnknawin* 45 with Scots loss of *g*, *byndand* 101 and *Afferand* 145, both most likely original (see notes), *lyvand* 197. *35.5* The regular Weak preterit as in Northern English has one form in all numbers and persons, without inflectional -*e*(*n*) or -*st* 2 sing., and in *Strong Verbs* the preterit has the same vowel in pl. as sing. Apart from *rynsid* and *heved* 1, *plaid:arraid* 35, the Weak Verbs end in -*it*(-*yt*), with frequent loss of the vowel. Typical Northern preterits are *begouth* (:*couth*) 16, *drewe* sing. 42, *flawe* sing. 61, *sawe* (:*drawe*) 82 sing. and pl. but once replaced in rhyme by *sye* 159, *faucht* pl. 85, *Lap* pl. 153, *maid* sing. and pl., *sat* pl. 163, 197 *35.6.* The past part. in Weak Verbs does not differ from the pret. (*Enbroudin* 152 is in the Scots poem *King Hart* and is from the Strong part. -*brogden*); -*ed* shows only in *Ensured* 9, *Despeired* 30, *Depeynted* 43, *Maked* 110. In Strong Verbs the long form prevails as in the North, though both are used, *cum* 192, *cummyn* 40, *tak* 193, *takin* 24, etc.; *dryve* (*dryven*) 92, *bore* (*boren*) 181 are Midland rhymes borrowed by other Scots poets, e.g. Douglas. Scots shortened participles from the infinitive occur: *forget* 120, *fricht* (*fyrhtan*) 162, *present* 179, *commyt* 196. The ending direct from the Latin participle is more affected by Scots than English writers, though common to them: *consecrat* 33, *vnquestionate* 125, *laureate:ornate* 197; in *infortunate* 24, *astonate* 98, 162 it is unstressed or lightly stressed and probably disguises -*it*. The Chaucerian prefix *y*- is sometimes conveniently adopted. *35.7.* Preterit-present and irregular verbs. The former have Northern uninflected forms for the sing. and pl., notably in the 2nd sing.: *sall* 128, *suld* 59; *may* 114, *myght* 14; *durst* pret. 128, *most* pret. 15 (but see *mosten* 2 pl. under 35.2); *wate* 129, *wist* 14. Exceptions are before the pronoun: *maist thou* 57, 120, and the contractions noted in para. 34.2. The auxiliary preterits *can* 4, frequent *gan*, are preferred to Midland *con*; *will* (never Midland *wol*) is uniform in the Northern way for the present, *wald/wold* for the preterit. Like other Scots poets the author uses Midland *done* 69, *doon* 97 for the infinitive along with normal *do*; *dois* 166 is the Northern 2nd sing. but for the 3rd sing. there is Midland *dooth* 12, 44. On the special use of *dooth* for the pl. see 35.2 above. Midland *gone* occurs for the infin., pres. pl. (but *go* after the pronoun, e.g. *ʒe go* 63) and past participle. The verb 'to be' 3 plur. is *ar* mainly but also *ben* and once peculiarly Northern *is* 120; the pret. pl. is usually *were*, less frequent in Northern texts than *war*, once as a metrical expletive *weren* 24, and Northern *was* 45, 50, 121. The Midland use of negative contractions appears: *nas* (*ne was*) 75, *nyl* (*ne will*) 142, *Nald* (*ne wald*) 140.

36. *Adverbs.* Some are formed in the Chaucerian way by sounding the final *e* of adjectives; *twise* 25 is probably Scots *twis* with added *ë* and not concealed Midland *twies*. For metrical insertion and more frequent omission of *ë* in trisyllabic adverbs see para. 20; *hennsfurth* MS 69, 144, 181 is given in the text the medial *ë* which it mostly has in both Scots and English despite the spelling. Beside usual *nought* (see para. 4.2) occur Midland negative forms, e.g. *Ne myght I nat* 10. On prepositions and conjunctions see 'Vocabulary' (6).

Vocabulary

The following are the characteristically or mainly Northern words and forms that are used in the *Quair*. (1) Nouns: *werdes* 9, *sanct(is)* 23, 191, *falowe* (*fēlagi*) 23, *wandis* 31, *beugh* 35, *bewis* 32, 191, *eyne* 35, 89, *lowe* (ON *logi*) 48, dissyllabic *remede* 69, 138, *busk* (ON *buskr*) 135, *foynʒee* 157, *glewis* (for *glees*) 160, *calk* 177 (but *chalk-* 157), *remyt* 195. (2) Adjectives: *poleyt* 4, *wilsum* 19; all but regular *mony*, *ony*, regular *sum* pl.; the several forms with *seker-* (*sicor*) 6, 15, etc.; *ʒalow* 95, *riall* 125, 157, *brukill-* (for *brotel-*) 134, 194; *fery* (ON *fóerig*) 156, *vgli* 162. (3) Pronouns: *tham, thair, thir, quhilk(is), ʒoure alleris* gen. pl. 113. (4) Verbs: regular *sall, suld* (both merely sporadic in the scribe's other work); *cleuer-* (ON *klifra*) 9, 159, *rele* (*hrēol*) 9, 165, *begouth* pret. (:*couth*) 16; *regne* (ON *hringja*) pronounced 'ring' (*benigne:digne*) for which see paras. 13, 25; *sen*, 'would that', 'grant' (*sendan*) 57; with one exception regular *sawe* pret. sing. and pl., *flawe* pret. sing. (*flæh*) 61, *pleye*, 'plead' (OF *plai*) 86; *hyng(en)* pres. pl. (ON *hengja*) 88, 89 (:*repenting*) with *hang* pret. pl. 81 (see para. 2.2); *traist* (ON *treysta*) 130 but with *trust* (*trystan*); *haue* pl. regularly preferred to Midland *han, junyt* past part. (:*fortunyt*) 133, *Afferand* (OF *afferir*) 145, *repellyng* vbl. sb. 145, *Lap* pret. pl. (ON *hlaupa*) 153, *fricht* past part. (*fyrhtan*) 162, *hailsing* pres. part. (*halsian*, ON *heilsa*) 166, *defade* 170, *call*, 'drive' (ON *kalla*) 172, *blissit* past part. (from *bliss* sb.) 189, *commyt* past part. 196, *present* past part. 199. (5) Adverbs: *seildin* (for *seldom*) 9, *quhare* usually preferred to *quhere*, *toforowe* (*-forwith*) 23, 48, 105; *airly* (*ar-*) 23, 29, *eneuch* 47, *furth* (*forð*), 'onward', 'out', 67, 191 etc., *halflyng* 49, *this* (for *thus*) 65; *amang* with the sense 'at times' 33, 66, 81; *ʒa* (*geā*) 68, *ylike* 70, 154, dissyllabic *endlang* adv. and prep. 81, 152, 167, *maist* 182, *syne* (*siððan*) 192, 196. (6) Prepositions and conjunctions: *but* (*būtan*) prep. 8 distinguished from *bot* conj.; *atoure* 81, *furth* prep. 'out (of)' 75, 158, *nouthir* 139; regular *sen* (*siððan*) for Midland *sith*, *gif* for *ʒif*; *als . . . as* regularly, 109 129, 151, 174, 182. Scots *till* is not used.

The Midland words and forms can be more briefly listed. (1) Nouns: *eyën* (see above), *brid*(*is*) 65, 135 but more often *bird*(*is*), *fone* 71. (2) Adjectives: *euery* 9 etc. (for *euerilk*), *thrid* 95, *streighte* 112 (but see para. 4). (3) Pronouns: *eche* pron. and adj., *euirich* 27, *euerichone* 64, *quhiche*, *the quhiche*. (4) Verbs: *trust*(*en*) 130, 137 (but see above); *besech*(*ing*) 113, 184 but *beseke* 114; *sprad* pret. pl. (*:glad*) 121 (see para. 8), *sye* pret. sing. 159, *clothit* past part. (*clāþian*) 96 for Northern *clethit* (*clǣþan*); the Strong participles without *-n*, *dryve* (*:gyve*) 92, *bore* (*:lore*) 181; *ben* pres. pl. but with more frequent *ar*; for *done*, *gone* and prevailing but irregular *were*, see para. 35.7; contracted forms in *-ow* such as *artow* etc. (see para. 34.2), the negative forms *nas* 75, *nyl* 142, *Nald* 140. (5) Adverbs: regular *suich*, *mich*, *moch*; *bet* 101 for *better* 50, 120, *wers* 95 for more usual Northern *war*; negative *ne*, *nat* occasionally.

DATE AND AUTHORSHIP

Language—Sources—History—Tradition

These topics are naturally discussed together. If King James can be shown to be the author, the content of his poem, which is a review of 'how I gat recure/ Off my distresse and all myn auenture' (st. 10), will give a date of composition between the marriage of February 1424, or more probably the return to Scotland in April of the same year, and his death at Perth in February 1437. If he is demonstrably not the author, we must imagine a contemporary poet doing his king the service of writing his autobiography or a later poet, who knew the horrific manner of his end and yet chose to write as if the events leading to the marriage and return were 'all myn auenture'. To the present writer both alternatives are incredible, yet the second at least has been seriously argued, particularly by J. T. T. Brown, and has found acceptance by scholars such as A. Lawson and J. M. Mackenzie. Other critics have retreated to a neutral view-point, neither for James nor for his enemies.

Plainly the sceptics' case will have to be answered and necessarily in some detail; linguistic, literary and historical kinds of evidence will have to be examined for their testimony concerning date and author.

Because of its mixed character the poet's language gives less indication of date than might be expected. Phenomena that would normally suggest a particular period of fifteenth-century Scots writing may alternatively be given an English explanation. Thus strong southern influence in a more decidedly Scots composition would be proof of lateness but not so where such English elements are more or less integral in the author's speech. The facts that $\bar{a}$ does not rhyme on *ai/ei*, that rhymes of *-as*, *-es* do not occur, and *i* as a mark of vowel-length is only notable in the forms *maid*, *ourehayle*, which are frequent with the scribe elsewhere—the rhyme-spellings *maid: glade: schade* 62 should be noted—cannot be adduced as marks of early work, since the poet's familiarity with, and frequent use of, Midland open $\bar{o}$ would naturally make him avoid such practices. Similarly the reluctance to rhyme *eu*, *ew* from OE $\bar{o}g$, $\bar{o}h$ with the same diphthong from $\bar{e}ow$ or French final *u* could be referred to early Scots procedure only if we were sure that he did not follow English usage in this respect. Again, with one exception, $\bar{e}ʒ$ is represented by Midland $\bar{\iota}$ and not Scots close $\bar{e}$, so that no deduction from the absence of rhymes with simple $\bar{e}$ from other sources is possible. The failure of the late Scots rhyming of *-y* with $\bar{e}$ (occasional in Hary, Dunbar, Douglas and a sign of the development of $\bar{e}$ to $\bar{\iota}$) could also have an English explanation. And the agreement of the single case of coincidence of $\ddot{u}$ with $\bar{u}$ (see para. 17) with the comparative rarity of such rhymes in early fifteenth-century Scots verse may be equally accounted for by Midland influence. A more suggestive feature is the poet's sounding or unsounding of the vowel for purely metrical reasons in inflectional *-es/-is* and *-it/-yt*, since this reflects a departure from English models; here it may be significant that he follows the more sober use of this freedom by the earlier Scots poets.

Southern influence is joined with the further complication of possible and probable scribal changes when considering the significance of spelling features. Little weight, therefore, can be given to the sporadic appearance of certain late Scots forms—the single case of loss of final *d* after *n*, *sen* 57; *nʒ* for liquid French *n* in *foynʒee* (OF *foine*, where it oddly intrudes) 157; *l* as a sign of length in preceding *a* in MS *walking* (*wācian*) 173; intrusive *t*, *g*, in *thought* conj. 5, *witht* 178, *coutht* 196, *gardyng* sb. 33, *fallyng* 45. It must be thought likely, however, that a Scots poet of the later period, naturally acquainted with native as well as foreign writing, would have introduced more such spellings, particularly that he would have occasionally written the almost regular late Scots *ocht*—that he consistently writes *ought* may be simply his English habit but in respect of *ou* also conforms with early Scots usage (see 'Language' para. 4). A further point is that the regular, as distinct from the occasional or even prevailing preference of *u* to *ui* as a spelling for the characteristically Scots sound *ü*, developed from close *ō* (see para. 16), belongs to the first half of the century.

English influence forbids any deductions from word-forms that would elsewhere be significant according to their frequency. *Rynsid* 1 is an early Northern spelling of the preterit, but the scribe and the fact of exceptional recurrences of *-id* throughout the century have to be remembered. In the *Quair quhilk*(*is*) 62, 180 (dissyllabic here) is the only distinctively Scots form of the relative, *that* and less frequent *quhiche* being normal. Usually absence of *the quhilk*(*is*) should indicate a date not much earlier than mid-century (see R. Girvan, p. liv) but in the present text, as in *Lancelot of the Laik*, it may well have an English substitute in *the quhiche* 120, 181. The Scots form *at* is increasingly rare as the century advances, being easily replaced by *that*; thus it is completely absent from the Hay MSS. and Girvan's explanation of its absence from *The Buik of Alexander* 1438, also by Hay, as due to interference by the printers is needless. Its failure to appear in the *Quair* may therefore have no significance. Frequent use of *ane* for *a* as the indef. art. before consonants other than *h* would be a late sign, but this occurs only thrice and may be scribal. *Quho* (*Quha*) appears in a relative function towards the close of the fifteenth century both in English and Scots and is absent as such from the *Quair*. Extended uses of the auxiliary *do* such as *has done rune*, 'has whispered', '*doing spring*', 'springing', are characteristic of later Scots and are not found.

Vocabulary in a courtly poem should yield a general indication of date in respect of the smaller proportion of Latinate words that an early work would show, and particularly the lesser endeavour to flourish such words in rhyme. This is indeed what the poem shows. Although *OED* assigns a surprising number of so-called first appearances to the *Quair*, the words that convey an 'aureate' effect are few— *poleyt* 4, *indegest* 14, *consecrat* 33, *stellifyit* 52, *facture* 66, *Signifere* 76, *plumyt* 94, *aduertence* 108, *vnquestionate* 125, *consequent* sb. 189, *marciall* 191. Of these perhaps only *marciall*, 'pertaining to March', and not as in 'martial deeds', would have struck the educated reader as being particularly *recherché* and literary. Certainly we do not see the verbal display-cabinet of Lydgate and the Scots rhetoricians.

One can only conclude that the author's Scots habits, though qualified and compromised by English ones, are such as best agree with a writer in the earlier half of the century. Later, with the same proportion of native and foreign elements in his language, the characteristic sounds, forms and vocabulary of the Scots literary community must have betrayed themselves more decidedly.

A comparison has been attempted, where a contrast would have been more instructive, of *The Kingis Quair* with those late compositions, *Lancelot of the Laik* and *The Quare of Jelusy*, because of the extraordinary efforts of the author of these two works to give an English appearance to his writing. It is, however, only an appearance, a matter of spellings rather than sounds, the concealment of Scots usages by similar English ones, rather than the adoption, however irregular, as in the *Quair*, of values that produce rhymes only possible in Midland speech and forms that have no Scots equivalents. Freakish forms that the author of the *Quair* would never have perpetrated flourish, and they are not to be charged to scribes, either English or Scottish. It may be that the writer had some experience of English speech, as he certainly had of English writing; he can hardly have studied either carefully. Perhaps his literary dialect was a unique response to the arrival of an English queen. Here he must be noticed mainly because he gave G. T. T. Brown the notion of a late fifteenth-century school of anglicizing poets, though no other Scots member of this school can be found, and Lawson the equally fantastic idea of a single author (not James, of course) for all three poems. Mackenzie does not reject the latter theory and agrees that all have 'like characteristics of language' and an equally 'artificial dialect'. The latter phrase he borrows from Skeat, who did not believe in a common authorship but unintentionally encouraged such opinions by limiting his treatment to formal aspects. Simon, who gives a more thorough discussion of the *Quair* but within the same general limits, does not mention the poems that were first invoked to support the theory and offers no conclusion upon the topics that concern us here. It is time that *Lancelot* and *The Quare of Jelusy* were considered historically, brief as such a discussion must be in this place.

All the sound-changes characteristic of the fully developed Middle Scots system are freely evidenced in the poet's rhyming habits and not only those noticed in my analysis of *The Kingis Quair*. Northern $\bar{a}$ can be proved outside of the special groups to which it is consistently confined in the *Quair*—*Infortunate*: *wate* L 1012–13, *ta*: *Prosperpina* Q 73–4. There is a striking contrast with the practice of the *Quair* in the fact that in the whole extent of the two poems Midland open $\bar{o}$ can only be proved in about a dozen cases, e.g. *before*: *sore* L 1116, *tofore*: *mor* Q 31, etc., the *o*- spelling being otherwise merely an orthographical substitution, e.g. *know* (*cnāwan*): *low* sb. (*lagu*) L 1640, *lowe* sb.: *unknowe* Q 63. Proofs of the Northern coalescence of $\bar{a}$ and *ai/ei* are frequent but in the *Quair* are only represented by internal spellings: *bare* pret.: *disspar* vb. L 890, *hate* sb. (hatian): *consate* (OF *conceite*) Q 151. The further development of $\bar{a}$ towards an open $\bar{e}$ sound, which is only common in rhyme after the first half of the fifteenth century, and in that use at least is absent from the *Quair*, is plain: *has*: *besynes* L 3131, *vas* in rhyme with both *cussynece* L 2799 and *Ras* sb. (ON *rās*) L 3086, *manhed*: *raid* pret. 3167 L, *care* (*caru*): *lufare* Q 316, *lufare*: *contrare*: *nevermare*: *dedliare* Q 500–4. Guttural *eʒ* develops *ī*- as well as the more usual $\bar{e}$-sounds in Scots, the former by the influence of forms with -*gh* such as *high*, *nigh*, hence *hee* (*hēah*): *cry* vb. L 13, *sobirly*: *ny* (*nēah*) Q 47 (see 'Language' para. 14); but a more general change of *ẹ* to *ī*, which is only apparent with any frequency in late Middle Scots texts, is also involved and is evidenced in *hee* pron.: *Ee* (*ēage*) L 3137 alongside *eye* (*ēage*): *thareby* Q 534, *denyed* past part. (*dénier*): *ded* (*dēad*) L 216 alongside *misgyit* (-*guier*): *denyit* L 1662. In the *Quair* there is no proof of the change *ẹ* to *ī*—apart from that of *ẹʒ* to *ī*, which can be referred to Midland usage, though Scots influence may be present (Scots close $\bar{e}$ is indicated only in *deye*, st. 86; see 'Language' paras. 11, 14). The Scots changes, $\bar{o}$ to $\ddot{u}$, $\bar{o}g/\bar{o}h$ to *eu/ew* (see para. 16) are present in the *Quair* but only evidenced in rhyme in the first case, whereas *Lancelot* illustrates both: *bure* (*bōr*): *discomfitoure* L 1576, *destitude* adj.: *gud* (*gōd*) Q 523; *hewis* (*hēow*): *bewis* (*bōgas*) L 337, *persew* (*pursuer*): *slew* pret. sing. (*slōh*) L 279. Rhymes of *eu* from OE *ōg*, *ōh* with the same diphthong from other sources are naturally very intermittent and it is not surprising that they do not occur in the much shorter *Kingis Quair* and *Quare of Jelusy*.

Vocalization of *l*, which in verse first shows in Hary's *Wallace* c. 1478 and *Golagros and Gawain*, *l*. 1278, perhaps only a year or two earlier, also appears in *Lancelot* 1316–7, *vall* sb. (ON *vāgr*, 'wave'): *fall* vb. The change of final *d* to *t* in the groups *nd*, *rd* may occur in the *Quair* but is definitely illustrated once in *Lancelot*, *hart*: *bastart* 2603–4, a rhyme which also shows the coalescence of *er* with *ar*, a development in the *Quair*. Also shared with the latter poem is the Scots unvoicing of final *v* as in *The Quare of Jelusy*, *life* sb.: *dryve*: *arryve* 547–51. An important point is that if this poet sounds Chaucerian final *e*, which is not certain, it is only in adjectives and proportionately much less often than the author of the *Quair*.

It will be patent from the sound-system illustrated above that despite certain features the *Quair* cannot be the work of the author of the other poems, and that its language cannot be said to represent their late stage of development. The same conclusion is required by the different use of grammatical forms and inflections in *Lancelot* and the *Quare*. For *the quhilk* and *quhilk* is regularly substituted *the quhiche*, *quhich* and even *the quhich that*; except for this last odd construction, such substitution also occurs in the *Quair* but its plural form, *quhilkis*, with sounded -*is* (apparently an earlier practice) is absent. The few occurrences of *at* as the relative show that a later date than the one proposed by me is most unlikely but does not speak for an earlier one. The indefinite article *ane/one* occurs as in late Middle Scots before consonants as well as vowels, in contrast with the all but regular use of *a/o* before consonants in the *Quair*. In later Scots writing, as a compromise with English *sh*, the forms *schull*, *schulde* often replace *sal*, *suld*; they are regular in the two anglicizing poems, while the older spellings appear with only two exceptions, probably scribal, in the *Quair*. Notably in the latter the early Scots spelling *ou* in *ought* from OE *oht* appears in all the uncontracted forms but in *Lancelot* the later *oght*, *ocht* are regular.

Other comparatively late features not in the *Quair* are the various forms of *do* with the infinitive in a participial use—*haith done . . . expell*, 'has expelled', L 78, *hath do . . . constreyne*, 'has constrained', Q 26, etc.—and the free use of the Anglo-Scots formation *tone* as participle of *ta(k)*. Although the *Quair* has a few cases of false substitution in the present indicative, first person singular and third person plural, of -*(i)th* for correct Scots -*(i)s* (see 'Language', para 35), the other pieces use -*ith* consistently for all numbers and persons and as a spelling at least even for the endings of the preterit and past participle of the Weak verb. There is no question of scribal responsibility here. Imitation of Chaucer, beside whose work, says this writer, 'our ryming is al bot derysioune', has become a matter of undiscriminating literary archaisms. The author of the *Quair* imitates with more knowledge and at closer range.

The literary materials out of which *The Kingis Quair* is made are almost wholly provided by Chaucer, Gower and their most influential disciple, Lydgate. Similarities of conception and expression found in such works as *The Cuckoo and the Nightingale*, probably written in the first decade of the fifteenth century (see note to st. 39), *The Flower and the Leaf* and *The Assembly of Ladies*, for both of which a date somewhat after 1450 has been suggested on general grounds by D. A. Pearsall in his edition of 1962, illustrate only the period's common style of love rhetoric, though one descriptive passsage of the *Assembly* indicates a more direct relationship. With these poems the *Quair* has no substantial connection, as it certainly has with its avowed models and the unacknowledged Lydgate. It is difficult to believe that any writer not near in time to the famous three could have established his work so firmly in their tradition, with so little strangeness in the treatment. There are important differences but they are such as a truly organic development produces. The late fifteenth-century *Court of Love*, on the other hand, a poem once thought to be a main source of the *Quair* because of their common reference to *The Temple of Glas*, represents a radical break with the great tradition; the sensibility of the latter is lost in it and it makes no more than a clever use of its conventions.

Between 1424, the year of the marriage that provided the theme of the poem, and the close of the century when some lines of Robert Henryson's *Trial Of The Fox* appear to echo the *Quair* (see notes to sts. 156, 158), the only poems that suggest a textual relationship are

The Assembly Of Ladies and Lydgate's *Pilgrimage of the Life of Man*, 1426–8, a translation of the second recension of *Le Pelerinage de la Vie Humaine* by Guillaume de Guileville. In the first case it is a style of dress that is to be considered, in the second the terms in which the poet conceives his total experience.

The lady Attemperaunce in the *Assembly* is a stately personage, as befits her name, but she has the same taste for brilliant dress as the more youthful and lively heroine of the *Quair*, and her choice of adornments is sufficiently like the latter's for us to ask which is the copyist.

> And furthermore to speke of hir aray . . .
> Aftyr a sort the coler and the vent,
> Lyke as ermyn ys made in purfelyng,
> With gret perles ful fyne and oryent
> They were couched all aftyr oon worchyng . . .
> Abowte hir nekke a serpe of fayre rubies
> In white floures of right fyne enemayle;
> Upon hir hede sette in the fresshest wise
> A cercle with grete balays of entaile . . .
> It was a world to loke on hir visage (*A. L.* 519–39)

> Of hir array the form gif I sall write,
> Toward hir goldyn haire and rich atyre,
> It fret-wise couchit was with perllis quhite
> And grete balas lemyng as the fyre . . .
> And aboue all this there was, wele I wote,
> Beautee eneuch to mak a world to dote.

> About hir nek, quhite as the fyne amaille
> A gudely cheyne of smale orfeuerye,
> Quhareby there hang a ruby without faille . . .
> (*K. Q.* sts. 46–8)

Changes of fashion are not easily dated in a period when they did not make the same immediate and general impact as they do today. However, if I understand correctly the historians of such matters, the following points have to be made. The 'vent' or V-neck, mentioned in the first case and implied by the pendant ruby in the second, reflects some period before the last quarter of the century, at which time square necks came in, and the chain-necklace was most affected in the first half of the century. Outside of these passages are other such indications: decorative plumes like those worn by the king's future bride were almost solely displayed by men throughout the reign of Edward IV (W. M. Webb, *The Heritage of Dress*, 1912, p. 88); and in the second half of the century it would have been unusual for a woman of fashion to show her hair, so that we may think it significant that the king mentions the colour of his mistress's hair and the authoress of the *Assembly* in her several descriptions does not even use the word. Significant or not, the alleged facts point to Attemperaunce as the copyist.

It seems certain that the symbolism of events and description in the *Quair*, which is itself the story of a spiritual journey, is influenced by Lydgate's version of the French narrative. A guiding theme of the *Pilgrimage* is, of course, the body's obstruction of the spirit; the latter seeks its freedom and happiness in God but can only reach Him through the use of right reason and the intervention of grace. Since the two principals in the conflict are imagined to have opposite movements a favourite source of illustration in the poem is Sacrobosco's commentary on the planets, 'Ech in his mevyng circuler' (*l.* 2343). Thus the lady Grace Dieu shows to the Pilgrim the Wheel of Lust, that is, man's sensual will, and explains how it turns westwards, as does Primum Mobile, and with it an inner wheel whose movement, like the contrary orbits of the planets, is to 'the party opposyt' (*l.* 12230), the east; this different direction would be almost undiscernible but for the butterfly that flits to and fro on the second wheel, gaining only fractionally each day on the contrary course imparted by the outer wheel. This is the winged soul striving towards 'the marke that he kam fro', his 'ownë duë place,/Reste in god' (*ll.* 12408–9). The Pilgrim must remember these comparisons, says Grace Dieu (*ll.* 12327–34):

> "For thy lyff, yt is no doute,
> Is lyk a cercle that goth aboute,
> Round and swyfft as any thouhte,
> Wych in his course ne cesseth nouht,
> Yiff he go ryht and wel compace
> Till he kome to hys restyng place,
> Wych is in god, yiff he wel go,
> Hys ownë place wych he kam fro."

The Pilgrim has been frustrated of his aim 'Almost the space of thritty yer' (*l.* 12448). Repeatedly he despairs and is rescued from his despair by Grace Dieu. Once he finds the wheel of Fortune amidst the world's waves and is cast from it but is saved again by the white dove of his protectress, which brings to him 'a lytel bylle' of counsel (*l.* 19730). Each of these picturesque concepts might have been found in use elsewhere but nowhere all together or with the same simple and consistent application as they are given here. The 'hevynnis figure circulere' (as James terms it) with its opposite movements, and the parallel earthly circle of life with a similar backward and forward turn, are also essential in the vision of the *Quair*, and the likeness there in expression as well as meaning seems most easily explained by direct recourse to the *Pilgrimage*.

Like the Pilgrim the king, as history and the poem tell us, had been almost thirty years on his voyage 'Amang the wawis of this warld' before winning 'The rypënesse of resoune . . ./To gouerne with my will', st. 16, his enemies having been the same ones, Fortune and youth's 'appetitis' (st. 6) or 'lust'. Before setting him on the upward turn of her wheel Fortune compares his long repulse from his natural goal to that of a planet opposed by the westward sweep of Primum Mobile, st. 170:

> "Though thy begynnyng hath bene retrograde,
> Be froward opposyt quhirlit aspert,
> Now sall thou turne and luke vpon the dert".

Chaucer's lament for the baneful effects of retrogradation on Constance's marriage voyage is remembered here (see note to st. 170) and the king's happier fate is indicated by De Guileville's notion of a return to 'natural east'. Waking to reality from his dreams of good fortune James despairs, st. 173:

> O besy goste, ay flikering to and fro,
> That neuer art in quiet nor in rest
> Till thou cum to that place that thou cam fro,
> Quhich is thy first and verray proper nest;
> From day to day so sore here artow drest,
> That with thy flesche ay waking art in trouble,
> And sleping eke, of pyne so has thou double.

Here there is a very interesting fusion of Troilus's lament for Criseyde, 'O soule lurking in thy wo unneste' (see note to st. 173), and Lydgate's above-quoted description of the course of man's life. The epithet 'flikering' may even imply a memory of De Guileville's butterfly (the soul), as well as Chaucer's bird nesting in its grief. The application in the *Quair* is, of course, the religious one of the Frenchman; for Troilus heaven is Criseyde herself. The white dove's scroll (st. 178 and note) containing confirmation of the dream certainly derives from De Guileville's poem, almost certainly from Lydgate's version.[1]

If these Lydgatian parallels are accepted as amounting to a proof, or at least a probability of indebtedness, the *Quair* should be dated after 1426–8, and if the previous arguments pertaining to language and the other literary source are conceded to have some force, between 1428 and 1450. Of course, if King James is the author, the limits of composition are then 1428 to 1437, the year of his death, and a likely date is about 1435. It should not be surprising that so popular a work as Lydgate's *Pilgrimage* was influential in Scotland so soon after its completion; certainly the author of *Ratis Raving*, which has a number of interesting points of contact with the *Quair* and was written in the second quarter of the century, uses *ll*. 11, 181–208 of the *Pilgrimage* for his description in *ll*. 1242–8 of the sports of reasonless youth. Those who interpret the *Quair* as a romantically immediate response to courtship, rather than a mature consideration of experienced marriage and its meaning within a total review of the writer's life ('all myn auenture'), will have to reserve their objections to this dating till the interpretation of the poem's theme has been attempted elsewhere.

What has now to be debated are the historical arguments that have been brought against the authenticity of the *Quair's* narrative and its claim to be autobiography. The statements of historical fact that are made in the poem are these. The prince sailed from his native land when the sun was on its northern course in Aries and had 'passit mydday bot fourë greis evin' (st. 21), that is, had passed the equinoctial line and, more precisely, the fourth degree of the sign Aries, which should mean that he sailed on the 15th of March or the following day, since in James's time the equinox occurred on 12 March (see note to

[1] Several prose versions of the first recension of the *Pelerinage* are extant, but the longer second one is represented only by Lydgate's *Pilgrimage*. It is the second recension that describes the Wheel of Lust, the planetary motions, and has the cited comparison of these with man's journey of life.

sts. 20–1). He was then 'nought ferre passit the state of innocence,/ Bot nere about the nowmer of ȝeris thre' (st. 22 and note), and was thus three years or so past the seven-years stage of infancy, as it was then legally reckoned. His capture took place at sea, 'Vpon the wawis weltering to and fro' (st. 24). He was 'In strayte ward and in strong prisoune . . . Nere by the space of ȝeris twisë nyne' (st. 25). At the time when he learned that he was to have both his future bride and freedom it was 'Ane houre and more . . ouer prime' so that 'the half' of his day of life was 'nere away' (st. 171 and note); more exactly it was something more than an hour past 9 a.m. in that twelve-hour day of life, which was then equated with the seventy years of the Psalmist, and he was therefore not quite thirty years old. When he wrote his verse-narrative he was no longer a youth and had attained to 'The rypënesse of resoune' (st. 16), a state that was then supposed only to be reached with one's thirtieth year. The time of year in which the king is said to tell his story is winter (st. 17) and from the mention of Aquarius apparently between 11 January and 10 February, by the reckoning of that day (see st. 1 and note).

Our examination begins conveniently with the representation of the king's age at the time of writing, since that factor must qualify any expectations of accuracy in his memories. James was born in the summer of 1394 and completed his thirtieth year some months after his marriage in February 1424, a figure which agrees with the indicated age of the writer. Furthermore, the stated time of composition (if not merely conventional[1]) makes the year 1423, proposed by Skeat, unacceptable, since 'The newis glad that blisfull bene and sure' (st. 179) of the arranged marriage and liberation were only received in the last month of that year, when the treaty was signed. Equally, if it is a married man who reviews his career, as the total attitude and particular phrases make evident, January or February of 1425 would be the earliest possible dating. In fact, it is plain that the author writes as one who looks back to the occasion of his marriage from a distance of years.[2]

---

[1] In its context 'the wynter nyght' of st. 17 impresses as factual statement.

[2] James's review of 'all myn auenture' 10 includes Minerva's discourse on marriage as the goal of love 129–44; the dove 177–9 announces it; in 179 it is 'decretit' by heaven and the final thanksgiving to heaven is for the decree's fulfilment; it is referred to as 'full plesance' in 185, is the joyous state that only death can end in 188, and as an event of some years past is indicated by the 'long and trew contynuance' of 192 and the 'blisfull auenture/In ȝouth, of lufe' of 193.

History and the statements of the poem thus agree in presenting the royal author at an age when the correct placing of childhood events is not to be expected. What is surprising is the relative correctness with which they are given, superior at certain points to that of the chroniclers from whom the sceptical Brown wilfully supposed the writer to derive his information.

Andrew Wyntoun's sole error in narrating the sailing and capture of the young prince is the day and month to which he assigns the latter event, 4 April (ix, ch. 21). In Walter Bower's *Scotichronicon* (1447) the day preferred is 30 March. We know now that the ship which carried James was taken by merchant-pirates of Great Yarmouth and Cley in Norfolk on the 22nd of March (E. W. M. Balfour-Melville, *James I, King of Scots 1406–1437*, 1936, p. 31). The author of the *Quair* achieves the best approximation to the above, and the date intended by him, as we shall see, may even be the same. He is very positive that the month was March, referring to it several times (see notes to stanzas 20–1, 170, 178, 194). That there is still a discrepancy of almost a week, between the time that his astronomical reference specifies for the departure and the known time of capture, troubles us only because of the mode of dating, which suggests a precision that may not really be intended. It is possible that the four degrees were introduced only as a poetical way of explaining why on that March day the sun was particularly bright; for in Chaucer's *Squieres Tale*, ll. 385–6, the brightness of the princess Canacee is compared to that of the morning sun, 'That in the Ram is four degrees upronne'. And if we do not include the four degrees, equivalent to four days, in our calculation, it becomes notable that according to the Church's calendar, which the writer is most likely to have had in mind, the spring equinox always fell on the 21st, the historically correct day of the ship's sailing.

Much has been made of the boy's age being represented as somewhere 'nere about' three years past 'the state of innocence', when it was in fact somewhere 'nere about' four, his birth-year being 1394, probably in July. Had the chronicle-inspired poet of Brown's imagining consulted Wyntoun, collating the scattered year-dates of the latter more carefully and correctly than Brown chose to do, he would of course have got it right (ix, chs. 13, 22, 23), and not wrong as Brown states; just as, if he had consulted Bower, the preferred authority for all writers after 1447 since he made his mistakes in Latin, he would have been out by three years. Whatever the source of information it was not the histories. The error, if such an approximate statement can be charged with error, would be quite natural to the king at his distance of time from the voyage—one may recall the time of year and sometimes even the day of an important happening, if there is special reason to do so, and be mistaken in the less significant or less easily visualized year—and the common vagueness and generality of medieval reckonings of age must be borne in mind. Of course, a question in the right quarters would have got the right answer, but there was no special reason for getting the age just right; it may have seemed more vital at that point to give a figure that let him introduce in his rhyme such significant words as 'casualtee', 'contree'.

A mistake that the poet avoids and Hector Boece does not is the report that James was taken during a landing on the English coast (*Scotorum Historia*, Paris, 1526, lib. XVI). The period of captivity, which Wyntoun naturally does not give, is correctly stated.

From the above examination the simple conclusion results that if the poet had followed the chroniclers in their statements (as did their successor, John Mair, in 1518) there would have been certainty that he was *not* King James. That he differs from Wyntoun correctly in one case and at least understandably in another does not prove that he was the king, but does agree with that opinion. The further objections, that the marriage was a political arrangement and (by an unwarrantable implication) nothing more, and that the king was not always the prisoner of the poem, can impress only the simple-minded and need no discussion here.

What does deserve notice is the assertion of Brown and Craigie that after eighteen years in England the Scottish king could not have spoken or written Scots. For Brown this was an argument against his authorship, since he found little English speech in the poem—in one place, p. 30, he remarks on the cautious avoidance of English rhymes by the *Quair*'s author! For Craigie it was an argument in James's favour that he found only two characteristic Scots rhymes, and nothing Scottish elsewhere that could not be explained by the hypothesis of scribal re-writing. The falsity of both findings about the language has been fully demonstrated. Here I am only concerned to notice what history tells us of James's use, and opportunities for use, of the Scots dialect before the period to which I have assigned the poem.

Its date is an important consideration. If he wrote about 1435, as I have maintained, he would then have been busy for a decade with Scotsmen and Scots affairs, and if at the time of his return he had to a considerable extent abandoned Scots habits of speech, he would naturally have resumed them to some degree. A mixture of dialects such as this account of his experience suggests is actually what the *Quair* displays. The resumption of Scots ways would, of course, be facilitated by previous use and the occasion given for it by the company of Scots speakers.

It is one of the pleasanter moral myths of that inspired chronicler, Walter Bower, aimed at the king's successors, that James received a prodigious education in England. In poverty and exile, which last is itself a first step to knowledge, says Bower,[1] he found an opportunity to satisfy his love of learning, so that he was instructed by a succession of brilliant scholars and duly became the philosopher-king of his nation (*Scotichronicon*, lib. XVI, cap. xxx). In later times, more friendly to England, the story was given an unintended turn to the credit of James's captor, Henry IV, who now figured as his paternally solicitous educator. The tradition persists in Balfour-Melville's history, and editors of the *Quair* have imagined James's speech as well as his ignorance being corrected.[2] English sources, however, are silent about this enlightened treatment of the captive. What is really known of the young king's residences and circumstances in the early years of his exile can be stated very briefly.

Immediately after his capture he was placed in the Tower of London, moved thence in June 1407 with his fellow prisoner, Griffith of Wales, to Nottingham castle, which he left about July 1409. If he was about the court in the next two years the records do not show it and he may equally have been in Pevensey castle (the only prison mentioned by Bower) or have followed Griffith to the Tower in the last mentioned year. In 1412 he appears at the side of King Henry on two occasions when Scots business had to be transacted, in January at Stratford Abbey in Essex and in November at Croydon. He was in the Tower again in

[1] This remark has Boethius and almost certainly James's Boethian poem in view.

[2] Norton-Smith, p. xxi, extends Bower's moral tale: 'Henry saw to it that James was given a good education, possibly at the hands of the royal tutors . . .', and speculates, p. xxix, on 'the effect of an exclusively English court education of some seventeen years on James's pronunciation'.'

March 1413, brought to Windsor during August and September because of a recurrence of the plague which had earlier been the cause of his removal to Nottingham, then returned to the Tower. He was in Pevensey castle from February 1415, and for the whole of 1416 once more in the Tower. What living conditions could be like there is glimpsed in the complaint made in 1414 by his cousin and companion in prison, Murdoch Stewart, the son of the Governor of Scotland, that the mattress and blankets issued to him ten years before were now rotten and tattered, and the sheets had not been changed these two years (Balfour-Melville, p. 60). Whatever these scraps of knowledge indicate, it is not a liberal concern for James's welfare. That the boy was visited for a few years by English tutors—his own tutor and some other unfortunate Scots scholar may equally have been employed—is not unlikely, but without the later support of regular courtly example and company their anglicizing influence must have been limited, especially if there was regular or even frequent Scots companionship to counteract it, as indeed there was.

From the scattered indications can be pieced together a clear enough picture of the captive in more or less continuous contact with his countrymen. The Earl of Orkney, who was originally in charge of James, and Sir Archibald Edmonstone contrived to ransom themselves within a few years, but Murdoch Stewart was his fellow-prisoner throughout the period noticed above, and William Giffart, marshal of his mother's household, remained with him for seven years and more. There were doubtless other Scots prisoners and hostages there, who had sailed with James, or come south after the disastrous defeat at Homildon Hill less than four years before the king's capture. Most important, however, a small retinue of Scots, that Giffart must have directed for a time, was always with the king. When Henry V, the day after his accession on 13 March 1413, sent James, Murdoch, Giffart and William Douglas of Dalkeith to the Tower, they were joined there for a period by twenty-five Scots, some of whom are known to have been his regular retainers. Names that recur in his service at different times are those of his secretary John Lyon, his chaplains Dougal Drummond and Thomas Myrton (later his Treasurer), Alexander Fullarton, styling himself keeper of the privy seal (in a petition to the pope that mentions the king's inability to pay his servants), Michael Ouchtre an ecclesiastical 'familiar', and John of

Alway his squire. Of course there was a succession of noble Scots
visitors. Though his relations with the English court seem to have
become closer after 1420 (when Henry haled him off to France to
disturb the French loyalties of his Scots subjects, quite ineffectually),
so that we find him on display at a few state functions, for the greater
part of his exile his Scots household ('My folk' as he calls them in the
Quair, st. 27) must have provided his most regular company. Contrary
to the assumptions of Brown and Craigie, therefore, there was little
likelihood of the poet-king forgetting his own speech in the process of
partially learning another.

We have one letter out of 'Egypt' (Bower's colourful name for his
Joseph's land of bondage) that purports to be written with his 'propre
hand'; it is a charter dated at Croydon 30 November 1412, confirming
certain lands to Sir William Douglas of Drumlanrig and, surprisingly,
it is in the vernacular. William Fraser prints it in facsimile in his
Scotts of Buccleuch (vol. 2, 1878, between pp. 22, 23). J. M. Thomson,
author of *Public Records of Scotland*, 1922, and James's biographer,
Balfour-Melville, find nothing suspicious in its occasion, contents or
style, but J. T. T. Brown does (pp. 24-7). He suggests that it is a
Douglas forgery—a theory which should mean that the forger ex-
pected the king to write good Scots but not good Latin,[1] the usual
language of such charters—and makes a number of objections that
would only have force if it were what it does not claim to be, the usual
form of confirmatory charter passed by the Great Seal. On the con-
trary, it is issued under the king's private signet, to be 'selit with oure
grete sele in tyme to come', and by implication to be then published
in Latin and duly attested. Brown is also wrong in believing this to be
the only sovereign act of the king in exile in this kind and form
(Balfour-Melville, p. 51). More important for the present discussion, he
is almost certainly wrong in his other suggestion that it is a copy of a
secretary's draft which would reveal only the secretary's writing
habits.

The handwriting (which is certainly not that of his current secretary,
John Lyon) is neat, even artistic, beyond the ordinary appearance of
such productions, but the writer, more intent perhaps on his calli-
graphy than his spelling, has perpetrated some odd slips that no

[1] We have indeed no evidence, even Bower does not make the claim, that the
king understood Latin.

secretary or professional scribe would have let stand. Contractions
are not indicated in several places; there are the uncorrected forms
possiouns (*possessiouns*), *chanusselar* which may betray hesitation between
Scots *an* and Midland *aun*, the inexplicable *fonorne* (not *fourme* as
Brown and others read it) which represents *form* and may have got
muddled in the laborious writer's mind with *suorne*, *unde* without final
r. One notes Midland *wh* twice in *whilkis*. All this might be expected
from James writing with his 'propre hand' but certainly not from a
competent Scots scribe. Had the secretary whose draft the king is
supposed to be copying been available, the charter would certainly
have been in Latin. Also, the few simple phrases of conveyancing that
are used would not have been unfamiliar to him, even at the age of
eighteen. There were, after all, others to consult. That the letter is
consistently Scottish, except for the above-quoted spelling, and
therein unlike the *Quair*, could merely reflect the difference between
six and eighteen years of English residence.

One must conclude that in view of these factors—the Scots company
that he kept throughout his experience of England, the enforced limits
of that experience, the evidence of the charter of 1412, the years in
Scotland that preceded the *Quair*—it is by no means unlikely that
James should have spoken and written the mixed speech of the
poem.

Granted that there are no valid historical objections to James putting
in a claim for the authorship of his autobiography, what specific
authority have we for considering him as a poet and the poet of the
Quair? There is firstly the writer's own representation of the king as
the poet of other work than the *Quair* (st. 13)—'And in my tyme more
Ink and paper spent/ To lyte effect'—who now undertakes a 'newe
thing'. Presumably the sceptics have noted this testimony and seen it
as a clever fiction to support the anonymous author's larger fiction of
James's authorship. But there is other testimony.

Ten years after the king's death Walter Bower, who had been much
involved in government business, penned a lengthy panegyric. James,
says Bower, was naturally active in mind and body, delighted to
learn from books, particularly books of moral philosophy, to practise
the crafts of workmen and the skills of athletes. More to our purpose,
he played many musical instruments, ranging from the harp and
church-organ (which he himself introduced into Scotland) to the

45

popular flute, and he composed music, talents that surely imply song-writing. Also he found time for literary labours (*operi artis literatoriæ et scripturæ*; *Scotichronicon*, lib. XVI, cap. xxx). We learn then from a contemporary that King James was a poet, and could be a serious-minded one, but we do not learn what poems he wrote. The reason may be the political moralist's eagerness to present a learned king, the glory of Scotland and a model to his successors; he may have thought that vernacular titles would spoil that impression. The two impromptu Latin verses that Bower quotes are almost certainly the chronicler's version of the king's Scots.

Another and later witness is Sir David Lindsay; in his *Testament and Complaynt Of The Papyngo*, after echoing st. 9, *l.* 5 of the *Quair* in a comment on the power of Fortune, 'And spairis nocht the prince more than the paige' (*l.* 411), he praises James as the 'flude of eloquence' (*l.* 432). That Dunbar in his *Lament for the Makaris*, listing the Scots poets, makes no mention of him might be variously explained; it may simply illustrate the fact that kings are most naturally remembered as kings, or be due to a feeling that too much would have to be said if he were cited at all. To this general evidence must be added the three moral stanzas in rhyme royal, of which the first line is 'Sen trew Vertew encressis dignytee', published by Skeat. The earliest version is in a manuscript of the last quarter of the fifteenth century but the first ascription is in *The Gude and Godlie Ballates* 1578. Subject-matter and language at least offer no objections.

Apart from the manuscript, whose testimony has yet to be con-sidered, the earliest and most important authority for attributing the *Quair* to the king is that of John Mair, writing in 1518 (*Historia Maioris Britanniæ Tam Angliæ Quam Scotiæ*, Paris 1521, lib. VI, cap. xiv). Mair was much interested in vernacular poetry and his other references are correct, for example his notice of Hary's *Wallace* (see my edition for the Scottish Text Society). His information comes in naturally as a gloss on Bower's account and appears to reflect his own reading as well as common knowledge. It may be translated thus— 'A skilled versifier in the vernacular, several of his poems and songs [*codices plurimi et cantilenæ*] are to this day remembered by the Scots and considered among the very best. When he was a captive, before he married her, he composed a book about the queen that shows much art—besides that other well made poem on the same person [so I interpret *cantilenam ejusdem*] *Yas Sen* etc., also that merry and clever song, *At Beltayn* etc., which other persons sought to alter so that it should be about Dalkeith and Gargeil[1] [the Latin reads *quem alii de Dalkeith & Gargeil mutare studuerunt* but my version makes the meaning more explicit]—for he was confined in the castle or lodging in which the lady dwelt with her mother'.

The fact that the comic set of verses known to us as *Peblis to the Play* begins with the words 'At Beltayn' and cannot be the king's work (the rhymes sufficiently forbid that supposition) does not have to mean that the tradition Mair cited was wholly mistaken in this case and therefore in the others. He may indeed have *Peblis* in mind but he has warned us not to accept every version as the king's poem. It is not unlikely that James did compose a substantially similar work for the court's amusement, and that its popularity soon provoked imitations that replaced it in the public memory. He was certainly capable of such rude humour; it was he who set the fashion of comic joustings, like those that Dunbar and Lindsay were later to celebrate (cf. Bower, lib. XVI, cap. xv). *Yas sen* has not been explained.[2] Lawson's ingenious suggestion that Mair condenses the first line of *Chrystis Kirk of the Grene*, 'Was nevir in Scotland hard nor sene', ignores the comparison of the subject-matter with that of the *Quair* and the distinction intended by the adjective, *jucundum*, as applied to *At Beltayn*. One other identification, John Pinkerton's in *Ancient Scottish Poems*, with the poem in the *Maitland Quarto MS.* (STS), 'Sen that Eine that werkis my weilfair', deserves notice here only because others have so often uncritically recorded his speculation; style, metre, vocabulary and phonology, alike require a date in the second half the the sixteenth century.

The *Quair*'s manuscript, which I have dated about 1505, has two ascriptions to the king, that of the second and final scribe, fol. 211, *Quod Jacobus primus scotorum rex Illustrissimus*, and the somewhat later one already noted, fol. 191 *verso*, 'Heirefter followis the quair Maid be King James of scotland the first Callit the kingis quair and Maid q*uhen* his Ma*iestie* wes In England'. It can not be objected to the scribe's attribution that the same person assigns other poems in the

---

[1] 'Gargeil' should be Cargill near Coupar Angus. It appears as 'Gargyll' in Hary's *Wallace* IV. 681, initial G, C, K being alternate spellings in such Celtic place-names at this period.

[2] *Yas* could be a slip for 'Alas'.

MS. wrongly—the first scribe's mistakes, if they are his, reflect only the common and understandable assumption that any good English verses of that period must be by Chaucer; there could be no compulsion to claim every good Scots poem for James—and the later ascription is almost certainly by a member of the Sinclair family. Both may be said to have the authority of that family, which had cause to be specially interested in the poem. The main scribe, James Gray, himself a student of Scots history and poetry as his notebook shows, was secretary of two archbishops of St Andrews who might well have had some knowledge of the matter—one, William Schevez, a notable collector of books, the other, James Stewart, brother of King James the Fourth—and should at least have known whether his assistant's statement agreed with the tradition of authorship.

As will have been noted, Mair and the late inserter of the above-quoted introductory note are in mistaken agreement on the time and place of composition. Their error, however, does not compromise the main tradition of James's authorship from which it derives. That is confirmed by all that can be observed of the poem: the consonance of its language with that of the king's period and with his special experience of both the Midland and Northern dialects of English; its literary connections; the conformity of its narrative with what James, at the indicated date of writing and within the conventions of his day, might be expected to say about the relevant events of his 'auenture'; the obvious consideration that no Scot save the king could have written that story during the latter's lifetime, and none would have been content to write so happily within its accepted terms—'In ʒouth, of lufe that now from day to day/ Flourith ay newe'—after his death.

THE TESTAMENT OF JAMES STEWART

The *Kingis Quair* is a poetical autobiography, a selective one of course, since the author reviews his life only in order to illustrate the single significant pattern that he has discovered in it. For such a purpose he needed to notice only a few relevant events and the ones that he chose were certainly critical in his career as historians know it. The meaning that he gave to these events in his poem is, however, not easily detachable and indeed the farther interpretation moves from them, in its

endeavour to make an independently meaningful statement, the more
it loses its way.

Too often critics have considered the poem simply as an attractive
collocation of topics, symbolized or conventionalized themes or doc-
trines, to be identified, abstracted, re-presented with much the same
significance as they have in works of a generally similar content.
What is individual tends not to appear as such; the application, which
is at least half the poem's meaning, is given less than proper attention
and the result is a too simple re-statement of what the poet has to say,
clarity being achieved by underplaying certain themes or even omit-
ting them from notice altogether. Examples of this defective treatment
are the studies of the *Quair* published by John Preston[1] and John
MacQueen.[2] Thus Mr Preston develops the topic of 'fortunys exiltree'
with an exclusiveness equal to that of the author of the *Epistola Con-
solatoria*, addressed to James by the University of Paris in 1414.[3] And
Professor MacQueen, relying on convention as a key to interpretation
rigorously seeks out and therefore finds only what is conventional.
Naturally he concludes that the 'attitude' of the poem is basically that
of *The Romance of the Rose*, and that its subject can be generally des-
cribed as 'the faire cheyne of love' in nature, more particularly, since
he has also in mind the precedent of De Guileville's *Pelerinage*, as the
action of divine grace in the king's life—not only the grace that is
already inherent in nature's order but also that which manifests itself
in direct intervention, for example, the saving sight of the beloved and
the arrival of the dove with good tidings. Each of these themes (except
the notion of special acts of grace) is undoubtedly in the poem but
they are presented out of context and therefore disproportionately
and misleadingly.

What is notably missing from these and other such accounts is the
author and subject of the *Quair*, James Stewart. Recent critics have

[1] 'Fortunys Exiltree: A Study Of *The Kingis Quair*', *The Review of English
Studies*, N.S., vol. VII, 1956, pp. 339–45.

[2] 'Tradition And The Interpretation Of *The Kingis Quair*', *ibid.*, vol. XIII,
pp. 117–31.

[3] *Chartularium Universitatis Parisiensis*, ed. H. Dénifle, A. Champellain, vol.
IV, pp. 285–6. He was to take heart from the number of men whom Fortune
had imprisoned or killed before his time and to think of bad fortune as the best
of teachers. The real object of the epistle was in its conclusion, an appeal to his
concern for a divided, schismatic Church.

indeed been reluctant to consider the *Quair* as a personal document at all. They do not actually say that the history it contains is irrelevant but they write as if it were, and they are quite clear that it is not what the poem is about. Preston objects to C. S. Lewis's praise of its originality as a real-life application of 'the allegory of love' ('the literal narrative of a contemporary wooing emerges from romance and allegory'[1]), and MacQueen asks us to observe that the poet 'does not mention the word marriage'. The latter thus chooses to omit from his discussion a subject that the historians, not to mention the goddess Minerva, think important in the king's life; and Preston prefers to illustrate the Boethian topic of fortune in the *Quair* without once referring to the question of free will which gives it significance—a mistake which Minerva naturally does not make—though it was a theme that had more than a philosophical interest for the Scottish king, as for his Roman teacher.

The contrary thesis will be maintained by the present writer in his approach to an interpretation: that the historical narrative, which includes the romantic one, does not merely answer, as Preston believes, 'the needs of the poem's developing thought', but directs it, and explains it to the reader. Not unless we bear firmly in mind that this is a spiritual autobiography, whatever conventions it may employ to tell its story, will we appreciate how impressive a statement it makes. An understanding involvement in the process of the king's narrative— 'Tell on, man, quhat the befell'—is therefore desirable, and as a necessary preliminary to further comment will be attempted in the following reconstruction of events, physical and spiritual. For the evidence supporting this series of interpretations the reader is referred to the editor's Notes.

The story of James begins with an explanation of how he came to tell it. (1:) On a winter's night, watching from his bed the circling course of the heavens, his thoughts turned to the workings of destiny, and how the planets are deflected so long from their right course before winning back to it eventually. (2–7:) Sleepless and disturbed— he could not yet say why—he took Boethius's book and read how that noblest of men was wronged by Fortune, reduced from high estate to poverty in exile, how he found in his own resources of virtue and philosophy something to rest on, so that he could take comfort

[1] *The Allegory of Love*, 1936, p. 237.

and rejoice that his peace was no longer at the mercy of wilful desire, selfish complaint and the restless world that provokes them. (8–13:) He put the book aside and thought of his own experience: a prince is as subject as his servant to this same Fortune, and specially in youth that lives only in the present. Thinking of this he heard the bell that rings to matins and words from the Office came to mind, 'Lord, thou wilt open my lips and my mouth will publish thy praise'. It seemed that they spoke to him. If any man had cause to praise God for his lot it was he. He took pen and paper, crossed himself, and began his tale.

(14–16:) He had been happy enough, as a boy, when he set out on that voyage to France, but not ready with a man's philosophy ('the rypĕnesse of resoune' 16) for the voyage of life; it would be many years before his will learned to listen to his reason. (17–19:) To tell the inward as well as the outward story, as he intended, of the pain and joy that befell him was going to be difficult. (20–8:) On the March day that he sailed, about the time of equinox, he was only three years or so past the thoughtless stage of 'innocence'. Whether it was by God's will in the stars, or some other cause, that his father's councillors had decided on the voyage, the event was his capture by an English ship and some eighteen years of life as a prisoner and exile. As the years passed and nothing was done for him by those who could have helped (27)[1] he knew bitterness; in prison he used to argue with his companions that there was no justice in this world. God's lesser creatures had their natural freedom and he, a man, was denied it. Other men went free; why should he, innocent of any offence, be an exception?[2]

(29–40:) It had been his lucky habit in his prison to rise early. Where there was nothing else to do he could at least watch the folk out there go about their business, and he could look down from the tower where they had put him to a garden and the arbour in one corner—particularly he remembered the juniper tree at its centre; from where he watched the branches seemed to spread all about it—and hear the birds sing their song, that was like a hymn to love and a call to lovers

[1] There is almost certainly an allusion here, not only to his English captors but also to his uncle, the Duke of Albany, Governor of Scotland, who made little effort to secure James's liberty.

[2] Calderon's imprisoned prince similarly questions divine justice (see note). In Hary's *Wallace*, II. 186, there is the same question from the captive hero, 'Quhi will thou giff thi handewerk for nocht?'

to love freely as they did. Love then could mean little to him: if it was as wonderful and powerful as the poets said, and nature too out there seemed to say, what crime had he committed that the freedom and joy they claimed for it were not for him? And it was as he rehearsed such thoughts, wishing that he too could know love, he saw the woman that he would love and marry enter the arbour with her two attendants.

(41–67:) She might have been Venus come to set him free of this restraint, or Nature herself, for everything in the arbour seemed to take its beauty from her. He knew then how beauty could hurt, and could wonder that God should let it be so, so much the feeling of that moment had changed him. Even so he could praise God for being a lover. He had even envied his beloved's little dog that played about her, and scolded the nightingale for its silence in such a golden hour, an hour that made all life seem worthwhile. On the spot he made up a song that said he would go through hell for her. Her going was like the coming of night.

(68–72:) Now that he was in love he felt fully what it was to be a prisoner, like knowing life and death together. Whatever peace of mind or comfort of friends had been his was gone. Now that he knew what joy could be, he knew real torment. [We are to understand, of course, that James, though treated as a prisoner, came to know his future queen well, and that among the events that befell him was the understanding of what love could and should mean, and, by the light of this knowledge and its confirmation in later years, how partial had been his view of life when his previous experience made him complain of Fortune. Now he would convey what he had learned in the form of a revelation, a visionary experience.]

(73–123:) With night-fall, tired with too much thought, too much feeling, his head against the cold stone of his window, he fell into a state between sleep and waking. There were suddenly a light and a voice and, no one preventing, he could leave his prison. Arms bore him through the heavens to the House of Venus, where the voice bade him look at all the kinds, ages and fortunes, of lovers. He was asked to notice that the highest honour was given to those who had kept their faith in love into old age (83–84). There were the lucky and unlucky lovers, and so many of the latter! There were churchmen who had violated their vows and the marriage sacrament. Fortune in all her changes was represented, and Venus, goddess of desire, was there upon her bed of love. He prayed her that the grace that had made him know love's pain should also grant its cure. She bade him be patient and consider the good reason that he had for hope (113), saying that the love and desire she had given him would not by themselves win their object; he needed to learn true service, and Minerva, goddess of reason, must teach him that: 'When you return to the world of men,' said Venus, 'rebuke the breakers of faith and all that take me lightly (115), for Nature herself grieves for a sin against love and rejoices in its service. Obey my law and when you have left the world you and your wife will share my heaven perpetually' (123).

(124–50:) With the reasons for hope that he had, and the patience to learn the true service of love, Divine Reason accepted him as her pupil. She told him that the love that is merely pleasure of sex ends in pain and repentance, that only the love that follows the teaching of Christ will endure (129-31). There were services to be rendered, not only words to be proffered, desire had to be joined with wisdom, and he must not be like those men who cared only for their appetite and not for the woman they professed to love. (139-45:) He assured the goddess that his love was sincere; he would have no joy till he had won his desire. Desire, she granted, had no fault in it if it proposed Christian marriage; let him say if this were so (142). When his intentions were understood Reason promised to help him with Fortune. (146-50:) 'Remember,' she said, 'that the stars do not determine everything, that you have free will and the ability to use the imperfect degree of knowledge and wisdom that you possess, to make at least some defence against Fortune's malice, even sometimes to make her turn, quite suddenly, in your favour.'

(151–58:) So he left the divine country of Love and Reason and was once more on earth, but still not in the world of Fortune, for this was the earthly paradise and he walked with delight by its river and knew the goodness of God in all His kinds of creation, just as Love and Reason had taught him to see it.[1] (159–72:) Now with real hope (158)

---

[1] MacQueen's identification of the river as 'a direct symbol of Fortune's dominion' is eccentric and removes the stage of meditation that logically follows the process of education and precedes the encounter with Fortune (see note to st. 152). His further connection of Fortune's tower with the walled garden as symbolizing her part in Nature's good order is ingenious, but it is easier to see the tower as denoting her earthly strength and contrasting with the celestial courts of Venus and Minerva.

he would seek out Fortune in her strong tower. To his new senses, when he came there and saw her crowded wheel, though it was still terrible and there was always the dreadful mystery of the pit beneath, as deep as hell itself (162), it was a smiling goddess that he found—not that her nature had altered, for change itself was her nature, but he saw now that she could help as readily as she had hurt before (165). 'In your beginning,' she said, 'like the planets themselves, you were turned from your natural goal. Now you will turn again and see it' (170). So the wish of all those years, and in so wonderful a way, was granted, and he stepped on Fortune's upward wheel. As he did, she reminded him: 'Almost half your life is gone by, so make good use of what is left (171), and remember me, that I can change.' And to make sure he did she struck him a blow on the ear, so smartly that he awoke.

(173-88:) But in the real world doubts and fears were still with him, specially the thought that waking or sleeping man has dreams but no certainty, not till the soul, always flitting between earth and heaven, finds its way finally to its true home (173-4). He prayed for reassurance and divine grace answered his prayer. The letter that brought him the certain news, he felt, should have been illuminated with gillyflowers, for some men call them the queen's flower and they are sown in March, the month that had been so fateful in his life (178). Heaven had indeed decreed that Fortune should grant what he had so long desired, for soon his beloved put away all the pains that love had first caused him, and now, at the time of writing, he lived freely and happily with his queen (181). It seemed to him that there could be no greater joy than to find love and freedom together. In his happiness he had to pray that other lovers would come to the same blissful state of marriage, where desire finds its full delight and is at one with conscience (184-5), and that those who seek another end to their desires should fail (186). Only death could now separate him from his beloved.

(189-97:) So much grace had been shown him. He must thank all flowers for the sake of his queen-flower (190). Fortune's wheel had turned so well, to bring him from that March day and his capture (191) to the sight of his queen and to their long continuance of love (192). She, if no one else, would take the present of his book and find no fault with it (195), as now he had no fault to find with his life, as God had written it so long ago (if only there had been understanding to read it) in the circling course of the heavens. Lastly he hoped that his hymn to love would find a place with those of his teachers, Gower and Chaucer.

Thus the thought of James, as I have ventured to spell it out, reviews a circular course of experience and learning, from a beginning in thoughtless innocence through self-willed and rebellious unreason to a new beginning in Christian reason. Youth 'that seildin ought prouidith' could not consider the whole and wanted the patience to wait and see the wheel come full circle. The circle of experience that he considers particularly is, of course, that of his life from his capture to his liberation, but this has reference also to the larger circle of life turning away from and eventually back to, its natural point of rest, in God—a conception that James might have found in many places, but most conveniently in commentaries on Boethius,[1] the moralizations in copies of Sacrobosco's *Sphere,* and especially in De Guileville's *Pelerinage de la Vie Humaine.*[2]

The controlling concept of the life-circle is not only in the opening and recurring allusion (sts. 1, 173, 195) to the return of the heavenly bodies from the unnatural westward course into which they are forced by Primum Mobile (the eastward movement being often compared to the soul's escape from the sensual will to reason and God), but also in the pervading theme of Fortune's wheel and its contrary motions and, most important of all, in the pattern of Boethius's experience, which is like that of the king's (4):

> Descryving first of his prosperitee
> And out of that his infelicitee,
> And than how he in his poleyt report
> In philosophy can him to confort!

Here the likeness in felicity consequent on infelicity is obvious, as also in the spiritual aspect of that felicity, which is an appreciation of providence or divine reason in the changing ways of fortune.

This 'figure circulere' in the poem's narrative has importance for its interpretation. It means that it is the whole of the poet's experience and not this or that particular part or aspect of it, however specially significant, that finally concerns him. Consequently it would be wrong

---

[1] A late example is the circular diagram of the spiritual life in the 1525 edition of John Walton's translation, EETS, 1927, pp. 369-71.

[2] See the discussion of the Frenchman's influence under 'Date And Authorship'.

for the critic to direct attention to the theme of love and marriage, which provides the main part of the poem's matter, except as it relates to the king's total comment on his experience. Similarly it would be a mistake to represent the introduction to love and confirmation of its happy future as direct interventions of divine grace, as Professor MacQueen does, when the king's concern is with grace as manifested in the whole course of his life. That this is what the reader is expected to perceive is externally suggested by the responses of both Walter Bower and Hector Boece to the king's English captivity; they see it, in Boece's words, 'non fortuna sed deo ducente'. Since the poet's purpose is to reveal, and not argue, the discovered pattern, the interpreter will simply follow him as he finds it.

It is, of course, as in Boethius and all Boethian poems or testaments, for example, *The Testament of Cresseid*, the complaint of Fortune's injustice that states the issue for comment. Like Boethius or Cresseid the king will cease to question, learn to accept. The main difference in his case, as we have seen, is that he discovers grace not through reasoning or painful correction, but by a change in Fortune's treatment of him that reveals how unhappiness can introduce happiness, even the greatest that can befall a man. He has seen the two faces of Fortune and found them fair.

It is here that his education through love begins. He has experienced something affected by, but more powerful than, Fortune, and in learning the serious duties of love learns also the reality of free will, from which choice of belief and conduct proceeds. The above-mentioned difference in procedure from the *Consolation* can thus be re-stated: that the enlightenment of reason comes to the king through a personal love which he learns to think of in Christian terms. What James finally preaches is, effectually, salvation through marriage, finding the love of God in the love of a woman, freedom from self in 'the ʒok that esy is and sure'. It need hardly be said that this is not a 'courtly' love, the love of a Troilus for his Criseyde; it has a doctrinal character that is more easily related to the known importance for the author of the event that inspired it than to any literary convention.

The element of doctrine is as apparent in the poet's Venus as in her sister Minerva, from whom she differs in no way in her thinking about the 'right true end' of love. If it is, admittedly, the quality and observance of love that concerns her most, she gives to her words on these subjects a moral and religious urgency that distinguishes her equally from the goddess Nature of *The Parlement of Foules*, the king and queen of love in the Prologue to *The Legend of Good Women* and the Venus of *The Temple of Glas*. The attitudes of the authors of *The Romance of the Rose*, widely differing as they are, agree in being much less evangelistic. The sacramental view of life and love that inspired these works (it is as basic to the rationalism of Jean de Meun as to the idealism of Guillaume de Lorris), and was the characteristically Christian interpretation of the Boethian 'faire cheyne of love', appears here in its dogmatic form. They exalt faithful love but, unlike King James, set it in the freedom of an ideal world where the bond of marriage need not be specified.

A remarkable instance of this treatment is provided by the monk of Bury's *Temple*. A careful reading is required to discover that its matter is the problem of a married woman and her lover. The heaven that the goddess of the temple offers to these worshippers is naturally indeterminate; it may be eventual marriage made possible by the death of the husband, or simply the consolation of reciprocated love. The problem need not be solved because it is not posed in real terms. In the *Quair*, of course, there is no such attempt to disguise, veil or ambiguously distance the subject-matter, and this is not only because the poem is an autobiography, and a marriage is part of its known personal story, but also because its author is frankly and sincerely interested in the meaning of marriage as a sacrament. His Venus accordingly avows that her 'lore' is incomplete without that of Minerva (111), and her promise of a perpetual heaven for the souls of the two lovers echoes the marriage service, and is clearly made to the faithful husband and wife that they will become (123).

It would be wrong to make more of Minerva's sermon than that of Venus, but without doubt it is she who most helps us to understand whatever doctrine or philosophy there is in the poem. Having at once identified herself with Christian teaching on the matter of love, that desire is not to be denied but is to be satisfied only in marriage, since all that men do must be done in the sight of God—'Tak him before in all thy gouernance/That in his hand the stere has of ʒou all' (130)—she proceeds to deal with the basic issue of free will and responsibility. God had foreseen all that would be done to the captive and all that he would do. All has happened by permission of His will and in that sense alone is He responsible for the whole; for His permission included the free choice of good and evil by James, as by others, so that his was the merit of acting according to divine reason, seeking to do 'trew seruis' in his loving, and thus deserving the full happiness denied to those that, in Venus's phrase, 'breken louse and walken at thaire large'. The point is not simply that had he chosen otherwise there would have been no marriage and no liberation, but that there would have been no 'long and trew contynuance' of married love. Yet, the goddess of reason admits, though such a choice was, especially in the captive's case, a pre-condition of his happiness, its full realization in this world was still dependent on the changes of Fortune.

This last very important qualification of reason's power in man has to be understood in the light of what Minerva says about foreknowledge. Since God possesses this faculty to an infinite extent, he is untouched by fortune. To the very limited degree that man has this knowledge he is also beyond her power and may influence her—*sapiens dominabitur astris*. Here Simon reads his Boethius less correctly than James, for the French critic attributes only a counsel of resignation to the philosopher and falsely contrasts this with the king's doctrine of action.[1] This knowledge itself depends on understanding the causes of happiness and unhappiness and these, as we have seen, James has learned, in so far as he now recognizes how the love of God for man works in the natural creation—an understanding that the birds outside the prisoner's window possessed 'in thaire wise'—particularly in the law of love and the necessity for the two faces of Fortune. This, however, is a knowledge of principles and if he has learned how the ones that specially concern love's observance should be applied, there is still the question of what can be done to win good fortune for it.

It is here that a personage in the poem who has been ignored by the critics, Gude Hope, plays his logical rôle. This guide, recommended by Venus (113) to help the lover on his way to Minerva, the support of his happiness in the earthly paradise, and still his companion when at last he encounters Fortune (158), is not only the confidence that comes from a new appreciation of life's happier possibilities, but also the confidence that is based on knowledge of particular favouring circumstances. Just as in theology Good Hope, as the opposite of 'Wanhope' or Despair, ensures God's mercy to the believing suppliant, in the practice of human love the same virtue ensures, to the extent that any

[1] *Le Livre du Roi*, pp. 242–3.

virtue in the earthly scene can do so, practical success. This help, according to the contemporary author of the Scots treatise, *Ratis Raving*, discussing the conditions of a successful courtship and marriage, is the same as reasonable expectation. Of 'dame resone' he says that 'gud hop is ay of hire assent' (1045). Gude Hope is thus the good reason a man has to expect success in his wooing and happiness in his marriage. When this guide is absent the object of love is beyond one's reach because of various impediments of character, kinship, rank, and by extension the kind of difficulty that historically beset James.

With this meaning in mind it can be understood that the king set his love where it was acceptable, where marriage was possible, and ensuing happiness might be expected. It is not therefore altogether miraculous that he eventually received the news 'that blisful bene and sure'. In respect of this personal relationship of fortunate love, as also in respect of the larger relationship of acceptance of God's will in the pattern of life, the theme of the poem may be described as the triumph of reason over foolish will.

With a final paean of thanksgiving, attributing the fortunate circle of his experience to 'the magnificence/Of him that hiest in the hevin sitt', the testament of James Stewart closes. It is patently the record of a man who has known love in marriage, 'that now from day to day/ Flourith ay newe', yet more patently the reflective statement of a mature mind whose chief concern is to give this central experience its place in a religious interpretation of 'all myn auenture'. It is neither the narration of a lover's wooing that Lewis assumes it to be—the absence of any of the conventional details or prescribed stages of such a courtship should have checked that reading—nor the impersonal if inspired treatise that Prescott and MacQueen present.

The inadequacy of the former view inevitably provoked the extreme reaction that the latter represents, and the second account was encouraged by mistaken doubts about the poem's claims to be autobiography. That kings do not love their queens seems to have been a wilful article of faith with the sceptics, though singularly unsupported in this case, and the historian's testimony will probably have little weight with them: 'Whether *The Kingis Quair* gives an historical version of the wooing or not, the marriage seems to have been of the happiest. The conjugal fidelity of the king is exceptional in early

Stewart history'.[1] He is said to have trusted his queen as a partner in the business of government to a quite remarkable extent. For the sincere interest in religion and philosophy, that would have made it natural for James to give to his experience the significance that it has in the *Quair*, we have the ample witness of his contemporary and biographer, Abbot Bower.[2]

The king's application of the Boethian theme to his own eventually happier lot has been said to want the profounder significance that a tragic narrative can possess.[3] It is true that Boethius's assertion of an ultimate goodness in the universe to be accepted by any reasonable mind can only be fully tested and illustrated by a more painful account of experience, such as Robert Henryson gives of his unfortunate Cresseid. Her self-criticism, 'Nane but my self as now I will accuse', is made the more impressive by its circumstances. None the less, James's 'divine comedy' is a legitimate and effective treatment.

More, perhaps, might have been made of the eighteen years of exile and frustration in order to give greater weight to the consequent happiness, yet the result might have been only to divide the poem and weaken the celebratory effect, and the change would still not have met Simon's point. The true answer must be that to the Boethian faith the acceptance of fortune for what she is, always the agent of God whichever face she shows, is all that counts. That James learned such acceptance only when the happier face was turned should not deprive his statement of its authority. The vital point is his success in seeing the new friend in the old foe, the two as complementary aspects of the single worthwhile experience of living. Most readers should recognize that the king understands and feels what he says, and that it is personal experience and conviction that allows him to give so significant a pattern to his life's story.

APPRECIATION

Form—Image and Attitude—Style

More than one 'deficultee' of 'enditing' confronted King James when he undertook a discussion and illustration of divine grace in the whole

---

[1] Balfour-Melville, *op. cit.*, p. 248.   [2] *Scotichronicon*, lib. XVI, cap. xxx.
[3] Simon, *op. cit.*, p. 248.

course of his life. There was the problem of giving a symbolic or allegoric character to actual events, physical and mental. The youthful voyager, the prisoner in the tower, the lover and the liberated man, had each to be given his significant rôle in the Boethian and Christian drama. The lover would be the most difficult to direct intelligently, for though his was the most attractive part and, of course, the decisive one in the developing argument, yet the *persona* that mattered most was that of the prisoner. It was his problem and his discovery of a solution that the story was first and last about. For this reason, to make his scene central, even the appearance of a possible action is sacrificed. In prison he makes his complaint against Fortune, from it he has his glimpse of an answer in the girl outside, in it that same night he has the vision that represents both his successful courtship and his education in the serious meaning of love, and there too next morning he has the miraculous confirmation of his dream. It is the freed and reconciled prisoner who celebrates the 'figure circulere' of unhappy past and happy present. Of course, there was the complementary problem of ensuring that romance and allegory did not lose their effect as history, the authentic statement of personal experience, but if he were indeed a poet that would be the least of his difficulties.

The greatest problem was the right balancing of the different rôles or aspects of his story. They might be presented in such a way that the larger shape and meaning were obscured: the early part of his experience that questioned the goodness of God might be given too little space and weight, and so be insufficiently remembered in the reconciling experience of love; and the final thanksgiving might similarly forget the occasion that 'first causit hath this accident'. In brief, the prisoner had to be seen to be comforted not only by his fortunate love but also by the Boethian 'vertew' and 'philosophy' that James set out to illustrate and confirm in his own person. It is a truism of criticism that treatment is everything and here an attempt will be made to appreciate the poet's varying degree of success in dealing with these problems, particularly that of overall relevancy.

At the beginning of the *Quair* the stance of moralist and philosopher is established for the poet by the traditionally appropriate winter setting, the destinal stars, the book of Boethius that would be so clear a pointer to the reader. The latter introduces in the most natural way James's own good reasons for being concerned with the theme of

Fortune's power, and the matin-bell that bids him talk about them also tells us that his story will be a religious one. This will not be like other poems he has written, 'of lyte effect' (13). Nothing so far specifically suggests the lover or the matter of love. The poet introduces himself as a mature man looking back on 'my tyme', reflecting on the vulnerableness of youth, 'of nature indegest', and its ignorance of 'payne to cum' and 'this warldis rage'. The invocatory stanzas 17–20, which have been objected to by Simon as delaying the personal story, by their confession of difficulties in commencing add to our awareness that the tale to be told will be no simple one. The first hint of its having to do with love is in the ambiguous phrase, 'my turment and my joye' (19).

When the Spring sunshine of the day of sailing is followed by the discomfort on the waves, 'weltering to and fro', the effect is of a continued allegory because of the previous imagery of life's treacherous sea and those 'Rokkis . . . Off doubilnesse' that daunt the writer. And with this preparation and the abruptly, briefly given account of the prince's capture, 'By strong hand, by fors schortly to say', Fortune's procedure of sudden reversals has been so well established that the direct transition to the 'strayte ward' of 'ʒeris twisë nyne' appears quite natural. There is also our consciousness of the mature author reminiscing selectively to help us to accept the yet more abrupt change of perspective when, in st. 26, he speaks as a prisoner of many years.

The ensuing picture of the complainant, weary of 'the long dayes and the nyghtes eke', resenting his separation from 'the warld and folk that went forby', his recreation reduced to the freedom 'to luke', arguing fruitlessly with his attendants about Fortune's injustice, realizes his prisoner's state sufficiently for us to be able to glimpse the meaning that the love-vision in the arbour held for him when it came, a moment of miraculous grace, at once a possible answer to his bitterness and provision of fresh cause for complaint. The reviewer of the past, not having the ordinary story-teller's task, need not hesitate to tell us what it will mean—'By the come I to joye out of turment' (29)—and here at least it is still a prisoner's and not a lover's torment of which he speaks.

In the arbour scene that follows the life and brightness do not efface the previous picture of the complainant. There is continued awareness of the spectator, the 'lyf without'. Thus the nightingale's song is of

freedom—"away winter, away!/Cumsomer, cum"—and we are not
allowed to forget that it is an outsider's description, a view from a
tower—'As I beheld and kest myn eyne alawe' (35). Especially we
understand that the effect of this alien love and joy in nature has to be
further questioning, whether it can be genuine, whether he can share
it as he would like to do (39).

These thirty-nine stanzas (and not merely, by Simon's count, the
nineteen that precede the prince's voyage) are the poem's substantial
introduction to its Boethian argument. The hymnal purpose of the
midnight writer has been hinted rather than stated. What has been
most apparent is the concern with Fortune as 'my fo'. We know that
later he will deal with her as 'my frende', but meanwhile he has con-
sistently illustrated the first relationship, so that the second can be
really meaningful as it develops. There have been no digressions, no
description for the sake of description.

The business of the ensuing scene is to intensify the prisoner's
complaint by making it also a lover's complaint. James's future queen
enters the arbour as 'the freschest 3ong floure', bringing the pang of
full awareness of his deprivation. His response has been compared with
that of Palamon to the appearance of Emilye but it has a further signifi-
cance. To Palamon's merely romantic and rhetorical question, whether
Emilye is a woman or Venus herself, James adds 'Or ar 3e verray
Nature the goddesse . . . ?', and this is not felt as conventional rhetoric.
The girl is effectually the Nature whose joy he had questioned come to
convince him in her own person, and her place in the context of the
argument is evident. The sudden violence of the change in the lover's
outlook is, of course, traditional, but the language of self-debate that
expresses it has an effect of intellect along with passion that is less usual,
for its terms echo main themes of the poem: his heart 'become hir
thrall/For euer of free wyll'; there is a suggestion of divine grace in her
coming, since she is a 'hevinly thing in liknesse of nature'; the ques-
tioning of God's goodness does not lapse but is given a new form—
'Quhy lest god mak 3ou so, my derrest hert,/To do a sely presoner
thus smert?' (44).

It has been observed by Simon that apart from the golden hair and
the face 'quhite as ony snawe' there is no attempt at bodily description;
the ornamentation of many-hued plumes and dazzling jewels is
chiefly noticed. A heightened sense of colour may be supposed to

reflect the lover's excitement but a main reason for this restraint is that she is less a woman than a revelation, an apparition of beauty and goodness. Illogically since James presents himself only as a prisoner, but relevantly in view of his moral theme, he appreciates her 'mesure/ In word, in dede' (50). One notes also that the nightingale, scolded for its silence at such a golden hour in his life's calendar, brings in the thought of Tereus's crime and 'thir husbandis that are false' (56), a topic that Venus will glance at and Minerva consider directly. In fact the symbolic character of the story-situation is manifest, and it is plainly assumed that the reader will be conscious throughout of the real-life reference and the author's intention to present the future marriage as the practical answer to the prisoner's Boethian complaint.

The complete identification of the frustrated prisoner with the fearful lover is the concern of the present scene and it is effected by the dramatic conveyance of fluctuating delight and anxiety. The complainant is now the supplicant to the 'sanct' who will intercede for him. His agitation over the nightingale's silence, and fear that anything he does to make it sing will drive it away, are not decorative poses but language for his anxiety lest the hope glimpsed in the girl should vanish; in which case there would be 'nought ellis than' but to follow her with his heart (63).[1] With her departure, after these twenty-six stanzas of description, we are returned to a more explicit treatment of the questioner's theme, with his distressful debating of the contraries of 'deth and lyf', 'turment and joye' (68–71), but now in the more challenging context of a prisoner's apparently hopeless love. The statement of the Boethian problem has for a time, admittedly, become less direct and general because of the new love-terms in which it is posed, but finally is the clearer and more urgent for them.

The visionary level of treatment in the garden scene makes the transition to the celestial one more natural than it might have been. The heavenly reference of the life-story had been indicated at the outset, made clear in the prisoner's lament, and continued in the response, at once idealizing and despairing, to the sight of the beloved;

[1] Since the above was written Mr Norton-Smith, *op. cit.*, pp. xv–xvii, has published a patronizing appreciation of James as poet that identifies his success with a 'naive, authorial charm' and 'amateurish quality', which he finds illustrated in 'his indulgent concern about the nightingale's failure to sing, and in his serious and irrelevant search for the reason'. This critic consistently undervalues the logic and art of *The Kingis Quair*, a defect also of his editing.

now it is given the form of a pilgrimage of instruction. Whether this didactic treatment of one central experience interrupts awareness of the theme of God's governance in the life as a whole has now to be considered.

It is very much a religious vision that comes to the distressed prisoner and response is expected in that kind, much more so than is the case with its source in Lydgate's *Temple of Glas*, where a triangular love affair is treated in a discreetly secular, if dignified, fashion. In the king's poem Biblical phenomena precede and accompany the Macrobian aerial journey: the blinding light of a supernatural revelation, the assurance of 'confort and hele', the miraculous liberation and the supporting arms. The disembodied voice that guides has the tones of The Book of Revelations—'Tak hede, man, and behold' (83)— and once, not incongruously, recalls the unearthly vision in *Thomas The Rhymer*: 'And seis thou now ʒone multitude on rawe' (90). The spectator is distanced from what he sees by the brief phrases that introduce each aspect, 'there I fand', 'there I sawe', and his strangeness to the scene conveyed by suggestions of puzzlement or uncertainty, 'Wist I nought quhy' (81), 'Thair hertis semyt' (82), etc. There is nowhere, as there is in Lydgate, the sense of merely literary device, securing a conveniently abstract frame for description and comment on an earthly situation. Pains are taken to make clear that this is indeed an after-world and that these are indeed the spirits of dead lovers in Venus's court. Thus reference to their earthly situations is qualified by reminders of the place of view-point, 'In all thaire dayes' (91), 'tuke thame of this warldis companye' (93).

In many ways we are made to recognize the intended affinity of this lovers' heaven with the Christian one. The pagan blind Cupid loses even the residual lightness of character that he had in *The Romance of the Rose* and becomes a figure of 'estate' and judgment, fit to be associated with the spiritually conceived Venus to whom we are now presented. She is still the 'goddesse of delyte' (96) but has no kinship with De Guileville's lustful hag and only a cousinship with the secular goddesses of Chaucer and Lydgate. Her values are those of her sister Minerva and she has much of the latter's judicial character. Simon stresses especially her pity for sinners and sufferers, but equally she represents justice and can threaten punishment to the obdurate. Her servants have names familiar to the tradition of courtly love, 'Secretee' and 'Fair Calling' (Bel Acceuil), but they serve a different delight, and when this is said to come 'by ordynance eterne' the phrase refers to the order of grace, as well as the order of nature that is more particularly celebrated in *The Parlement of Foules*. To the latter order belongs James's discovery of love, but to the former his 'trew seruis' and the 'Gude Hope' which depends on Minerva's counsels. The concept of sin more than breach of good custom informs her scolding of those that 'breken louse and walken at thaire large', and it is plainly the reward of the Christian heaven that she offers 'perpetualye' (123) to her faithful worshippers. If she leaves it to Minerva to make doctrinal statements, these obviously have her assent, so that earthly love means to her married love. It is in her Christian aspect, of course, as representing the experience of divine love, that her relevance to the prisoner's complaint of an unjust Fortune is to be found.

The court of Minerva has more of state, 'ordour digne', than that of Venus, for as the goddess of reason authority specially becomes her, and it is her characteristic business to be right and to instruct to right rather than to be merciful. If she is 'the pacient goddesse' and her porter is Patience, this is not because she is long-suffering but because she teaches the will of God and admits 'vnquestionate' all those who, like the prisoner and lover, are prepared to learn and accept it. It was a lesson that Venus too had taught ('Paciently thou tak thyne auenture', 106), though in her case with more direct reference to love's fortunes and observances than to its commandments. These are specifically Christian as Minerva teaches them. She allows only the love that, 'in Cristin wise', seeks marriage. Since she speaks of duties she turns naturally to the subject of free will and affirms it as the basis of all responsibilities. When the lover, assisted by Gude Hope, leaves the goddess to seek out Fortune, it must be understood that he has accepted the divine will and his complaints have ceased. It is naturally at this point that, symbolizing his reconciled spirit, he enters the 'lusty plane' and appreciates its beauty and variety of life. If the pious point that any bestiary was supposed to make is made somewhat weakly here—its meaning developed enough to secure understanding but not full appreciation—it is not because it is made in the wrong place. James should now be ready to meet that very various goddess, Fortune, as he had not been when he lacked 'the rypënesse of resoune'.

His readiness, however, is not conveyed. There is nothing of the

Boethian self-possession in his approach to her; the conventional fearfulness of the petitioning lover and the more dreadful association of the wheel with death and hell replace it. Despite Minerva's lecture on the real, if limited, power of reason and 'Gude Hope' to influence the fickle goddess, nothing in the traditional picture given here encourages us to see her new kindness as an effect of the instruction that he has received. Also nothing about her suggests the intervention of grace; that this is involved we only learn later. On the other hand, if an intractable tradition has obscured the significant connection of Fortune's action with previous events in the visionary sequence, it has also prevented the danger of reason seeming to be given the credit that must eventually go to Grace; and, more immediately, it allows an easier transition to the awakened dreamer's very natural reassertion of Fortune's power in this world, where man's 'besy goste' can enjoy no greater 'sekirnes' than dreams (173-4).

Here we are with the prisoner-complainant again, but now he makes a statement that the repentant Everyman might have made, one that is not meant to be controverted: only in 'the place that thou cam fro' is there real surety. What follows, the lighting on his hand of the dove bearing good tidings, signifies this source of true comfort: whatever reason or virtue he has acquired, the change to good fortune must finally be recognized as the work of Grace. It is in this sense, and not with some deterministic reference, that the statement is to be understood, 'For in the heuyn decretit is the cure' (179). That is how the Christian is supposed to see events, and we are to think that James is now able to do this. This supernatural representation has been objected to by Simon for having a real rather than a visionary context, but the act of grace had to be placed in the waking world if it was to have an effect of reality, and most readers will respond to it on the level of symbolic language rather than actual event. A more serious objection to it, as language, will be considered later.

In st. 181 the prisoner is a free man and happy with his 'souirane' and can now say that his good fortune day by day quickens his 'lore'. By his different route he has reached the same destination as did Boethius by his philosophy; he has found the 'faire cheyne of lufe' in the marriage-bond, 'lufis ȝok that esy is and sure' (193).

The ensuing celebration does not forget the larger in the immediate theme, the lifetime pattern of good within which the temporary evil was contained. Not only is the past celebrated along with the happier present but the attitude of review is established by distancing the marriage from the writer as a remembered event, 'In zouth, of lufe' (193). The conventional valediction to the book is equally addressed to the events it records. The penultimate stanza returns to the significant image of the first, the heavenly circle, now explicitly a circle of grace. The last stanza maintains this viewpoint by defining the poem as a hymn and recommending the souls of the poet's masters 'vnto the blisse of hevin'.[1]

In *The Kingis Quair* the author has succeeded, for the most part, in relating the selected events or stages of his experience to the significant shape that they comprise as a whole. His partial failure to develop his intention in two scenes, those of the earthly paradise and Fortune's wheel, has not prevented an overall success. Particularly notable is the effective balance of his composition: the sense of an argument with a beginning, a middle, and an end that reflects the beginning, is stronger in the reader's response than is the case with most medieval poems.

*   *   *   *   *

How this well-patterned argument is impressed on the reader's consciousness by a suitable and memorable choice of situation, attitude and expressive image is worth some study.

It has been objected that it is easy to imagine the writer who speaks at the outset as being in the same position as the prisoner who makes his lament, though the writer's words make clear that this is not so.[2] That he can be so imagined is, however, a convenience of the narrative, for it helps to give a unity of impression to all that precedes the beloved's appearance, defining its introductory character and setting up a striking contrast with the brighter life she introduces. The unity comes of the common concern of the reflective poet and protesting prisoner with the Boethian problem of Fortune. It is established by a consistency in the kinds of imagery used to convey that concern.

Its seriousness for James in both rôles is expressed by a series of pictures all indicative, in their various kinds, of Fortune's power and the subject's weakness—the stars viewed high in heaven by a sleepless

---

[1] The 'Amen' which follows 'hevin' in MS may well be the king's.
[2] Simon, *op. cit.*, p. 204.

author, restless he does not know why, turning naturally to the conso-
latory reflections of the philosopher-prisoner which explain his mood
to him, the bell of midnight matins heard as an expression of his own
thoughts on 'this matere new'. This significant scene-setting is de-
veloped by a sequence of connecting images. Mental unrest is indicated
by images of restless movement, weakness by images of opposing
power and finally by contrasts of static frustration and dynamic joy,
The unfledged bird 'wayke and vnstable' (14), the rudderless ship,
the fruit prevented from ripening by 'windis variable', the empty sail
that must wait for a favouring wind, the rocks that menace the good
ship, the 'bryght lanternis' that the traveller needs by night (19)
cumulatively and impressively prophesy the fate of vulnerably
inexperienced youth about to put forth on life's voyage.

In st. 21 the angel-like sun with its comforting spread of wings above
the opening flowers, contrasting with the pictures of night and dark-
ness and failure of fruition that had preceded it, symbolizes hopeful
beginnings and cheerful innocence. Along with the friendly bustle of
departure—'With mony "fare wele" and "sanct Johne to borowe"'—it
sketches a pleasant picture that is to be rudely effaced by ideas of
violence, 'wawis weltering to and fro', the 'strong hand' of enemies. A
brusque alternation of suggestions of harsh confinement, weary
endurance, succeeds—'in strayte ward and in strong prisoune,' 'the
heuy lyne' of Lachesis' distaff, the same heaviness of spirit conveyed in
the way the years of captivity are expressed, 'twisë nyne'.

The symbolic thinking thus developed in the introductory section
has been of one controlling mood, sombre in its reminiscence and
reflection. It has been very much of a generalizing, even allegorizing,
tendency, directing attention to the author as philosopher even more
than subject. This changes when the single picture of prison and
prisoner replaces the many images, when the prisoner speaks from his
particular situation.

His complaint—'I, a man, and lakkith libertee!'—is then supported
by the purely picturesque argument of the free and bright creatures
outside, the sunlit arbour and its birds. They define by simple contrast
his isolation and frustration, more effectively than does his own
rhetoric, though the conceit of being a zero among figures—'I suffere
allone amang the figuris nyne'—has a bleak force. Admirable use is
made of the thick hedges and branching juniper of the arbour to

suggest both a private world of delight and his exclusion from it. Bird-movements—'From beugh to beugh thai hippit and thai plaid'— and bird-song, welcoming winter's passing and spring's coming, are at once a celebration of nature and statement of his alienation from it. The conception of 'Venus chapel clerkis' is conventional enough, but their hymnal chanting to love is unusually meaningful because of the questioning of the prisoner who listens. Something like a declaration of faith in the creative goodness of God is being made in the birds' song of love. Love's papal powers, both 'To bynd and louse and maken thrallis free', are what the prisoner is about to test. In effect, the birds assert what he would like to believe and cannot since his experience gives no warrant for it.

The answering appearance of the beloved makes a brilliant effect. Described in purely external terms of fiery jewels and dazzling metals ('spangis bryght as gold'), it has the unnatural clarity of one of Dunbar's allegoric descriptions and is thus suitable to its semi-visionary character. Yet there are attractively human and dramatic touches. Despite the jewelry her dress is 'halflyng louse for haste', a suggestion of impulse and innocence; and the conveyance of delighted shock in the watching prisoner, who abruptly draws back his head as if to recover and debate the reality of what he sees, is admirably done (42). A convincing tenderness enters his references to the 'lytill hound' and 'lytill nyghtingale'; and his distress that the nightingale is silent, that anything he does may drive it away, that he must wait for a wind to wake it to song on its branch, and meanwhile the girl will find no reason to stay, expresses dramatically his impotence and painful dependence on the hope that she brings. With her departure the images of the bucket that goes to the well in vain, the day that is turned to night, and the now for the first time mentioned cold of the prison walls, answer well to the heightened frustration that the 'vision' leaves.

As already remarked, the Biblical features of the following dream are suitable to its character of an instructive revelation. The dreamer leaves his prison effortlessly, the door of Venus's palace opens, 'as quho sais, "at a thought"', and the remoteness and symbolic nature of the figures described, like groups of statuary or scenes in an illuminated manuscript, are emphasized by the incorporeal voice that comments. Quite properly nothing here is at the level of life and a want of decorum is only briefly sensed with the rhetorical attempt to put real passion into the lover's appeal. Here a confusion of imagery, rare in the *Quair*'s poetical logic, makes an impression of artifice (100)—Venus is at once 'suete well', 'blisfull havin and sure', 'anker and keye', and feudal mistress of her 'man'. She herself, however, is given a fitting dignity. The supplicant must wait a while before she turns her face to him, slowly, so that an effect of deliberation is given to her words. In her speech there is an alternation of aspects of her character: she is first presented in her destinal function of planetary goddess; next as critical judge of the lover's merits; then as a cosmic mercy, represented in this last rôle by the tears (showers) of Spring (117), responsive flowers and sunshine, 'the lightis in the hevin round', all symbols of her services in the world of nature to un-appreciative man; and finally, by her association with Saturn (in one tradition equated with divine justice and perfection), in her first-mentioned rôle as the executrix of law (122–3). One might describe the impression made by her as that of an unusually austere Virgin, as much the voice of a Christian heaven as is the wholly judicial Minerva, who is next to be approached in her 'court riall' and 'ordour digne'.

In the latter there is much of the preacher and something of the confessor and even theologian. She is authority itself, the 'stern daughter of the voice of God', emotion is not found in her as it is in Venus, only right reason. Her language is Biblical when it is not weightily repetitive in the deliberate, judicial way—'I haue wel herd and vnderstond', 'thy request, to procure and to fond' (127). She is least impressive when, somewhat academically, she states opposing opinions on free will instead of simply asserting the one correct view. Deliberately formal rather than natural and spontaneous as her 'court dyvine' is, as a significant image it is central in one's picturing of the supplicant; it defines him as not simply the romantic lover but the Christian lover.

By contrast, in the description of the joyous plain to which the visionary descends the symbols are of abundance and vitality. His sensuous response to the happiness it represents is conveyed chiefly by his heightened awareness of light, movement and sound. The pebbles in the river are 'bryght as ony gold', the fishes' scales 'As gesserant ay glitterit in my sight', the fish 'Lap, and playit, and in a rout can swym', the tumble of the stream is heard 'mellit with armony'. There are green-leaved, fruit-bearing trees 'delitable to sene'. And in the catalogue of creatures seen some few descriptions capture at least a characteristic life. However, the symbolism of the plain is largely wasted, especially in the bestiary, because of the hasty, snapshot character of its references. It appears too briefly and is left too abruptly—'Bot now to purpose' (158)—for its proper significance of joyous meditation to be clearly conveyed.

This cursoriness is all the more regrettable for the inevitable inadequacy of the ensuing picture of the many-coloured, 'cheer-changing' goddess and her wheel, as symbolic language for the important meaning that they should carry. No medieval poet succeeds in making much of this pictorial theme, but it had its logical place in the procession of visionary events, and he does succeed more than most poets in suggesting something of Fortune's menace, her busyness and 'sudayn weltering'. His best stroke of judgment in the presentation, however, is undoubtedly the rude dispatch with which she receives and dismisses the supplicant's case. Her significance is much better realized in the reaction of the rudely awakened dreamer. The bird image that had first expressed vulnerable youth (14), then the freedom and joy of life outside the prison, and the prisoner's anxieties lest he should lose his chance to participate in that life, now focuses unforgettably the ancient theme, 'here is no abiding place' (173).

Much less expressive as symbolic language is the reassuring picture of the dove with its illuminated scroll, not because the marvellous thus intrudes in a supposedly real context, which is Simon's objection, or because an image from art proclaims artifice, for the symbolic character of situation and action has been sufficiently patent elsewhere, but because, *in its context*, the first-person address—'I bring, lufar, I bring/ The newis glad', etc.—is not easily related to any imagined speaker or writer. James tries to make the episode say too much: the bird lighting on the prisoner's hand represents both Grace with its gift of faithful love (the most common meaning of the turtle-dove) and the beloved herself. The illuminated scroll is both a charter of divine confirmation and a love-letter; its gillyflowers are flowers of March, the month of the unhappy event that made happiness possible, and, as their popular names of 'queen's flower' and 'cherisaunce' signify, tokens of affection and the marriage to come.[1] What is clearly and happily articulated is not the logical meaning of the episode itself, but the subject's emo-

[1] See notes to sts. 177, 178.

tional response to it; to his feelings the good tidings that mean so many things are indeed miraculous.

In the concluding part of the poem the initial stance of the reviewer of events is resumed but now with reference to the delighted present rather than the sombre past. The hymnal purpose, only hinted in the allusion to the midnight matins, is now effected. The hymn simply but very effectively recapitulates the poem's significant images, stressing the happier meaning that they have since acquired—'the blisfull goddis all,/So fair that glitteren in the firmament!' (189), 'fortunys exiltree/ And quhele, that thus so wele has quhirlit me!' (189), 'the fairë castell wall', 'the sanctis marciall', 'the suete grene bewis bent' (191), 'lufis ӡok that esy is and sure' (193), and finally 'the hevynnis figure circulere' where long ago God's will might have been read and seen to be good.

In the 'faire cheyne of lufe' that James has fashioned from events and the symbols that represent them some links are less strong than others but the chain holds and the whole can be admired for its workmanship.

✻　　✻　　✻　　✻　　✻

The developing logic of event, attitude and symbol, in the *Quair* is supported by a correspondingly various style. Changes of scene and thought and mood in the mental drama are mostly represented in a convincingly appropriate way. Yet the basic character of the style is one of extreme simplicity. It is sober and almost prosaic, prevailingly colloquial, and it is this excellent plainness that controls and sets off the author's special effects when they come.

The opening manner is factual and introspective, that of a man quietly talking his way towards his serious subject, his observations keyed to the mood that has caused his sleepless state, 'Forwakit and forwalowit, thus musing,/Wery, forlyn' (11). The bell that breaks in on his thoughts echoes their heaviness—'Tell on, man, quhat the befell'. The address to inexperienced youth that follows is not felt as rhetoric but as reflective remembrance—'Wist thou thy payne to cum and thy trauaille/For sorow and drede wele myght thou wepe and waille!'

With so deliberate a start the development of pace in the recollective narrative, to its abrupt climax in the capture—'With strong hand, by fors schortly to say', 'Fortune it schupe non othir wayis to be' (24)—

is the more impressive. And the argumentation of the prisoner's complaint comes in with the same effect of facts that speak for themselves—'The bird, the beste, the fisch eke in the see,/They lyve in fredome, euerich in his kynd,/And I, a man, and lakkith libertee!' (27). Details of description take on a force that a less restrained, more overtly poetical manner might have wanted. An excellent example of how this restriction to an almost prosaic level of observation can convey feeling is the picture of the arbour's screened privacy (32), which paints into its subject both the observer's confinement and admiration of the spreading life outside.

> So thik the bewis and the leues grene
> Beschadit all the aleyes that there were;
> And myddis of the herbere myght be sene
> The scharp, grene, suetë jenepere,
> Growing so faire with branchis here and there,
> That, as it semyt to a lyf without,
> The bewis spred the herbere all about.

Similarly, when the singing voice enters, the difference of key and pitch is the better appreciated: 'And sing with vs, away winter, away!/Cum somer, cum, the suete sesoune and sonne!' Lyrical movement is always qualified by mention of detail or an appearance of reasoning, and gains body by this. The sense of a real movement of mind and feeling owes to this factualness and argumentativeness. Phrases like 'vnto my self I thought', 'For gif he be', 'Eft wald I think', etc., secure the impression of a truthful narrative, much as the contrary physical responses of the watching prisoner—'And in my hede I drewe ryght hastily,/And eftsones I lent it forth ageyne' (42)—make convincing the mental shock of the first sight of the girl in the arbour. By such simple touches actual recollection of the moment is suggested.

In particular cases the plainness underlines a delightful felicity of phrasing—'This gardyn full of flouris as thai stand' (43.5), 'Beautee eneuch to mak a world to dote' (47.7)

It is, of course, a suitable manner for the introverted melancholy that colours the first section of the poem, and marries well with the sober lyricism that the melancholy introduces, as in the expression of the prisoner's helpless anxiety over the nightingale's sleepy silence, when its song might serve to keep the girl in the garden: 'Bot, blawe wind, blawe, and do the leuis schake,/That sum twig may wag, and mak hir to wake' (60). The rhetoric used to list the depressive effects of the beloved's going derives most of its success from the simple final clause, 'Sen sche is gone' (71).

In the introducing of the vision the sympathy of this well-maintained simplicity with the Biblical echoes—'I bring the confort and hele, be nought affrayde'—and with the supernatural circumstances—'I went my weye, nas nothing me ageyne'—contributes to their acceptance. Perhaps no other manner could have fitted so well with matter that was at once religious and autobiographic. At this point the plain style of the descriptive commentary is used to establish the authority of the incorporeal commentator, as later of the didactic goddesses, the dignity of the unearthly scene and the importance of what is being said. When emphasis is intended it is usually conveyed only by a heavier stress in the rhythm or by the simplest of all rhetorical devices, that of the dramatic repetition of words and phrases: 'Here bene' is thrice repeated within st. 85 and 'Sum' five times in st. 87. The poet's best moments indeed have little or nothing of 'literary' effect; these lines are 'prose-speech' so sensitive that they are fine poetry (103):

> that suetë hevinly sight,
> That I, within the wallis cald as stone,
> So suetly saw on morow walk and gone,
> Law in the gardyn, ryght tofore myn eye.

The style's varying success in giving a characteristic utterance to the three goddesses is instructive. It gives sensitive expression to the aspect of Venus defined in the phrase rightly admired by Simon, 'My femynyne and wofull tender hert', but over so long a speech its fresh plainness, despite the occasional lyrical movement, shades into the monotone that is too often characteristic of medieval prose rhythms. In the description of Minerva's court it displays the dignity and nobility of which it is capable (125):

> the perfyte excellence,
> The sad renowne, the state, the reuerence,
> The strenth, the beautee and the ordour digne,
> Off hir court riall, noble and benigne.

And in her sermon a colloquial directness and proverbial crispness does much to ward off the mere prosiness that does intrude. A favourable

example is her dictum, 'Gif the ne list thy lufe on vertew set,/Vertu
sal be the cause of thy forfet' (129). Again something of the plain
excellence of Biblical idiom is intermittently captured, particularly in
the second of these two lines—'Ground thou thy werk therefore vpon
the stone,/And thy desire sall forthward with the gone' (131). If the
pronouncement on free will is entirely devoid of poetic quality—one
cannot expect all such matter to be transmuted by style—it has an
economy and clarity unusual in such expositions.

The earthly paradise, of course, asked for impressionistic effects of the
simplest kind and here the style was naturally employed (152):

> The cristall water ran so clere and cold,
> That in myn ere maid contynualy
> A maner soune mellit with armony.

Even in the catalogue, whose method of definitions is at odds with the
desired sense of nature, life is momentarily caught in a word or phrase,
as in these: 'the clymbare gayte' 'the herknere bore', 'The lytill
squerell full of besynesse', 'The haire also that oft gooth to the wortis'.

The goddess Fortune, celebrated for her sudden change of face to
favourite and foe alike, had always been a figure of dreadful mystery,
brooking no question, brusque and peremptory in speech, seldom
accorded any dignity of manner. Accepting the traditional portrait
James was able to render her in both her main aspects. The pit that he
imagines beneath her wheel conveys the first of them: 'Bot o thing
herd I, that quho therein fell/Come no more vp agane tidingis to
telle'. The second is captured in equally graphic 'prose': ' "Fare wele,"
quod sche, and by the ere me toke/So ernestly that therewithall I woke'.

Stanza 173, in which the awakened dreamer speaks, is unquestionably
the finest demonstration of the style's aptness for significant comment:

> O besy goste, ay flikering to and fro,
> That neuer art in quiet nor in rest
> Till thou cum to that place that thou cam fro,
> Quhich is thy first and verray proper nest;
> From day to day so sore here artow drest,
> That with thy flesche ay waking art in trouble,
> And sleping eke, of pyne so has thou double.

This is quintessential expression, with the qualities of form and spirit
that Arnold's canon of 'high seriousness' requires, such as Chaucer

achieves in the commencement of his *Hous of Fame* and rarely elsewhere, such as Henryson's epitaph for Cresseid is, and Dunbar matches for a classic moment in his *Meditation on Winter*: 'Thou, tending to ane othir place,/A journey going euery day'. What follows, the verses of exultation, almost touch this quality at points, as in the excellent stanza 193.

The perfect round that James finally conceives his experience to have been, 'Quho coutht it red, agone syne mony a ʒere', is not felt to be a mere play of fancy; not only because the concept is a natural one and, though optimistic, involves no denial of the circle's less happy half, but also because style as well as structure and symbol has prepared the reader for its imaginative acceptance. At its best the king's language shares the fine simplicity of its argument.

The Kingis Quair

Heigh in the hevynnis figure circulere
The rody sterres twynklyt as the fyre;
And in Aquary Cinthia the clere
Rynsid hir tressis like the goldin wyre,
That late tofore in faire and fresche atyre
Through Capricorn heved hir hornis bright.
North northward approchit the myd-nyght.

2   Quhen as I lay in bed allone waking,
New partit out of slepe alyte tofore,
Fell me to mynd of mony diuerse thing,
Off this and that, can I nought say quharefore
Bot slepe for craft in erth myght I no more;
For Quhiche as tho coude I no better wyle
Bot toke a boke to rede apon a quhile.

3   Off quhiche the name is clepit properly
Boece, efter him that was the compiloure,
Schewing the counsele of philosophye,
Compilit by that noble senatoure
Off Rome, quhilom that was the warldis floure,
And from estate by fortune for a quhile
Forjugit was to pouert in exile.

4   And there to here this worthy lord and clerk,
His metir suete full of moralitee,
His flourit pen, so fair he set awerk,
Descryving first of his prosperitee
And out of that his infelicitee,
And than how he in his poleyt report
In philosophy can him to confort!

5

For quhiche though I in purpose at my boke
To borowe a slepe at thilkë tyme began,
Or ever I stent my lest was more to loke
Vpon the writing of this noble man,
That in him self the full recouer wan
Off his infortune, pouert and distresse,
And in tham set his verray sekirnesse.

6

And so the vertew of his ʒouth before
Was in his age the ground of his delytis.
Fortune the bak him turnyt, and therefore
He makith joye and confort, that he quitis
Off thir vnsekir warldis appetitis;
And so aworth he takith his penance
And of his vertew maid it suffisance.

7

With mony a noble resoune, as him likit,
Enditing in his fairë Latyne tong,
So full of fruyte and rethorikly pykit,
Quhich to declare my scole is ouer ʒong;
Therefore I lat him pas, and in my tong
Procede I will agayn to the sentence
Of my mater, and leve all incidence.

8

The long nyght beholding, as I saide,
Myn eyen gan to smert for studying,
My buke I schet and at my hede It laide
And doune I lay but ony tarying,
This matere new in my mynd rolling,
This is to seyne, how that eche estate
As Fortune lykith thame sche will translate.

9

For sothe It is, that on hir tolter quhele
Euery wight cleuerith in his stage,
And failyng foting oft quhen hir lest rele,
Sum vp, sum doune; is none estate nor age
Ensured more, the pryncë than the page,
So vncouthly hir werdes sche deuidith,
Namly in ʒouth that seildin ought prouidith.

10   Among thir thoughtis rolling to and fro
Fell me to mynd of my fortune and vre,
In tender ȝouth how sche was first my fo,
And eft my frende, and how I gat recure
Off my distresse; and all myn auenture
I gan ourehayle, that langer slepe ne rest
Ne myght I nat, so were my wittis wrest.

11   Forwakit and forwalowit, thus musing,
Wery, forlyin, I lestnyt sodaynlye
And sone I herd the bell to matyns ryng,
And vp I rase, no langer wald I lye.
Bot now, how trowe ȝe, suich a fantasye
Fell me to mynd, that ay me thought the bell
Said to me, "Tell on, man, quhat the befell".

12   Thought I tho to my self: "Quhat may this be?
This is myn awin ymagynacioune.
It is no lyf that spekis vnto me.
It is a bell, or that impressioune
Off my thought causith this illusioune,
That dooth me think so nycely in this wise".
And so befell as I schall ȝou deuise.

13   Determyt furth therewith in myn entent,
Sen I thus haue ymagynit of this soune,
And in my tyme more ink and paper spent
To lyte effect, I tuke conclusioune
Sum newë thing to write. I set me doune,
And furth-withall my pen in hand I tuke
And maid a croce, and thus begouth my buke.

14   Thou sely ȝouth, of nature indegest,
Vnrypit fruyte with windis variable,
Like to the bird that fed is on the nest
And can nought flee, of wit wayke and vnstable,
To fortune bothe and to infortune hable,
Wist thou thy payne to cum and thy trauaille
For sorow and drede wele myght thou wepe and waille!

15   Thus stant thy confort in vnsekirnesse,
And wantis it that suld the reule and gye;
Ryght as the schip that sailith sterëles
Vpon the rokkis most to harmes hye,
For lak of it that suld bene hir supplye,
So standis thou here in this warldis rage
And wantis that suld gyde all thy viage.

16   I mene this by my self as in partye.
Though nature gave me suffisance in ȝouth,
The rypënesse of resoune lakkit I
To governe with my will, so lyte I couth,
Quhen sterëles to trauaile I begouth,
Amang the wawis of this warld to driue.
And how the case anone I will discriue.

17   With doutfull hert, amang the rokkis blake
My feble bote full fast to stere and rowe,
Helples, allone, the wynter nyght I wake
To wayte the wynd that furthward suld me throwe.
O empti saile, quhare is the wynd suld blowe
Me to the port, quhare gynneth all my game?
Help, Calyope, and wynd, in Marye name!

18   The rokkis clepe I the prolixitee
Off doubilnesse that doith my wittis pall.
The lak of wynd is the deficultee,
Enditing of this lytill trety small.
The bote I clepe the mater hole of all,
My wit vnto the saile that now I wynd
To seke connyng, though I bot lytill fynd.

19   At my begynnyng first I clepe and call
To ȝow Cleo, and to ȝow Polymye,
With Thesiphone, goddis and sistris all,
In nowmer nyne as bokis specifye;
In this processe my wilsum wittis gye,
And with ȝour bryght lanternis wele conuoye
My pen to write my turment and my joye.

20 In Vere that full of vertu is and gude,
   Quhen nature first begynneth hir enprise,
   That quhilum was be cruell frost and flude
   And schouris scharp opprest in mony wyse,
   And Synthius begynneth to aryse
   Heigh in the est, a morow soft and suete,
   Vpward his course to driue in Ariete;

21 Passit mydday bot fourë greis evin,
   Off lenth and brede his angel wingis bryght
   He spred vpon the ground doune fro the hevin,
   That for gladnesse and confort of the sight,
   And with the tiklyng of his hete and light,
   The tender flouris opnyt thame and sprad
   And in thaire nature thankit him for glad.

22 Nought ferre passit the state of innocence,
   Bot nere about the nowmer of ȝeris thre,
   Were it causit throu hevinly influence
   Off goddys will, or othir casualtee,
   Can I nought say, bot out of my contree,
   By thaire avise that had of me the cure,
   Be see to pas tuke I myn auenture.

23 Puruait of all that was vs necessarye,
   With wind at will, vp airly by the morowe,
   Streight vnto schip, no longer wald we tarye,
   The way we tuke—the tyme I tald toforowe—
   With mony "fare wele" and "sanct Johne to borowe"
   Off falowe and frende; and thus with one assent
   We pullit vp saile and furth oure wayis went.

24 Vpon the wawis weltering to and fro,
   So infortunate was that fremyt day
   That, maugre playnly quhethir we wold or no,
   With strong hand, by fors schortly to say,
   Off inymyis takin and led away
   We weren all, and brought in thaire contree.
   Fortune it schupe non othir wayis to be.

25 Quhare as in strayte ward and in strong prisoune,
  So fereforth of my lyf the heuy lyne,
  Without confort, in sorowe and bandoune,
  The secund sistir lukit hath to twyne
  Nere by the space of ȝeris twisë nyne,
  Till Jupiter his merci list aduert
  And send confòrt in relesche of my smert.

26 Quhare as in ward full oft I wold bewaille
  My dedely lyf, full of peyne and penance,
  Saing ryght thus: "Quhat haue I gilt to faille
  My fredome in this warld and my plesance,
  Sen euery wight has thereof suffisance
  That I behold, and I, a creature,
  Put from all this? Hard is myn auenture!

27 The bird, the beste, the fisch eke in the see,
  They lyve in fredome, euerich in his kynd,
  And I, a man, and lakkith libertee!
  Quhat schall I seyne, quhat resoune may I fynd
  That fortune suld do so?" Thus in my mynd
  My folk I wold argewe, bot all for nought;
  Was none that myght that on my peynes rought.

28 Than wold I say, "Gif God me had deuisit
  To lyve my lyf in thraldome thus and pyne,
  Quhat was the cause that he me more comprisit
  Than othir folk to lyve in suich ruyne?
  I suffere allone amang the figuris nyne,
  Ane wofull wrecche that to no wight may spede
  And ȝit of euiry lyvis help hath nede!"

29 The long dayes and the nyghtis eke
  I wold bewaille my fortune in this wise,
  For quhiche agane distresse, confort to seke,
  My custum was on mornis for to ryse
  Airly as day. O happy excercise!
  By the come I to joye out of turment.
  Bot now to purpose of my first entent.

30   Bewailing in my chamber thus allone,
Despeired of all joye and remedye,
Fortirit of my thought and wo begone,
Vnto the wyndow gan I walk in hye
To se the warld and folk that went forby.
As for the tyme, though I of mirthis fude
Myght haue no more, to luke it did me gude.

31   Now was there maid fast by the touris wall
A gardyn faire, and in the cornere set
Ane herbere grene, with wandis long and small
Railit about; and so with treis set
Was all the place, and hawthorn hegis knet,
That lyf was none, was walking there forby,
That myght within scarse ony wight aspye.

32   So thik the bewis and the leues grene
Beschadit all the aleyes that there were;
And myddis of the herbere myght be sene
The scharp, grene, suetë jenipere,
Growing so faire with branchis here and there,
That, as it semyt to a lyf without,
The bewis spred the herbere all about.

33   And on the small grene twistis sat
The lytill suete nyghtingale and song,
So loud and clere, the ympnis consecrat
Off lufis vse, now soft, now lowd among,
That all the gardyng and the wallis rong
Ryght of their song, and of the copill next
Off thaire suete armony, and lo the text:

34   "Worschippe, ӡe that loueris bene this May,
For of ӡour blisse the kalendis ar begonne,
And sing with vs, away winter, away!
Cum somer, cum, the suete sesoune and sonne!
Awake, for schame, that haue ӡour hevynnis wonne,
And amorously lift vp ӡour hedis all.
Thank lufe that list ӡow to his merci call."

35 Quhen thai this song had song a lytill thrawe,
    Thai stent a quhile, and therewith vnaffraid,
    As I beheld and kest myn eyne alawe,
    From beugh to beugh thay hippit and thai plaid,
    And freschly in thaire birdis kynd arraid
    Thaire fetheris new, and fret thame in the sonne,
    And thankit lufe that had thair makis wonne.

36 This was the planë ditee of thaire note,
    And therewithall vnto my self I thought:
    "Quhat luf is this that makis birdis dote?
    Quhat may this be, how cummyth it of ought?
    Quhat nedith it to be so dere ybought?
    It is nothing trowe I bot feynit chere
    And that men list to counterfeten chere."

37 Eft wald I think, "O Lord, quhat may this be,
    That lufe is of so noble myght and kynde,
    Lufing his folk, and suich prosperitee
    Is it of him as we in bukis fynd?
    May he oure hertes setten and vnbynd?
    Hath he vpon oure hertis suich maistrye?
    Or all this is bot feynyt fantasye?

38 For gif he be of so grete excellence
    That he of euery wight hath cure and charge,
    Quhat haue I gilt to him, or doon offense,
    That I am thrall and birdis gone at large,
    Sen him to serue he myght set my corage?
    And gif he be nought so, than may I seyne,
    Quhat makis folk to jangill of him in veyne?

39 Can I nought elles fynd bot gif that he
    Be lord, and as a god may lyue and regne,
    To bynd and louse and maken thrallis free.
    Than wold I pray his blisfull grace benigne
    To hable me vnto his service digne,
    And euermore for to be one of tho
    Him trewly for to serue in wele and wo."

40   And therewith kest I doune myn eye ageyne
        Quhare as I saw walking vnder the toure,
        Full secretly new cummyn hir to pleyne,
        The fairest or the freschest ʒong floure
        That euer I sawe, me thought, before that houre;
        For quhich sodayne abate anone astert
        The blude of all my body to my hert.

41   And though I stude abaisit tho alyte,
        No wonder was, for quhy my wittis all
        Were so ouercome with plesance and delyte,
        Onely throu latting of myn eyen fall,
        That sudaynly my hert become hir thrall
        For euer of free wyll, for of manace
        There was no takyn in hir suetë face.

42   And in my hede I drewe ryght hastily,
        And eftsones I lent it forth ageyne
        And sawe hir walk, that verray womanly,
        With no wight mo bot onely women tueyne.
        Than gan I studye in my self and seyne:
        "A, suete, ar ʒe a warldly creature,
        Or hevinly thing in liknesse of nature?

43   Or ar ʒe god Cupidis owin princesse,
        And cummyn are to louse me out of band?
        Or ar ʒe verray Nature the goddesse,
        That haue depaynted with ʒour hevinly hand
        This gardyn full of flouris as they stand?
        Quhat sall I think? Allace, quhat reuerence
        Sall I minister to ʒour excellence?

44   Gif ʒe a goddesse be and that ʒe like
        To do me payne, I may it nought astert.
        Gif ʒe be warldly wight that dooth me sike,
        Quhy lest god mak ʒou so, my derrest hert,
        To do a sely presoner thus smert,
        That lufis ʒow all, and wote of nought bot wo?
        And therefore, merci, suete, sen it is so."

45   Quhen I a lytill thrawe had maid my moon,
        Bewailling myn infortune and my chance,
        Vnknawin how or quhat was best to doon,
        So ferre I fallying was in lufis dance
        That sodeynly my wit, my contenance,
        My hert, my will, my nature and my mynd,
        Was changit clene ryght in ane othir kynd.

46   Off hir array the forme gif I sall write,
        Toward hir goldin haire and riche atyre,
        It fret-wise couchit was with perllis quhite
        And gretë balas lemyng as the fyre,
        With mony ane emeraut and fair saphire,
        And on hir hede a chaplet fresche of hewe,
        Off plumys partit rede and quhite and blewe;

47   All full of quaking spangis bryght as gold,
        Forgit of schap like to the amorettis,
        So new, so fresch, so plesant to behold;
        The plumys eke like to the floure jonettis
        And othir of schap like to the margarettis,
        And aboue all this there was, wele I wote,
        Beautee eneuch to mak a world to dote;

48   About hir nek, quhite as the fyne amaille
        A gudely cheyne of smale orfeuerye,
        Quhareby there hang a ruby without faille,
        Lyke to ane hertë schapin verily,
        That as a sperk of lowe so wantounly
        Semyt birnyng vpon hir quhytë throte.
        Now, gif there was gud partye, god it wote!

49   And for to walk that freschë mayes morowe
        Ane huke sche had vpon hir tissew quhite,
        That gudeliar had nought bene sene toforowe
        As I suppose, and girt sche was alyte.
        Thus halflyng louse for haste, to suich delyte
        It was to see hir ʒouth in gudelihed,
        That for rudenes to speke thereof I drede.

50 In hir was ȝouthe, beautee, with humble aport,
 Bountee, richesse and wommanly facture,
 God better wote than my pen can report,
 Wisedome, largesse, estate and connyng sure.
 In euery poynt so guydit hir mesure,
 In word, in dede, in schap, in contenance,
 That nature myght no more hir childe auance.

51 Throw quhich anone I knew and vnderstude
 Wele that sche was a warldly creature;
 On quhom to rest myn eye, so mich gude
 It did my wofull hert, I ȝow assure,
 That it was to me joye without mesure;
 And at the last, my luke vnto the hevin
 I threwe furthwith, and said thir versis sevin:

52 "O Venus clere, of goddis stellifyit,
 To quhom I ȝelde homage and sacrifise,
 Fro this day forth ȝour grace be magnifyit,
 That me ressauit haue in suich a wise,
 To lyve vnder ȝour law, and do seruise.
 Now help me furth, and for ȝour merci lede
 My hert to rest, that deis nere for drede."

53 Quhen I with gude entent this orisoune
 Thus endit had, I stynt a lytill stound,
 And eft myn eye full pitously adoune
 I kest, behalding vnto hir lytill hound,
 That with his bellis playit on the ground.
 Than wold I say, and sighe therewith alyte,
 "A, wele were him, that now were in thy plyte!"

54 Ane othir quhile the lytill nyghtingale
 That sat apon the twiggis wold I chide,
 And say ryght thus: "Quhare ar thy notis smale,
 That thou of loue has song this morowe tyde?
 Seis thou nought hir that sittis the besyde?
 For Venus sake, the blisfull goddesse clere,
 Sing on agane and mak my lady chere.

And eke I pray for all the paynes grete,
That for the loue of Proigne, thy sistir dere,
Thou sufferit quhilom—quhen thy brestis wete
Were with the teres of thyne eyen clere
All bludy ronne, that pitee was to here
The crueltee of that vnknyghtly dede,
Quhare was fro the bereft thy maidenhede.

56 Lift vp thyne hert and sing with gude entent,
And in thy notis suete the tresoune telle
That to thy sistir, trewe and innocent,
Was kythit by hir husband false and fell;
For quhois gilt, as it is worthy wel,
Chide thir husbandis that are false, I say,
And bid thame mend, in the twenti deuil way!

57 O lytill wrecche, allace, maist thou nought se
Quho commyth ȝond? Is it now tyme to wring?
Quhat sory thought is fallin vpon the?
Opyn thy throte. Hastow no lest to sing?
Allace, sen thou of resoune had felyng!
Now, suete bird, say ones to me 'pepe'.
I dee for wo. Me think thou gynnis slepe!

58 Hastow no mynde of lufe? Quhare is thy make?
Or artow seke, or smyt with jelousye?
Or is sche dede, or hath sche the forsake?
Quhat is the cause of thy malancolye,
That thou no more list maken melodye?
Sluggart, for schame, lo here thy goldin hour
That worth were halë all thy lyvis laboure!

59 Gyf thou suld sing wele euer in thy lyve,
Here is in fay the tyme and eke the space.
Quhat, wostow than sum bird may cum and stryve
In song with the, the maistry to purchace?
Suld thou then cesse? It were grete schame, allace.
And here, to wyn gree happily for euer,
Here is the tyme to syng, or ellis neuer!

60   I thought eke thus, gif I my handis clap,
Or gif I cast, than will sche flee away;
And gif I hald my pes, than will sche nap;
And gif I crye, sche wate nought quhat I say.
Thus quhat is best wate I nought be this day,
Bot, blawe wynd, blawe, and do the leuis schake,
That sum twig may wag, and mak hir to wake.

61   With that anone ryght sche toke vp a sang,
Quhare come anone mo birdis and alight.
Bot than to here the mirth was thame amang!
Ouer that to, to see the suetë sicht
Off hyr ymage, my spirit was so light
Me thought I flawe for joy without arest,
So were my wittis boundin all to fest.

62   And to the notis of the philomene
Quhilkis sche sang, the ditee there I maid,
Direct to hir that was my hertis quene,
Withoutin quhom no songis may me glade;
And to that sanct, there walking in the schade,
My bedis thus, with humble hert entere,
Deuotly than I said on this manere:

63   "Quhen sall ʒour merci rew vpon ʒour man,
Quhois seruice is ʒit vncouth vnto ʒow?
Sen, quhen ʒe go, there is nought ellis than
Bot, hert, quhere as the body may nought throu,
Folow thy hevin. Quho suld be glad bot thou,
That suich a gyde to folow has vndertake?
Were it throu hell, the way thou nought forsake!"

64   And efter this the birdis, euerichone,
Tuke vp ane othir sang full loud and clere,
And with a voce said, "Wele is vs begone,
That with oure makis are togider here.
We proyne and play, without dout and dangere,
All clothit in a soyte full fresch and newe,
In lufis service besy, glad and trewe.

65   And ʒe, fresche May, ay mercifull to bridis,
Now welcum be ʒe, floure of monethis all;
For nought onely ʒour grace vpon vs bydis,
Bot all the warld to witnes this we call,
That strowit hath so playnly ouer all
With new, fresche, suete and tender grene,
Oure lyf, oure lust, oure gouernoure, oure quene."

66   This was thair song, as semyt me full heye,
With full mony vncouth suete note and schill,
And therewithall that faire vpward hir eye
Wold cast amang, as it was goddis will,
Quhare I myght se, standing allone full still,
The faire facture that nature for maistrye
In hir visage wrought had full lufingly.

67   And quhen sche walkit had a lytill thrawe
Vnder the suete grene bewis bent,
Hir faire fresche face, as quhite as ony snawe,
Scho turnyt has and furth hir wayis went.
Bot tho began myn axis and turment,
To sene hir part and folowe I na myght.
Me thought the day was turnyt into nyght.

68   Than said I thus, "Quhareto lyve I langer,
Wofullest wicht and subiect vnto peyne?
Of peyne, no! God wote, ʒa, for thay no stranger
May wirken ony wight, I dare wele seyne!
How may this be, that deth and lyf, bothe tueyne,
Sall bothe atonis in a creature
Togidder duell, and turment thus nature?

69   I may nought ellis done bot wepe and waile,
Within thir caldë wallis thus ilokin.
From hennesfurth my rest is my trauaile,
My dryë thrist with teris sall I slokin,
And on my self bene all my harmys wrokin.
Thus bute is none, bot Venus of hir grace
Will schape remede, or do my spirit pace.

70   As Tantalus I trauaile ay but-les,
That euer ylike hailith at the well
Water to draw with buket botemles,
And may nought spede, quhois penance is ane hell.
So by my self this tale I may wele telle,
For vnto hir that herith nought I pleyne;
Thus like to him my trauaile is in veyne.

71   So sore thus sighit I with my self allone
That turnyt is my strenth in febilnesse,
My wele in wo, my frendis all in fone,
My lyf in deth, my lyght into dirknesse,
My hope in feere, in dout my sekirnesse,
Sen sche is gone—and god mote hir conuoye,
That me may gyde to turment and to joye!

72   The long day thus gan I prye and poure,
Till Phebus endit had his bemes bryght
And bad go farewele euery lef and floure;
This is to say, approchen gan the nyght
And Esperus his lampis gan to light,
Quhen, in the wyndow, still as any stone,
I bade at lenth and kneling maid my mone.

73   So lang till evin, for lak of myght and mynd
Forwepit and forpleynit pitously,
Ourset so sorow had bothe hert and mynd,
That to the coldë stone my hede on wrye
I laid and lent, amaisit verily,
Half sleping and half suoune, in suich a wise.
And quhat I met I will ʒow now deuise.

74   Me thought that thus all sodeynly a lyght
In at the wyndow come, quhare that I lent,
Off quhich the chambere wyndow schone full bryght,
And all my body so it hath ouerwent,
That of my sicht the vertew was iblent,
And that withall a voce vnto me saide,
"I bring the confort and hele, be nought affrayde."

75   And furth anone it passit sodeynly
      Quhere it come in the ryght way ageyne,
      And sone, me thought, furth at the dure in hye
      I went my weye, nas nothing me ageyne.
      And hastily, by bothe the armes tueyne,
      I was araisit vp into the aire,
      Clippit in a cloude of cristall clere and faire;

76   Ascending vpward ay fro spere to spere,
      Through aire and watere and the hotë fyre,
      Till that I come vnto the circle clere
      Off Signifere, quhare fairë, bryght and schire,
      The signis schone, and in the glade empire
      Off blisfull Venus, quhare ane cryit now—
      So sudaynly almost I wist nought how!

77   Off quhiche the place, quhen as I come there nye,
      Was all, me thought, of cristall stonis wrought,
      And to the port I liftit was in hye,
      Quhare sodaynly, as quho sais 'at a thought',
      It opnyt and I was anon in brought,
      Within a chamber largë, rowm and faire,
      And there I fand of peple grete repaire.

78   This is to seyne, that present in that place
      Me thought I sawe, of euery nacioune,
      Loueris that endit had thaire lyfis space
      In lovis seruice, mony a mylioune,
      Off quhois chancis maid is mencioune
      In diuerse bukis, quho thame list to se,
      And therefore here thaire namys lat I be.

79   The quhois auenture and grete labouris
      Aboue thaire hedis writin there I fand,
      This is to seyne, martris and confessouris,
      Eche in his stage and his make in his hand;
      And therewithall thir peple sawe I stand
      With mony a sad and solempt contenance,
      After as lufe thame lykit to auance.

80   Off gude folkis that faire in lufe befill
There saw I sitt in ordour, by thame one,
With hedis hore, and with thame stude Gude Will
To talk and play, and after that anone
Besyde thame, and next there, saw I gone
Curage amang the freschë folkis ʒong,
And with thame playit full merily and song.

81   And in ane other stage, endlong the wall,
There saw I stand in capis wyde and lang
A full grete nowmer, bot thaire hudis all,
Wist I nought quhy, atoure thair eyen hang,
And ay to thame come Repentance amang
And maid thame chere, degysit in his wede.
And dounward efter that ʒit I tuke hede.

82   Ryght ouerthwert the chamber was there drawe
A trevesse thin and quhite, all of plesance,
The quhich behynd standing there I sawe
A warld of folk, and by thaire contenance
Thaire hertis semyt full of displesance,
With billis in thaire handis, of one assent
Vnto the juge thaire playntis to present.

83   And therewithall apperit vnto me
A voce, and said: "Tak hede, man, and behold.
Ʒond there thou seis the hiest stage and gree,
Off agit folk with hedis hore and olde,
Ʒone were the folk that neuer changë wold
In lufe, bot trewly seruit him alway,
In euery age, vnto thaire ending day.

84   For fro the tyme that thai coud vnderstand
The exercise, of lufis craft the cure,
Was none on lyve that toke so moche on hand
For lufis sake, nor langer did endure
In lufis seruice, for, man, I the assure,
Quhen thay of ʒouth ressauit had the fill
Ʒit in thaire age thame lakkit no gude will.

85   Here bene also of suiche as in counsailis
        And all thare dedis were to Venus trewe.
        Here bene the princis, faucht the grete batailis,
        In mynd of quhom ar maid the bukis newe.
        Here bene the poetis, the sciencis knewe,
        Throwout the warld, of lufe in thaire suete layes,
        Suich as Ouide and Omere in thaire dayes.

86   And efter thame, downe in the nextë stage,
        There as thou seis the ȝongë folkis pleye,
        Lo, thise were thay that in thaire myddill age
        Seruandis were to lufe in mony weye,
        And diuersely happinnit for to deye,
        Sum soroufully for wanting of thare makis,
        And sum in armes for thaire ladyes sakis;

87   And othir eke by othir diuerse chance,
        As happin folk all day as ȝe may se—
        Sum for dispaire without recouerance,
        Sum for desyre surmounting thaire degree,
        Sum for dispite and othir inmytee,
        Sum for vnkyndënes without a quhy,
        Sum for to moche, and sum for jelousye.

88   And efter this, vpon ȝone stagë doune,
        Tho that thou seis stond in capis wyde,
        Ȝone were quhilum folk of religioune,
        That from the warld thaire gouernance did hide
        And frely seruit lufe on euery syde
        In secrete, with thaire bodyis and thaire gudis.
        And lo quhy so thai hingen doune thaire hudis:

89   For though that thai were hardy at assay
        And did him seruice quhilum priuely,
        Ȝit to the warldis eye it semyt nay,
        So was thaire seruice halflyng cowardy;
        And for thay first forsuke him opynly
        And efter that thereof had repenting,
        For schame thaire hudis oure thaire eyne thay hyng.

90   And seis thou now ʒone multitude on rawe
                Standing behynd ʒone trauerse of delyte?
                Sum bene of thame that haldin were full lawe,
                And take by frendis, nothing thay to wyte,
                In ʒouth from lufe into the cloistere quite;
                And for that cause are cum vnreconsilit,
                On thame to pleyne that so thame had begilit.

91   And othir bene amongis thame also
                That cummyn are to court on lufe to pleyne,
                For he thaire bodyes had bestowit so
                Quhare bothe thaire hertes gruchë there-ageyne;
                For quhiche in all thaire dayes, sothe to seyne,
                Quhen othir lyvit in joye and in plesance,
                Thaire lyf was nought bot care and repentance;

92   And quhare thaire hertis gevin were and set,
                Were coplit with othir that coud nought accord.
                Thus were thai wrangit that did no forfet,
                Departing thame that neuer wold discord."
                Off ʒong ladies faire and mony lord,
                That thus by maistry were fro thair chose dryve,
                Full redy were their playntis there to gyve.

93   And othir also I sawe compleynyng there
                Vpon Fortune and hir grete variance,
                That quhere in loue so wele they coplit were,
                With thaire suete makis coplit in plesance,
                Scho sodeynly maid thaire disseuerance
                And tuke thame of this warldis companye,
                Withoutin cause, there was none othir quhy.

94   And in a chiere of estate besyde,
                With wingis bright, all plumyt bot his face,
                There sawe I sitt the blyndë god Cupide,
                With bow in hand that bent full redy was,
                And by him hang thre arowis in a cas,
                Off quhiche the hedis grundyn were full ryght,
                Off diuerse metals forgit, faire and bryght.

95   And with the first that hedit is of gold
      He smytis soft, and that has esy cure.
      The secund was of siluer, mony-fold
      Wers than the first and harder auenture.
      The thrid of stele is schot without recure.
      And on his long ʒalow lokkis schene
      A chaplet had he all of levis grene.

96   And in a retrete lytill of compas,
      Depeyntit all with sighis wonder sad,
      Nought suich sighis as hertis doith manace
      Bot suich as dooth lufaris to be glad,
      Fond I Venus vpon hir bed, that had
      A mantill cast ouer hir schuldris quhite.
      Thus clothit was the goddesse of delyte.

97   Stude at the dure Fair Calling, hir vschere,
      That coude his office doon in connyng wise,
      And Secretee, hir thrifty chamberere,
      That besy was in tyme to do seruise,
      And othir mo I can nought on avise.
      And on hir hede of rede rosis full suete
      A chappellet sche had, faire fresch and mete.

98   With quaking hert, astonate of that sight,
      Vnnethis wist I quhat that I suld seyne,
      Bot at the last febily, as I myght,
      With my handis, on bothe my kneis tueyne,
      There I begouth my caris to compleyne
      With ane humble and lamentable chere.
      Thus salute I that goddesse bryght and clere:

99   "Hye quene of lufe, sterre of beneuolence,
      Pitouse princes and planet merciable,
      Appesare of malice and violence
      By vertew sure of ʒour aspectis hable,
      Vnto ʒour grace lat now bene acceptable
      My pure request, that can no forthir gone
      To seken help bot vnto ʒow allone.

100   As ȝe that bene the socoure and suete well
Off remedye, of carefull hertes cure,
And in the hugë weltering wawis fell
Of lufis rage blisfull havin and sure,
O anker and keye of oure gude auenture,
Ȝe haue ȝour man with his gude will conquest.
Merci therefore and bring his hert to rest!

101   Ȝe knaw the cause of all my peynes smert
Bet than my self, and all myn auenture.
Ȝe may conuoye and as ȝow list conuert
The hardest hert that formyt hath nature.
Sen in ȝour handis all halë lyith my cure,
Haue pitee now, O bryght blissfull goddesse,
Off ȝour pure man, and rew on his distresse.

102   And sen I was vnto ȝour lawis strange
By ignorance and nought by felonye,
And that ȝour grace now likit hath to change
My hert to seruen ȝow perpetualye,
Forgeue all this, and schapith remedye
To sauen me, of ȝour benignë grace,
Or do me steruen furthwith in this place.

103   And with the stremes of ȝour percyng lyght
Conuoy my hert, that is so wo begone,
Ageyne vnto that suetë hevinly sight,
That I, within the wallis cald as stone,
So suetly saw on morow walk and gone,
Law in the gardyn, ryght tofore myn eye.
Now, merci, quene, and do me nought to deye!"

104   Thir wordis said, my spirit in dispaire,
A quhile I stynt, abiding efter grace,
And therewithall hir cristall eyen faire
Sche kest asyde, and efter that a space
Benignëly sche turnyt has hir face,
Towardis me full plesantly conueide,
And vnto me ryght in this wise sche seide:

105   "ʒong man, the cause of all thyne inward sorowe
Is nought vnknawin to my deite,
And thy request, bothe now and eke toforowe,
Quhen thou first maid professioune to me.
Sen of my grace I haue inspirit the
To knawe my lawe, contynew furth, for oft
There as I mynt full sore I smyte bot soft.

106   Paciently thou tak thyne auenture.
This will my sone Cupide, and so will I.
He can the stroke, to me langis the cure
Quhen I se tyme, and therefore humily
Abyde and serue and lat Gude Hope the gye.
Bot for I haue thy forehede here present
I will the schewe the more of myn entent.

107   This is to say, though it to me pertene
In lufis lawe the septre to gouerne,
That the effectis of my bemes schene
Has thaire aspectis, by ordynance eterne,
With otheris byndand mynes, to discerne
Quhilum in thingis bothe to cum and gone.
That langis nought to me to writhe allone.

108   As in thyne awin case now may thou se,
For-quhy, lo, that by otheris influence
Thy persone standis nought in libertee;
Quharefore, though I geve the beneuolence,
It standis nought ʒit in myn aduertence
Till certeyne coursis endit be and ronne,
Quhill of trew seruis thow have hir graicë wonne.

109   And ʒit, considering the nakitnesse
Bothe of thy wit, thy persone and thy myght,
It is no mache, of thyne vnworthynesse,
To hir hie birth, estate and beautee bryght.
Als like ʒe bene as day is to the nyght,
Or sek-cloth is vnto fyne cremesye,
Or doken foule vnto the fresche dayesye.

110   Vnlike the mone is to the sonnë schene,
       Eke Januarye is vnlike to May;
       Vnlike the cukkow to the phylomene,
       Thaire tabartis ar nought maid of one array;
       Vnlike the crow is to the papë-jay,
       Vnlike in goldsmythis werk a fischis eye
       To prese with perll or maked be so heye.

111   As I haue said, vnto me belangith
       Specialy the cure of thy seknesse;
       Bot now thy matere so in balance hangith,
       That it requerith, to thy sekirnesse,
       The help of othir mo that bene goddesse,
       And haue in thame the menes and the lore
       In this matere to schorten with thy sore.

112   And for thou sall se wele that I entend
       Vnto thy help, thy welefare to preserue,
       The streight weye thy spirit will I send
       To the goddesse that clepit is Mynerue.
       And se that thou hir hestis wele conserue,
       For in this case sche may be thy supplye,
       And put thy hert in rest als wele as I.

113   Bot, for the way is vncouth vnto the,
       There as hir duelling is and hir sojurne,
       I will that Gud Hope seruand to the be,
       ʒoure alleris frend, to letë the to murn,
       Be thy condyt and gyde till thou returne,
       And hir beseche that sche will, in thy nede,
       Hir counsele geve to thy welefare and spede;

114   And that sche will, as langith hir office,
       Be thy gude lady, help and counseiloure,
       And to the schewe hir rype and gude auise,
       Throw quhich thou may, be processe and laboure,
       Atteyne vnto that glad and goldyn floure
       That thou wald haue so fayn with all thy hart.
       And forthir-more, sen thou hir seruand art,

115   Quhen thou descendis doune to ground ageyne,
        Say to the men that there bene resident,
        How long think thay to stand in my disdeyne,
        That in my lawis bene so negligent
        From day to day, and list thame nought repent,
        Bot breken louse and walken at thaire large?
        Is nought left none that thereof gevis charge?

116   And for," quod sche, "the angir and the smert
        Off thaire vnkyndënesse dooth me constreyne
        My femynyne and wofull tender hert,
        That than I wepe and, to a token pleyne,
        As of my teris cummyth all this reyne,
        That ʒe se on the ground so fastë bete
        Fro day to day, my turment is so grete.

117   And quhen I wepe and stynten othir quhile,
        For pacience that is in womanhede,
        Than all my wrath and rancoure I exile,
        And of my cristall teris that bene schede
        The hony flouris growen vp and sprede,
        That preyen men, ryght in thaire flouris wise,
        Be trewe of lufe and worschip my seruise.

118   And eke in takin of this pitouse tale,
        Quhen so my teris dropen on the ground,
        In thaire nature the lytill birdis smale
        Styntith thaire song and murnyth for that stound;
        And all the lightis in the hevin round
        Off my greuance haue suich compacience,
        That from the ground they hiden thair presence.

119   And ʒit in tokenyng forthir of this thing,
        Quhen flouris springis and freschest bene of hewe,
        And that the birdis on the twistis sing,
        At thilkë tyme ay gynnen folk renewe
        Thaire seruis vnto loue, as ay is dewe
        Most commonly has than his obseruance,
        And of thaire sleuth tofore haue repentance.

120   Thus maist thou seyne that myn effectis grete,
       Vnto the quhiche ʒe aught and mosten weye,
       No lyte offense, to sleuth is all forget;
       And therefore in this wisë to thame seye,
       As I the here haue bidden, and conueye
       The matere all the better tofore said.
       Thus sall on the my chargë bene ilaid.

121   Say on than, quhare is becummyn, for schame,
       The songis new, the fresch carolis and dance,
       The lusty lyf, the mony change of game,
       The fresche array, the lusty contenance,
       The besy awayte, the hertly obseruance,
       That quhilum was amongis thame so ryf?
       Bid thame repent in tyme and mend thaire lyf.

122   Or I sall with my fader old Saturne,
       And with al hale oure hevinly alliance,
       Oure glad aspectis from thame writhe and turne,
       That all the warld sall waile thaire gouernance.
       Bid thame by tyme that thai haue repentance,
       And thaire hertis halë renew my lawe,
       And I my hand fro beting sall withdrawe.

123   This is to say, contynew in my seruise,
       Worschip my law, and my name magnifye
       That am ʒour hevin and ʒour paradise,
       And I ʒour confort here sall multiplye,
       And for ʒour meryt here perpetualye
       Ressaue I sall ʒour saulis of my grace,
       To lyue with me as goddis in this place."

124   With humble thank, and all the reuerence
       That feble wit and connyng may atteyne,
       I tuke my leue; and from hir hie presence
       Gude Hope and I togider bothë tueyne
       Departit are, and, schortly for to seyne,
       He hath me led by redy wayis ryght
       Vnto Mineruis palace, faire and bryght.

125 Quhare as I fand full redy at the ȝate
  The maister portare, callit Pacience,
  That frely lete vs in vnquestionate.
  And there we sawe the perfyte excellence,
  The sad renowne, the state, the reuerence,
  The strenth, the beautee and the ordour digne,
  Off hir court riall, noble and benigne.

126 And straught vnto the presence sodeynly
  Off Dame Minerue, the pacient goddesse,
  Gude Hope, my gyde, has led me redily;
  To quhom anone, with dredefull humylnesse,
  Off my cummyng the cause I gan expresse,
  And all the processe hale vnto the end
  Off Venus charge, as likit hir to send.

127 Off quhiche ryght thus hir ansuere was in bref:
  "My sone, I haue wele herd and vnderstond
  Be thy reherse the matere of thy gref,
  And thy request, to procure and to fond
  Off thy pennance sum confort at my hond,
  Be counsele of thy lady, Venus clere,
  To be with hir thyne help in this matere.

128 Bot in this case, thou sall wele knawe and witt,
  Thou may thy hertë ground on suich a wise
  That thy laboure will be bot lytill quit;
  And thou may set it in anothir wise,
  That wil be to the grete worschip and prise.
  And gif thou durst vnto that way enclyne,
  I wil the geve my lore and disciplyne.

129 Lo, my gude sone, this is als mich to seyne,
  As, gif thy lufe be sett alluterly
  On nycë lust, thy trauail is in veyne,
  And so the end sall turne of thy folye
  To payne, and repentance. Lo, wate thou quhy?
  Gif the ne list thy lufe on vertew set,
  Vertu sal be the cause of thy forfet.

130   Tak him before in all thy gouernance,
That in his hand the stere has of ȝou all;
And pray vnto his hyë purueyance
Thy lufe to gye, and on him traist and call,
That corner-stone and ground is of the wall,
That failis nought; and trust, withoutin drede,
Vnto thy purpose sone he sall the lede.

131   For, lo, the werk that first is foundit sure
May better bere a pace and hyare be
Than othir wise, and langere sall endure
Be monyfald, this may thy resoune see,
And stronger to defend aduersitee.
Ground thou thy werk therefore vpon the stone,
And thy desire sall forthward with the gone.

132   Be trewe and meke and stedfast in thy thought,
And diligent hir merci to procure;
Nought onely in thy word, for word is nought
Bot gif thy werk and all thy besy cure
Accord thereto, and vtrid be mesure
The place, the houre, the maner and the wise,
Gif mercy sall admitten thy seruise.

133   'All thing has tyme', thus sais Ecclesiaste,
And 'wele is him that his tyme wele abit'.
Abyde thy tyme, for he that can bot haste
Can nought of hap, the wisë man it writ;
And oft gud fortune flourith with gude wit.
Quharefore, gif thou will be wele fortunyt,
Lat wisedome ay to thy will be junyt.

134   Bot there be mony of so brukill sort,
That feynis treuth in lufe bot for a quhile,
And setten all thaire wittis and disport
The sely innocent woman to begyle,
And so to wynne thaire lustis with a wile.
Suich feynit treuth is all bot trechorye,
Vnder the vmbre of ypocrisye.

135 For as the foulere quhistlith in his throte
     Diuersëly, to counterfete the brid,
     And feynis mony a suete and strangë note,
     That in the busk for his desate is hid,
     Till sche be fast lokin his net amyd;
     Ryght so the fatoure, the false theif I say,
     With suete tresoune oft wynnith thus his pray.

136 Fy on all suich! Fy on thaire doubilnesse!
     Fy on thaire lust and bestly appetite!
     Thaire wolfis hertis hid in lambis liknesse,
     Thaire thoughtis blak hid vnder wordis quhite!
     Fy on thaire laboure! Fy on thaire delyte,
     That feynen outward all to hir honour
     And in thaire hert hir worschip wold deuoure!

137 So hard it is to trusten now on dayes,
     The warld, it is so double and inconstant;
     Off quhich the suthe is kid be mony assayes,
     More pitee is, for quhich the remanant
     That menen wele, and ar nought variant,
     For otheris gilt ar suspect of vntreuth
     And hyndrit oft, and treuely that is reuth.

138 Bot gif the hert be groundit ferme and stable
     In goddis law thy purpose to atteyne,
     Thy laboure is to me than agreable,
     And my full help, with counsele trew and pleyne,
     I will the schewe, and this is the certeyne.
     Opyn thy hert therefore and lat me se
     Gif thy remede be pertynent to me."

139 "Madame", quod I, "sen it is ȝour plesance
     That I declare the kynd of my loving,
     Treuely and gude, withoutin variance,
     I lufe that floure abufe all othir thing,
     And wold bene he that to hir worschipping
     Myght ought auaile, be him that starf on rude,
     And nouthir spare for trauaile, lyf nor gude!

140 And forthirmore, as touching the nature
  Off my lufing, to worschip or to blame,
  I darre wele say, and there-in me assure
  For ony gold that ony wight can name,
  Nald I bene he that suld of hir gude fame
  Be blamischere, in ony point or wyse,
  For wele nor wo, quhill my lyf may suffise.

141 This is theffect trewly of myn intent
  Touching the suete that smertis me so sore.
  Giff this be faute, I can it nought repent
  All-though my lyf suld forfaut be therefore.
  Blisfull princes, I can seye ȝow no more,
  Bot so desire my wittis dooth compace
  More joy in erth kepe I nought bot ȝour grace".

142 "Desire?", quod sche, "I nyl it nought deny,
  So thou it ground and set in Cristin wise.
  And therefore, sone, opyn thy hert playnly."
  "Madame", quod I, "withoutin ony fantise
  That day sall I, trewly, neuer vprise,
  For my delyte to couate the plesance
  That may hir worschip putten in balance.

143 For oure all thing, lo, this were my gladnesse,
  To sene the freschë beautee of hir face,
  And gif I might deseruë, be processe
  For my grete lufe and treuth to stond in grace,
  Hir worschip sauf; lo here the blisfull cace
  That I wold ask, and thereto wold attend,
  For my most joye, vnto my lyfis end."

144 "Now wele", quod sche, "and sen that it is so,
  That in vertew thy lufe is set with treuth,
  To helpen the I will be one of tho
  From hennesforth; and hertly, without sleuth,
  Off thy distresse and excesse to have reuth
  That has thy hert, I will hir pray full faire
  That Fortune be no more thereto contraire.

145   For suthe it is, that all ȝe creaturis
      Quhich vnder vs beneth haue ȝour duellyng,
      Ressauen diuersely ȝour auenturis;
      Off quhich the cure and principall melling
      Afferand is, withoutin repellyng,
      Onely to hir that has the cuttis two
      In hand, bothe of ȝour wele and of ȝour wo.

146   And how so be it that sum clerkis trete,
      That all ȝour chancë causit is tofore
      Heigh in the hevin, by quhois effectis grete
      Ȝe movit are to wrething lesse or more,
      Quhare in the warld, thus calling that therefore
      'Fortune', and so that the diuersitee
      Off thaire wirking suld cause necessitee;

147   Bot othir clerkis halden that the man
      Has in him self the chose and libertee
      To cause his awin fortune, how or quhan
      That him best lest, and no necessitee
      Was in the hevin at his natiuitee,
      Bot ȝit the thingis happin in commune
      Efter purpose, so cleping thame 'Fortune'.

148   And quhare a persone has tofore knawing
      Off it that is to fallë purposely,
      Lo, Fortune is bot wayke in suich a thing,
      Thou may wele wit, and here ensample quhy:
      To god, that is the firste cause onëly
      Off euery thing, there may no fortune fall.
      And quhy?, for he foreknawin is of all.

149   And therefore thus I say to this sentence:
      Fortune is most and strangest euermore
      Quhare leste foreknawing or intelligence
      Is in the man; and, sone, of wit or lore
      Sen thou art wayke and feble, lo, therefore
      The more thou art in dangere, and commune
      With hir that clerkis clepen so 'Fortune'.

150   Bot for the sake and at the reuerence
        Off Venus clere, as I the said tofore,
        I haue of thy distresse compacience,
        And in confòrt, and relesche of thy sore,
        The schewit haue here myn avise therefore.
        Pray Fortune help, for mich vnlikly thing
        Full oft about sche sodeynly dooth bring.

151   Now go thy way, and haue gude mynd vpone
        Quhat I haue said in way of thy doctryne."
        "I sall, madame," quod I, and ryght anone
        I tuke my leve; als straught as ony lyne,
        Within a beme, that fro the court dyvine
        Sche, percyng throw the firmament, extendit,
        To ground ageyne my spirit is descendit.

152   Quhare in a lusty plane tuke I my way,
        Endlang a ryuer plesant to behold,
        Enbroudin all with freschë flouris gay;
        Quhare throu the grauel, bryght as ony gold,
        The cristall water ran so clere and cold,
        That in myn ere maid contynualy
        A maner soune mellit with armony;

153   That full of lytill fischis by the brym,
        Now here, now there, with bakkis blewe as lede,
        Lap, and playit, and in a rout can swym
        So prattily, and dressit thame to sprede
        Thaire curall fynnis as the ruby rede,
        That in the sonne, on thair scalis bryght,
        As gesserant ay glitterit in my sight.

154   And by this ilkë ryuer-syde alawe
        Ane hye-way fand I euer ylike to bene,
        On quhich on euery syde a long rawe
        Off treis saw I, full of leuis grene
        And fruyte, that delitable were to sene;
        And also, as it cummys vnto my mynd,
        Off bestis sawe I mony diuerse kynd.

155   The lyoune king and his fere lyonesse,
The pantere, like vnto the smaragdyne,
The lytill squerell full of besynesse,
The slawë ase, the druggare beste of pyne,
The nycë ape, the werely porpapyne,
The percyng lynx, the lufare vnicorne,
That voidis venym with his euour horne.

156   There sawe I dresse him new out of his hant
The fery tigere, full of felonye;
The dromydare, the standar oliphant,
The wyly fox, the wedowis inemye,
The clymbare gayte, the elk for alblastrye,
The herknere bore, the holsum grey for hortis,
The haire also that oft gooth to the wortis;

157   The bugill, draware by his hornis grete,
The martrik sable, the foynȝee, and mony mo;
The chalk-quhite ermyn tippit as the jete,
The riall hert, the conyng and the ro,
The wolf that of the murthir nought says ho,
The lesty beuer and the ravin bare,
For chamelot the camel full of hare;

158   With mony ane othir beste diuerse and strange
That cummyth nought as now vnto my mynd.
Bot now to purpose: straucht furth the range
I held away, ourehailing in my mynd
From quhenns I come, and quhare that I suld fynd
Fortune the goddesse, vnto quhom in hye
Gude Hope my gyde has led me sodeynly.

159   And at the last, behalding thus asyde,
A round place and a wallit haue I found,
In myddis quhare eftsones I haue spide
Fortune the goddesse, hufing on the ground,
And ryght before hir fete, of compace round,
A quhele, on quhich there cleuering I sye
A multitude of folk before myn eye.

160 And ane surcote sche werit long that tyde,
That semyt vnto me of diuerse hewis.
Thus quhilum, quhen sche wald hir turne asyde,
Stude this goddesse of fortune and of glewis.
A chapelet with mony fresche anewis
Sche had vpon hir hed, and with this hong
A mantill on hir schuldris, large and long;

161 That furrit was with eremyn full quhite,
Degoutit with the self in spottis blake.
And quhilum in hir cherë thus alyte
Louring sche was, and thus sone it wold slake
And sodeynly a maner smylyng make,
As sche were glad, for at one contenance
Sche held nought bot was ay in variance.

162 And vnderneth the quhele eke sawe I there
Ane vgly pit als depe as ony helle,
That to behald thereon I quoke for fere;
Bot o thing herd I, that quho therein fell
Come no more vp agane tidingis to telle;
Off quhich astonait of that ferefull syght,
I ne wist quhat to done, so was I fricht.

163 Bot for to se the sudayn weltering
Off that ilk quhele, that sloppare was to hold,
It semyt vnto my wit a strong thing,
So mony I saw that than vp clymben wold,
And failit foting, and to ground were rold;
And othir eke that sat aboue on hye
Were ouerthrawe in twinklyng of ane eye.

164 And on the quhele was lytill void space;
Wele nere oure-straught it was fro lawe to hye.
And they were ware that long sat in place,
So tolter quhilum did sche it to-wrye;
There was bot clymbe, and right dounward hye!
And sum were eke that fallyng had so sore,
There for to clymbe thaire corage was no more.

165 I sawe also, that quhare sum were yslungin
     Be quhirlyng of the quhele vnto the ground,
     Full sudaynly sche hath thame vp ythrungin,
     And set thame on agane full sauf and sound;
     And euer I sawe a newë swarme abound,
     That sought to clymbe vpward vpon the quhele
     In stede of thame that myght no langer rele.

166 And at the last, in presence of thame all
     That stude about, sche clepit me be name,
     And therewith apon kneis gan I fall,
     Full sodaynly, hailsing, abaist for schame;
     And smylyng, thus sche said to me in game:
     "Quhat dois thou here? Quho has the hider sent?
     Say on anone and tell me thyne entent.

167 I se wele by thy chere and contenance
     There is sum thing that lyis the on hert.
     It stant nought with the as thou wald perchance?"
     "Madame," quod I, "for lufe is all the smert
     That euer I fele, endlang and ouerthwert.
     Help, of ȝour grace, me, wofull wrechit wight,
     Sen me to cure ȝe powere haue and myght."

168 "Quhat help," quod sche, "wold thou that I ordeyne,
     To bringë the vnto thy hertis desire?"
     "Madame," quod I, "bot that ȝour grace dedeyne,
     Off ȝour grete myght, my wittis to enspire,
     To win the well that slokin may the fyre
     In quhiche I birn. A, goddesse fortunate,
     Help now my game that is in poynt to mate!"

169 "Off mate?" quod sche. "O verray sely wreche!
     I se wele by thy dedely colour pale,
     Thou art to feble of thy self to streche,
     Vpon my quhele to clymbë or to hale
     Withoutin help, for thou has fundin stale
     This mony day withoutin warldis wele,
     And wantis now thy veray hertis hele.

170 Wele maistow be a wrechit man ycallit,
That wantis the confòrt that suld the glade,
And has all thing within thy hert ystallit
That may thy ȝouth oppressen or defade.
Though thy begynnyng hath bene retrograde,
Be froward opposyt quhirlit aspert,
Now sall thou turne and luke vpon the dert.

171 And therewithall vnto the quhele in hye
Sche hath me led, and bad me lere to clymbe,
Vpon the quhich I steppit sudaynly.
"Now hald thy grippis", quod sche, "for thy tyme,
Ane hour and more it rynnis ouer prime;
To count the hole, the half is nere away.
Spend wele therefore the remanant of the day.

172 Ensample", quod sche, "tak of this tofore,
Fro that my quhele be rollit as a ball;
For the nature of it is euermore
After ane hicht to vale and geue a fall,
Thus, quhen me likith, vp or doune to call.
Fare wele," quod sche, and by the ere me toke
So ernestly that therewithall I woke.

173 O besy goste, ay flikering to and fro,
That neuer art in quiet nor in rest
Till thou cum to that place that thou cam fro,
Quhich is thy first and verray proper nest;
From day to day so sore here artow drest,
That with thy flesche ay waking art in trouble,
And sleping eke, of pyne so has thou double.

174 Touert my self all this mene I to loke.
Though that my spirit vexit was tofore
In sueuenyng, als sone as euer I woke
By twenti fold it was in trouble more;
Bethinking me, with sighing hert and sore,
That I nane othir thingis bot dremes had,
Nor sekirnes, my spirit with to glad.

175   And therewith sone I dressit me to ryse,
      Fulfild of thought, pyne and aduersitee,
      And to my self I said right in this wise:
      "A! merci, lord, quhat will ʒe do with me?
      Quhat lyf is this? Quhare hath my spirit be?
      Is this of my forethought impressioune,
      Or is it from the hevin a visioune?

176   And gif ʒe goddis, of ʒoure puruiance,
      Haue schewit this for my reconforting,
      In relesche of my furiouse pennance,
      I ʒow beseke full humily of this thing,
      That of ʒoure grace I myght haue more takenyng,
      Gif it sal be as in my slepe before
      ʒe schewit haue." And forth, withoutin more,

177   In hye vnto the wyndow gan I walk,
      Moving within my spirit of this sight;
      Quhare sodeynly a turture, quhite as calk
      So evinly vpon my hand gan lyght,
      And vnto me sche turnyt hir full ryght;
      Off quham the chere in hir birdis aport
      Gave me in hert kalendis of confort.

178   This fairë bird, ryght in hir bill, gan hold
      Of red jorofflis with thair stalkis grene
      A fairë branche; quhare written was with gold
      On euery list, witht branchis bryght and schene,
      In compas fair, full plesandly to sene,
      A plane sentence; quhich, as I can deuise
      And haue in mynd, said ryght apon this wise:

179   "Awak! awake! I bring, lufar, I bring
      The newis glad that blisfull bene and sure
      Of thy confort. Now lauch, and play, and syng,
      That art besid so glad ane auenture,
      For in the hevyn decretit is the cure."
      And vnto me the flouris fair present,
      With wyngis spred hir wayis furth sche went.

180   Quhilk vp anon I tuke and, as I gesse,
Ane hundreth tymes or I forthir went
I haue it red, with hert full of glaidnesse;
And, half with hope and half with dred, it hent,
And at my beddis hed with gud entent
I haue it fairë pynnit vp, and this
First takyn was of all my help and blisse.

181   The quhich treuly efter, day by day,
That all my wittis maistrit had tofore,
From hennesferth the paynis did away;
And schortly, so wele Fortune has hir bore
To quikin treuly day by day my lore,
To my larges that I am cumyn agayn,
To blisse with hir that is my souirane.

182   Bot for als moche as sum micht think or seyne,
Quhat nedis me aponn so littil evyn
To writt all this? I ansuere thus ageyne—
Quho that from hell war croppin onys in hevin
Wald efter o thank for joy mak sex or sevin!
And euery wicht his awin suete or sore
Has maist in mynde, I can say ʒou no more.

183   Eke quho may in this lyfe haue more plesance
Than cum to largesse from thraldom and peyne,
And by the mene of luffis ordinance,
That has so mony in his goldin cheyne
Quhich thinkis to wyn his hertis souereyne?
Quho suld me wite to write thar-of, lat se?
Now sufficiance is my felicitee.

184   Beseching vnto fair Venus abufe
For all my brethir that bene in this place,
This is to seyne, that seruandis ar to lufe
And of his lady can no thank purchase,
His pane relesch, and sone to stand in grace,
Boith to his worschip and to his first ese,
So that it hir and resoune nought displese;

185   And eke for thame that ar nought entrit inne
        The dance of lufe, bot thidderwart on way,
        In gude tym and sely to begynne
        Thair prentissehed; and forthirmore I pray
        For thame that passit bene the mony affray
        In lufe, and cummyng ar to full plesance,
        To graunt thame all, lo, gude perseuerance.

186   And eke I pray for all the hertis dull,
        That lyven here in sleuth and ignorance
        And has no curage at the rose to pull,
        Thair lif to mend, and thair saulis auance
        With thair suete lore, and bring thame to gude chance;
        And quho that will nought for this prayer turne,
        Quhen thai wald faynest speid that thai may spurne.

187   To rekyn of euery thing the circumstance
        As hapint me, quhen lessen gan the sore
        Of my foos rancoure and my wofull chance,
        It war to long. I lat it be tharefor.
        And thus this floure, I can seye ȝou no more,
        So hertly has vnto my help attendit
        That from the deth hir man sche has defendit.

188   And eke the goddis mercifull virking,
        For my long pane and trewe seruice in lufe,
        That has me gevin halë myn asking,
        Quhich has my hert for-euir sett abufe
        In perfyte joy, that neuir may remufe
        Bot onely deth; of quhom, in laud and prise,
        With thankfull hert I say richt in this wise:

189   "Blissit mot be the blisfull goddis all,
        So fair that glitteren in the firmament!
        And blissit be thare mycht celestiall,
        That haue convoyit hale, with one assent,
        My lufe, and to so glade a consequent!
        And thankit be fortunys exiltree
        And quhele, that thus so wele has quhirlit me!

190   Thankit mot be, and fair in lufe befall,
The nychtingale, that with so gud entent
Sang thare of lufe the notis suete and small,
Quhair my fair hertis lady was present,
Hir with to glad or that sche forthir went!
And thou, gerafloure, mot ithankit be
All othir flouris for the lufe of the!

191   And thankit be the fairë castell wall,
Quhare as I quhilom lukit furth and lent.
Thankit mot be the sanctis marciall,
That me first causit hath this accident.
Thankit mot be the suete grene bewis bent,
Throu quhom, and vnder, first fortunyt me
My hertis hele and my confòrt to be.

192   For to the presence suete and delitable,
Rycht of this floure that full is of plesance,
By processe and by menys fauorable,
First of the blisfull goddis purueyance,
And syne throu long and trew contynuance
Of veray faith, in lufe and trew seruice,
I cum am. And ȝit forthir in this wise:

193   Vnworthy, lo, bot onely of hir grace,
In lufis ȝok that esy is and sure,
In guerdoun dere of all my lufis space
Sche hath me tak hir humble creature.
And thus befell my blisfull auenture
In ȝouth, of lufe that now from day to day
Flourith ay newe. And ȝit forthir I say:

194   Go, litill tretisse, nakit of eloquence,
Causing simplesse and pouertee to wit,
And pray the reder to haue pacience
Of thy defaute, and to supporten it,
Of his gudnesse thy brukilnesse to knytt,
And his tong for to reulë and to stere
That thy defautis helit may bene here.

195   Allace! and gif thou cum in the presence
        Quhare as of blame faynest thou wald be quite,
        To here thy rude and crukit eloquens,
        Quho sal be thare to pray for thy remyt?
        No wicht, bot geve hir merci will admytt
        The for gud will, that is thy gyd and stere,
        To quhame for me thou pitously requere.

196   And thus endith the fatall influence
        Causit from hevyn, quhare powar is commytt
        Of gouirnance, by the magnificence
        Of him that hiest in the hevin sitt;
        To quhame we thank, that all oure lyf hath writt,
        Quho coutht it red, agone syne mony a ʒere
        Hich in the hevynnis figure circulere.

197   Vnto the impnis of my maisteris dere,
        Gowere and Chaucere, that on the steppis satt
        Of rethorike quhill thai were lyvand here,
        Superlatiue as poetis laureate,
        In moralitee and eloquence ornate,
        I recommend my buk in lynis sevin,
        Ane eke thair saulis vnto the blisse of hevin.

Notes

1. 1–2: the first line, repeated at the close of the penultimate stanza, introduces the theme of Providence. The sphere of the fixed stars includes the zodiacal signs, so important in judicial astrology. 2. *twynklyt*: *twynklyng* MS can be the Midland pres. part. or a Scots spelling with intrusive *g* of the pres. pl., but the poet does not elsewhere confuse tenses. 3–7: the heavenly picture uses similar descriptions in *The Parlement of Foules* 113–18, *The Temple of Glas* 1–9, but does not, therefore, have to be only literary. Attention to fact is a feature of the poem, and note how naturally 'wynter' is mentioned in st. 17. None the less, because of his Chaucerian source, it is possible that James wrote *Citherea* as in MS, though the name is properly given to Venus in the *Parlement* and here the moon is meant. For the reader's sake I accept Skeat's change to *Cinthia*. The Lydgatian reference to the moon being joined '*wiþ Phebus in Aquarie*' and the further mention of 'wynter' in st. 17 support my view that it is the solar year that is actually considered in the naming of the signs and in the statement of *l.* 7. James commenced writing when the sun was in Aquarius, i.e. between 11 January and 10 February as then reckoned. 4. *Rynsid hir tressis*: a play on the name Aquarius, 'the Water-bearer'. 5–6: recently the moon had been new (*in faire and fresche atyre* with *hornis bright*) in Capricorn, the southmost sign of the zodiacal circle. 7: the moon may be understood but the subject is more probably *myd-nyght*, which does not refer to the time of day but to the circle's northern half, as *mydday* st. 21 refers to the southern (see note to **20–1**).

3. Walton's 1410 version of Boethius's *De Consolatione Philosophiæ* (EETS) may have been used; it has *pouert* in st. 11, the references to Rome and the senatorship, which are not in Chaucer's work, the verb 'Foriuggen' in st. 374. 3. *the* om. MS. 6. *for* om. MS.

4. 1. *there to here*: 'there to hear' refers to 2. 7, *a boke to rede*. 2. *His metir suete*: Boethius closes each chapter with a *Metrum* but James seems to speak of a translation entirely in verse and this could only be Walton's. 3. *His flourit pen*: his 'flowers of rhetoric'; the relative is to be understood after *pen*. 4–7: the author of the *Consolatio* like the poet of the *Quair* had been a prisoner in exile. 6. *poleyt*: *poetly* MS is rightly amended by Lawson; cf. Robert Henryson's Prologue to the *Fables* 3, 'polit termys of sueit rethory'.

5. 1. *though*: MS *t* for the contraction after *tho* should give *thought* in this poem, with Scots intrusive *t*, but for clearness of meaning I have omitted *t*. 3. *lest*: *best* MS but see *lest* 57. 4. 7: he based his (true) stability on misfortune's lessons.

6. 1–2: the moral philosophy learned in his youth was later the source of his comfort (Part I, Prose II). 4–5. *quitis/Off:* lit. 'quits in respect of', i.e. 'abandons'. Skeat and others needlessly alter to *quit is*, thus spoiling the rhyme. *thir: their* MS. 6. *suffisance:* sufficiency equated with happiness, as in **16.** 2; cf. Walton III, Prose XII, st. 7, 'suffisaunce is blisfulnesse'.

7. 2. *Latyne tong:* seems to be contrasted with *my tong l.* 5, but 'polished speech' may be what is chiefly meant; cp. *Lancelot of the Laik* 327, where Chaucer's *laiting toung* is praised. 4. *scole:* 'learning', not 'skull' as preferred by Skeat; cp. Thomas of Usk, *The Testament of Love*, ed. Skeat, p. 123, *l.* 253, where Love says that Chaucer has 'no pere in scole of my rules'. 6–7. *my sentence/ Off my mater* MS seems awkward; Lawson reasonably amends to *the sentence*, 'the theme'.

8. 2. *eyen gan: eyne gan* MS. 4. *but:* 'without', is clear in MS yet misread by Skeat and his successors as *bot.* 7. *sche* om. MS, perhaps because of *eche* directly above. *translate:* 'change utterly', as poor Grisilde 'translated was in swich richesse' (*The Clerkes Tale* 385).

9. 5. *pryncë than:* Skeat needlessly inserts *nor* after *pryncë.* See 'Language' 32.

10. 4. *eft:* corrected in MS from *oft.* 5. *all myn auenture:* certainly includes the king's marriage and almost certainly his return to Scotland the same year.

11. These are the midnight matins. It has not been noticed that the poet alludes to the first verse of that office, 'Domine labia mea aperies Et os meum annunciabit laudem tuum', 'Lord thou will open my lips and my mouth will publish thy praise', *Psalm* 50. v. 15. James probably has in mind a Book of Hours such as 'The Hours of The Blessed Virgin Mary' in *Horæ Eboracenses* (Surtees Soc., vol. 132, p. 37). Excerpts from *Psalms* 50, 94, 18, 24 were sung in that order; the last of these begs forgiveness for the crimes and ignorance of youth. For a related but less effective use of the office see *The Court of Love* 1356, etc., and Skeat's note thereto. The significance of the above for the poet's theme will be clear.

13. 4. *To lyte effect:* he had written poems on comparatively trivial themes. 5. *newë: new* MS. 7. *maid a croce:* in place of the noun MS has the mark of a cross but this is probably the scribe's; a similar cross is drawn in the top left-hand corner of fol. 203 *verso.* We have thus the usual phrase, 'I made the sign of the cross', 'I crossed myself'. Whether the mark is original or not, its purpose is to indicate not merely a beginning but a pious intent.

14. 1. *sely:* 'weak' om. MS., supplied from, **134.** 4, **169.** 1. 2: 'Fruit that has not come to ripening because of the changeful winds of passion'. See *Ratis Raving*, STS, 1152–8, 'rutis of resone/That beris the froyt discressione/Bot thai ryp nocht sa hastily', etc. According to this poem the years seven to fifteen inclusively see the first period of reason's growth but only sixteen to thirty inclusively see its full ripening. James was approaching his thirtieth year at the time of his marriage.

15. 4. *rokkis: rok* MS.

16. 2. *suffisance:* see note to **6.** 6. 3: see note to **14.** 2; *lakkit: lak* MS. 6: a frequent metaphor, cp. Walton st. 123, 'We men that fortune dryueth vp and doun/Among the wawes of this worldly see'.

17. 7. *Calliope:* the Muse of eloquence. *Marye* as a weak gen. is common where the Virgin is meant. (James's ship bore the name 'Maryenknyght'.)

18. 1. *The rokkis* in **15** were the dangers that beset unready youth, they are now the complex difficulties and dangers in the storyteller's way. The invocation in *Troilus* I, sts. 1–2, is remembered. 4. *In enditing* MS but see **7.** 2; *In*, merely understood, has been supplied by the scribe. 6: 'the sail that now I hoist'.

19. 1–4: cf. *Anelida and Arcite* 7, 15–16. Clio and Polyhymnia are respectively the Muses of history and hymning; the poem becomes finally a hymn of thanksgiving. James loosely associates the Fury, Tisiphone, with the Muses because of her 'craft of eloquence' in tragic matters (Walton I, st. 8) and his intention to tell his *turment, l.*7. That he thought of her as one of the Muses is made unlikely by his correct reference to the second Fury, Lachesis, **25.** 4, and his recent study of Lydgate's *Temple of Glas*, which specifically distinguishes 'the famous Nine' from 'the three', 953–60. 4. *nyne: ix* MS.

20–1. It is a Spring morning, the sun, *Synthius*, moves *Vpward*, i.e. northward, having passed *mydday*, the southern half of the zodiacal circle, more exactly the fourth degree of the first northern sign, Aries. Its entrance into the first degree marked the vernal equinox, which occurred 12 March (H. G. Guiness, *Astronomic Tables*, 1895), not 11 March as stated by Skeat, so that James sailed 15 March or 16 March. He may, however, have in mind the ecclesiastical calendar which made the equinox always fall on 21 March; the latter would have been historically correct as the day of his departure. See Introduction. That *mydday* is not noon, as Skeat and Mackenzie assume, is made clear in st. **23** which specifies early morning and thereupon adds that the *tyme*, presumably not the time of day just given in the same stanza, had been told earlier. Lawson and Simon needlessly consider amending to 'mydway' as a conceivable term for the equator, though not given as such in *OED*. In fact, *mydday* corresponds to *Meridies*, 'south'—Macrobius in his Commentary, II, cap. 5, sect. 18, derives this from *medidies*—as inscribed beneath the southern half of the Sphere on some astrolabes and in some illustrations in Sacrobosco's *De Sphæra;* just as *myd-nyght l.* 7 corresponds to *Media Nox* marked above the northern half. Chaucer's *Astrolabe*, Part I, sect. 4, divides the meridian into 'the south lyne' and 'the north lyne or elles the lyne of midnight'. For *mydday* in common use for 'south' see *OED*.

20. 5. *gynneth* MS. 7. *Ariete* is from the accusative of *Aries*.

21. 1. *bot mydday* MS: however, *bot*, 'only', more naturally precedes *fourë greis evyn*. 2–3: cf. the Prologue of *The Legend of Good Women* 236, 'And aungellyke his winges saugh I sprede'. 4. *confort* in MS. margin corrects cancelled *freschnesse*.

22. The prince's guardians decided to send him abroad when he was 'three years or so' past *the state of innocence*. The phrase describes the first seven years of life (*Corpus Juris Canonicum*, cap. 88; *Ratis Raving* 1126–49), so that his age is given as around ten years or so. Since he was born in July or August 1394 and sailed 21 March 1406, his reckoning, if such an approximation is to be considered strictly, is out by a year and more. If he makes a rough count from the official beginning of the year, 25 March 1395, he would be a few days short of his eleventh calendar year. But see under 'Date and authorship' in Introduction. 4: is probably echoed in Hector Boece's comment on James's capture and eventual happiness, 'non in captivitatem forte fortuna incidisse videre debuit, sed deo ducente' (*Scotorum Historia*, Paris, 1526, lib. XVI, fol. CCCLIII).

23. 1: see Wyntoun's chronicle 2579, 'he was thare purwayde weile'. 3. *no longer wold we tary*: a stock phrase but there is perhaps an allusion to the month's delay at the Bass Rock before sailing. 5. *'sanct Johne to borowe'*: "Saint John be your safeguard", a common farewell greeting; the knights of St. John protected the passage to the Holy Land.

24. 2. *was: was vs* MS makes an irregular line. The scribe may have found *vs*, a fairly common shortening of *was*, read it as the pron. and added *was*. For *infortunate* with stressed *u* cp. *Troilus* IV. 744, *infortuned*, 'ill-starred'.

25. 1. Cp. the beginning of st. **26.** But for the poet's repetitive habit one might suspect that this factual stanza was written into the poem later. 3. *in sorowe and bandoune: in sorowe abandoune* MS. Other editors consider *abandoune* as a reduction of the adverbial phrase *at abandoune*. Skeat translates freely 'left to myself', Mackenzie and Simon offer 'without limit', Lawson prefers 'in the abandonment of sorrow', treating *sorowe* as a genitive. These are arbitrary extensions of the usual senses of the phrase, 'boldly', 'randomly', 'at will', none of which will do here. I make the obvious suggestion, proceeding from the prisoner's situation, that we have a corruption of *and bandoune*, 'and thraldom' (cf. *in thraldome* **28.** 2). 4. *The secund sistir*: Lachesis, the second of the Furies, who had spun out *the heuy lyne*, 'the sad thread', of the prisoner's life. 5: captured March 1406, James's liberty was ensured by his marriage in February 1424. *twisë*: see 'Language' 36. 6–7: 'till it pleased God to turn his mercy to me and (he) sent comfort'; *send* is probably a preterit (see 'Language' 22).

26. 3. *quhat haue I gilt to*: 'Of what have I been guilty that I should', etc. 6. *I, a creature*: 'I, though one of God's creatures'.

27. The Boethian and Christian theme of true liberty through reason inspires similar contrasts in Calderon's *La Vida es Sueño* 123–72, between its imprisoned prince and the free creatures of Nature, and as here raises the question of God's justice. 6. *My folk*: the king's retainers (see 'Date And Authorship' in Introduction on his prisons).

28. 3. *me* om. MS.   5–7: Skeat's note lengthily explains the quite simple conceit but not the contextual sense: 'I am like a cipher without accompanying figure, in that I have neither friend nor lover, am of no account to anyone, in need of help from any quarter'.   7. *hath nede:* is written above cancelled *in drede.*

29. 1. *long dayes:* strong stress on both words can dispense with final syllabic *e* in *long.*

30. 4. *Vnto: And to* MS.

31–2. Next to the tower was a *gardyn*, i.e. a small park and not the modern-style garden, and in the corner (nearest the tower) a *herbere* fenced and enclosed with trees and hawthorn-hedge. A *herbere* was chiefly a private wooded place with a scattering of shrubs and flower-beds. One such 'herber grene' was entered directly from Deiphebus's house in *Troilus*, II. 1705. Another is lengthily described in *The Flower and the Leaf.* It is to this enclosure that the heroine of the *Quair* comes, presumably from another quarter of the castle where James is confined. Skeat, misled by a corrupt text, and without contradiction from later editors, imagines there to be four such 'arbours'. James speaks only of one.

31. 2. *cornere: corneris* MS. Cp. 187.5 *flouris* for *floure* and 79.1, 3, final *e* for the *—is* contraction.   6. *was walking: was* om. MS; the relative is understood. Omission of *was* is a recurrent feature of MS; here it is due to the preceding *was.*

32–5. There is a general debt to the scenery of happy and beneficent nature in *Le Roman de la Rose* and *The Parlement of Foules.*
32. 3. *And myddis of the herbere: And myddis euery herbere* MS. See note to **31–2.** *myddis of* would be normal use, e.g. Lydgate, *Reson and Sensualyte* 5197, 'And myddys of the soote herbage'.   4. *scharp, grene, suetë:* as with *grene* in **33.**1, **67.** 2, the sharp and strong vowel stresses do not seem to require the final sounded *e* inserted regularly by Skeat, perhaps not even in *suete.* However, **65.** 6 makes one speculate whether some such omission as 'and gentil' occurs before *jenepere*, cp. *The Pistill of Susan* 71, 'The jwnipre gentill'.

33. 1: is not necessarily defective; see note to **32.** 4 and compare **67.** 2.   6. *of the copill next:* 'of the following stanza'; MS has *on.*

34. 1. *Worschippe:* is amended to *Worschippeth* by Skeat, who prefers a third syllable, but the hortatory stress on the first syllable removes the need for a third; see 'Language' 35.   3. Another hand writes *Cantus* in the margin.   2. *kalendis:* 'first days', since in the Roman calendar the Kalends fall on the first of the month.

36. 3. *luf:* in place of MS. *lyf*, the accepted reading, is indicated by the context and plainly by *l.* 5, with which compare *Troilus* I. 810, 'What, many a man hath love ful dere ybought'.   5: 'Why must it be so highly prized?' and not, '. . . so painfully purchased?'.

37. 5: see note to **39.** 3.   7. *feynyt fantasye:* invention of the story-tellers.

39. 1. *fynd:* 'I can only find in books that he is', etc.   2. *regne* and its rhymes are pronounced with—*ing;* see 'Language' 13.1.   3. *To bynd and louse:* the phrase used of the Papal powers as claimed from *Matthew* xvi. 19; cp. *The Cuckoo And The Nightingale* 9, 'And he can binden and unbinden eke'.   4. *Than:* 'If such is the case'.

40. 3. *pleyne:* an alternative form of *pleyen*, 'play'.   4. *ʒong:* as with *long* **29.** 1 a sounded final *e* does not seem necessary.   6. *abate*, sb., 'shock'. The past part. and pret. (OF *abatre*) is always *abated* in OED.

43. 1–2: similarly Palamon in *The Knightes Tale* 1101–7 sees Emilye in the garden and prays to her as Venus to give him his freedom.   3: the goddess Nature in Chaucer's *Parlement* is remembered.   7. *minister:* the MS contractions give the reading, *minster.*

44. 5. *do . . . smert:* 'cause . . . to suffer'.

45. On *Vnknawin*, pres. part., *l.* 3, and *fallyng*, past part., *l.* 4, see 'Language' 25. 4.   4. *I-fallyng into* MS is possible but dubious; *was* may be understood but is more likely to be omitted by the hasty scribe (as at **46.** 3), who had written the same word directly above; also Northern *into* for *in* occurs only once elsewhere in the poem.

46. 3. *It fret-wise couchit was with:* MS has *In* and omits *was.* The subject is *array;* the scribe's alterations are due to his mistaking *fret-wise*, 'by way of adornment', for a noun. In *The Assembly of Ladies* the 'array' of the lady Attemperaunce is 'couched', i.e. adorned, with 'grete perles' 528–9 and on her head is 'A cercle with grete balays' 536. The 'balas' is the spinel ruby, of a pale rose-red colour.

47. 1. *All* om. MS seems required by metre and sense.   2. *amorettis:* loveknots, signifying faithful love.   4–5. *the floure jonettis:* is the great St John's wort, a yellow or white flower with many species. James affects repetition of rhyme but not also of sense; accordingly in *l.* 5 for *floure jonettis* MS I propose *margarettis*, 'daisies', one of the flowers in the arbour described in the *Assembly* 57.   7: cp. the same poem 539, 'It was a world to loke on her visage'.

48. 1. *fyne amaille:* Skeat and other editors retain *fyre amaille* MS, to which they give the forced sense, 'enamel produced by fire', but the passage is explained by the *Assembly* 533–4: 'About her nekke a serpe of fair rubyes/ In whyte floures of right fyne enamayl'.   4. *hertë: hert* MS.   7. *gud partye:* a part or portion coveted, hence 'a fair prize'. Skeat gives no authority other than Cotgrove 1611 for the meaning 'match', and Mackenzie's suggestion that *partye* is the heraldic term for one of the coloured compartments on a shield, indicating here the contrast between the ruby and the white neck, seems much too clever.

49. 5. *Thus halflyng louse for haste:* she had dressed hurriedly, her frock being only loosely fastened about her (*girt . . . alyte*). Simon chooses to see this detail as inconsistent with the fine head-dress and display of jewelry.

50. 4–6: reflect later knowledge.

52. 1: 'among gods that are made stars'. Lydgate's *Temple of Glas* 136 has the form 'Istellified' and his *Pilgrimage* has 'stelleffyed' several times. 4. *a* om. MS.

53. 4–7: I do not know a precedent in poetry of this date for the lover's envy of his mistress's *lytill hound* but it was to become common in sonneteering, e.g. Ronsard's 'Petit barbet, que tu es bienheureux'.

55. It is Gower's version, vv. 5551–6052, of the tale of Philomene that is followed: sent for by her loving sister Progne, raped by the latter's husband Tereus who then cuts out her tongue, revenged by Progne and transformed by the gods into a nightingale. 1. *for:* 'because of'. 3–5: 'when thy breasts were wet with the tears shed so painfully from thy bright eyes that', etc. For *bludy* with this sense and application see Henryson's *Orpheus and Eurydice*, l. 150, 'The bludy teres sprang out of his eyne'. 2. *Proigne:* Procne, dissyllabic in Chaucer and Gower, is probably monosyllabic here and pronounced *Prūng* (see 'Language' 10.2, 25.5).

56. 7: in *The Legend of Ariadne* 292 Chaucer exclaims on the faithless Theseus who had abandoned his saviour, Ariadne, 'A twenty devil way the wind him dryve!'

57. 5: 'Alas, would that thou hadst knowledge (possession) of reason!' *sen* is the same as *send*, 'grant', and not, as editors have assumed, from *seoppan*, 'since'; for its frequent use with this spelling and meaning in Scots verse see *OED.*, also here 'Language' 22.

59. 3–7: James asks the nightingale if it knows that a bird may come and compete with it for superiority in song; it would be disgrace to cease singing for such a cause, especially when now is its greatest chance to win fame. Skeat considers *wostow* as contracted *woldest thou* but almost always it represents *wost thou*.

60. 3. *my: me* MS. 6–7: possibly from a north-country love-song but may be James's own words (see note in 'Language' 3.1).

61. 1. *sche: he* MS. 7. *wittis boundin all to fest:* 'senses wholly compelled to feast (upon the scene)'. Skeat's gloss, 'senses bound all too fast', is nonsense in the context. Mackenzie accepts Wischmann's comic 'all bounding to the feast', though the meaning 'bound' or 'spring' is only acquired by the French source, *bondir*, in the fifteenth century and was then unknown in England (*OED*).

62. 5. *there* om. MS. 7. *than* om. MS.

63. 3–5. *there is nought ellis than/Bot, hert . . . / Folow thy hevin:* 'there is nothing else to do then except for you, my heart (since the body cannot win through these walls) to follow your heaven'. Skeat separates the first three lines from what follows, puts an exclamation mark at the end of the third line and makes *Folow* an imperative. This may be more dramatic but *nought ellis* naturally connects with *Bot l.* 4.; cp. 39 *l.* 1.

64. 3. *a:* 'one', 'a united', but in *l.* 6 indefinite.

65. 1–4: Skeat misinterprets *bridis* 1 as 'brides', *bydis* 3 as 'abides'. The sense is plain: May is always kind to the birds, who now welcome her; not only does the bounty (*grace*) she lavishes upon them bid (*bydis*) them sing her praise but thus they call all the world as witness to it. From Roman times to our own day May has been popularly thought unlucky as a time for marrying (E. J. Wood, *The Wedding Day In All Ages*, vol. 1, pp. 57–8). 4. *this:* a Northern form of *thus.*

66. 4. *amang:* 'at times', a Northern sense.

67. 2: need not be considered a defective line. See note to **32.** 5 and compare **33.** 1.

68. 3: 'to pain no, yet, God knows, yes'. *thay* refers to love's contraries, delight and pain (e.g. *deth and lyf l.* 5); cp. the *Cantus Troili* I. 400–13.

69. 3: 'Henceforth what will give me rest is cause of my unrest'. 4. MS *sall I slokin* (identical with *sall islokin* in the script) is acceptable, though a participle as in *ll.* 2, 5 is more to be expected, with *be* for *I*; *teris* is most naturally dissyllabic. 5: 'And all my hurts are wreaked upon myself', i.e. are self-inflicted. 7. *pace:* 'pass', 'die'.

70. 1. *Tantalus:* his plight in the well that ever eludes his lips is confused with that of the Belides, the daughters of Danaus, who killed their husbands on the wedding night and were condemned in Hades endlessly to fill with water a jar with many holes.

72. 3. *ly(lyf)* MS is cancelled before *lef.* 5. *Esperus his lampis:* the masculine pron. has been objected to since Hesperus the evening-star is Venus but the usage is normal where 'planet' is understood; cp. *Bartholomeus*, VIII, cap. 26, 'Venus . . . a night Planet in his qualyteis', and the 'Glosse' to 'December' in *The Shepheardes Calender*, 'Venus starre otherwise called Hesperus . . . he seemeth to be one of the brightest starres'.

73. 4. *cold* MS. 5. *amaisit* (*amasian*), 'with senses dazed'. 6. *Half sleping and half suoune:* Macrobius in his Commentary on Cicero's *Somnium Scipionis* attributes his fifth category of dreams, the *phantasma* or apparition, to physical and mental distress along with anxiety about the future, and says that it comes between waking and slumber, in 'the first cloud of sleep'.

74. 5. *vertew was iblent:* editors have accepted *vertew hale iblent* MS but *was*, omitted several times in MS by the scribe, is wanted, and *hale* has been naturally inserted, the insertion facilitated by *hath* written just above; *hale* in the poem is always dissyllabic. The blinding light and comforting voice are Biblical echoes, possibly of the angels and good tidings at Bethlehem and Peter's visitation in prison by a light and angel, *Acts* xii. 7. Skeat's change in *l.* 6 to *ther-withall* becomes needless.

75. The poet may have in mind St Paul miraculously leaving prison unopposed, *Acts* xvi. 26. The ascension through the spheres owes something to Macrobius's Commentary and Chaucer's use of it in *The Parlement of Foules*, but it takes its tone, e.g. in the incorporeal voice, from visionary literature. 4. *nas nothing:* the double negative, 'there was nothing'.

76. 1–6: the spheres of the elementary or sub-lunar region in Ptolemaic order are water, air, fire. In the celestial region Venus would be in the third sphere but is here assigned to *Signifer*, the zodiac; presumably she is imagined in her special House, Taurus, for it is the beginning of May (**34, 65**), which coincides with the sun's entrance into the last 'face' or ten degrees of that sign. 6. *quhare* om. MS; *ane cryit*, 'one made proclamation'. 7: refers to the bewildering speed of arrival, not to the proclamation.

77. 1. *quhen as: as* om. MS.

78. 3. *had* om. MS. 5. *quhois:* is dissyllabic as also at **79.** 1.

79. 1–3. *laboure: confessoure* MS, but the pl. ending is suggested by context and *martris l.* 3. 6. *sad and solempt: sad and* om. MS. *solempt* shows Scots intrusion of silent *pt;* Skeat's emendation *solempnit* in spite of its spelling is not trisyllabic in any of the cases seen by me. For *sad,* 'sober', see **125.** 5. 7: 'According to the degree of happiness to which Love cared to advance them'. After *lykit* is cancelled *had* in MS.

80–93: make an individual use of the classification of lovers at Venus's court in Lydgate's *Temple of Glas* 143–246. The *Quair* has these classes—(**80**) no-longer-young lovers who are still well disposed to love, the young who show joy and enterprise (*Curage*) in loving, (**81**) priestly lovers sometimes visited by Repentance, (**82**) partitioned from all these the unlucky in love. Stanzas **83–93** comment on the above groups.

80. 2. *by thame one:* lit. 'by them alone', i.e. 'by themselves', 'apart'.

81. See note to **88–9.** 2: cf. *The Temple of Glas* 204, 'In wide copis perfeccion to feine'. 5. *amang:* 'at times'.

82. 2. *thin:* 'transparent'. The partition is white as symbolizing the pure *plesance* of love from which it separates those deprived of it. 6. *of one assent:* 'being all agreed'.

83. 3. *ȝond there:* 'Yonder where'. The scribe, not anticipating *there*, has added the *-er* contraction. 5. *changë:* French-derived final *-ge* can be syllabic in Scots as in English (Smith, *Specimens of Middle Scots*, p. xxxix).

84. 2: 'the exercise and cares of the art of love'. Only Simon avoids Skeat's natural enough mistranslation of *cure* as 'cure'.

85. 3–4: the warlike heroes who were subject to love, such as Alexander, Lancelot, etc.   3: the relative is to be understood before *faucht*, the Northern pret. sing, with pl. subject.   5. The Latin-stressed pl. (*scientias*) agrees with the stresses in *counsailis, batailis* and suggests omission of MS *that* after *poetis*, cp. *princis l.* 3.   7. *Ouide and Omere:* Ovid's poems were read in the original, for example, by James's acquaintance and biographer, Walter Bower, but his reputation owed much to the *Ovide Moralisé* of Nicole Bozon. Homer's association with love poetry is chiefly due to the romantic fictions of the very popular *Historia Destructionis Troiæ* of Guido delle Colonne.

86. 1. *next* MS.   2–3: *ȝongë folkis . . . in thaire myddill age:* they are young in comparison with the old lovers (**83**–**4**) and the great warriors and poets (**85**) who are all on the topmost level. They died in their 'middle age', i.e. in youth as distinguished from full manhood, presumably between the ages of 15 and 30 (cf. *Ratis Raving* 1274–5).   2. *pleye:* 'bring pleas to court' (see 'Language' 11). The young people here are the same as in **82**. 6–7, who come with petitions 'Vnto the juge thaire playntis to present'; see also **90**. 6–7. Previous editors understand 'play', a sense wholly at odds with the context.

87. 7. *Sum for to moche:* 'Some for loving too much'.

88–9. The expression is ambiguous but the sense clear; the clerical lovers are ashamed both of breaking their vows of holy chastity and of not professing love openly as in marriage.

89. 4. *halflyng* for *half* MS is suggested by **49**. 5.

90. 3. *haldin were full lawe:* 'were kept in extreme subjection'.   4. *nothing thay to wyte:* 'they (the lovers) being in no wise to blame'.   6. *cum vnreconsilit: cumyn recounsilit* MS. The spelling *recounsilit* points to confusion with *counsel*, suggested by *pleyne*, 'complain', *l.* 7. *reconsilit*, 'reconciled'—with their lovers according to Skeat, with Venus according to Mackenzie and Simon—does not make sense, since the young people are *full of displesance* (**82**.5) and come to lodge complaints in love's court (**82**. 6–7, **90**. 7). We are not told that their pleas have been heard and that they are now 'reconsiled . . . vnto Joy and ease', as is the case with the heroine of *The Temple of Glas* 475–6. Misunderstanding *vnreconsilit* a scribe might try to 'improve' sense and metre as in MS.

91. 2: cp. the *Temple* 209–14.   4. *gruchë:* read by Skeat and others as *gruch* though the stroke sometimes used for final *e* is perfectly plain. Lawson accepts Skeat's misreading and alters to *gruchit*.   6. *in plesance: in* om. MS.

92. 2. *Were coplit:* Skeat would omit *Were* but without reason.   6. *dryve:* without *-n* or participial prefix *y-* occurs in Chaucer; here it is probably a rhyme of convenience.

93. 5. *Scho: So* MS, misread from Scots *Scho.*

94. 1. *chiere:* is dissyllabic; *ie* represents close *ē*.   3. *blyndë: blynd* MS.

95. In *Le Roman de la Rose* (Anciens Textes Français, vol. 2, p. 303) Cupid has arrows of steel, gold, lead. In *The Hous of Fame* 683 enduring love is 'love of stele'.

96. As noted by Skeat such painted sighs, i.e. sighing looks, appear in Venus's temple in *The Knightes Tale* 1920; *sad*, *l.* 2, means 'serious', not 'sad'. It is also notable that Chaucer's naked Venus has acquired a mantle.

97. 1. *Fair Calling:* is the 'Bialacoil' (Bel Acueil), son of Courtesy, who admits the lover to view the Rose in the *Roman*. 3. *Secretee:* is a chief virtue in the discipline of *amour courtois*. 5. *mo: mo that* MS.

98. 4: other editors omit a comma after *handis* but the sense is surely, 'on my knees, with my hands outstretched in supplication'. *han* MS is scored out before *kneis*. 7. *salute:* a Northern form of *salued* pret. (*OED*).

99-103. More than most addresses to Venus the rhetoric echoes prayers to the Virgin Mary; compare the following in J.A.W. Bennett's *Devotional Pieces In Verse And Prose*, STS, 1955: 'Haill, quene of hevin and sterne of blis', p. 298; 'O Mary, sterne of the seye, port of heill, bowsum gidder of schip brokin', p. 281; 'O thou deipe well and fontane of all grace and marcy, haill', p. 285.

99. 3-4: Venus is now the planetary goddess capable of modifying the baleful aspect of Mars, who has been, and still is, responsible for the supplicant's imprisonment. In good aspect with Jupiter she represses the possible 'malice' of Mars in *The Legend of Hypermnestra* 23-32. In *Troilus* III. 22 she can 'fierse Mars apeysen of his ire'. 4. *sure:* MS *pure*, 'pure', is possible but most likely anticipates *pure*, 'poor', in *l.* 6. I have therefore substituted *sure* from **100.** 4.

100. 5. *anker and keye:* for *keye* Skeat offers 'quay', or 'key' with the odd meaning, 'helm'. He derives the latter sense from Chaucer's mistranslation of *clavus et gubernaculum* in Boethius, Book III, Prose XII, as 'a keye and a stiere' (rudder). This is merely ingenious. As noted, st. **3**, James seems to have used Walton's version. *keye* is the common word used figuratively as in *Anelida and Arcite* 323-4, 'the keye/Of al my worlde and my good aventure'.

102. 1. *sen: though* MS is just possible but agrees awkwardly with *that*, 'since', *l.* 3. 5. *schapith:* see 'Language' 35. 3.

104. 4. *Sche kest asyde:* 'She turned away'. For *Sche* MS has *me*.

105. 7. MS has *full* cancelled before *bot*.

106. The lover cannot have his reward from Venus without the aid of Good Hope. According to *Ratis Raving* 1039-92 he cannot have this help without consulting with 'dame resone' on the suitability of the match, for 'gud hop is ay of hire assent'; hence perhaps the comment on James as a *mache* in **109, 110**, and certainly Venus's recommendation of Good Hope as guide to, and adviser with, Minerva, **112-13**. To have good hope is to have good reason for hope, so that special knowledge is probably implied here. 1: cf. *The Compleynt of Mars* 21,

'And paciently taketh your aventure'. 3. *can the stroke:* 'has power to make the stroke'. 4. *humily* MS, as elsewhere in MS has its sign for *m* above *i*. 6: 'since you have shown your face here'; cp. Barbour's Troy Book, ed. Horstmann, 325–6, 'with forhede blith' ('fronte hylari'). *present* may be the past part., as at **179**. 6.

107–8. As Skeat says, this is a difficult passage and its crux is in **107**. 5, rendered by him, 'Which binds up my influence with others, to discern'. I prefer 'binding up mine with others' so as to give judgment'; *discerne* is a variant spelling of *decerne* (L. *decernere*), cf. *OED*, and there is no need to replace the absolute possess. pron. *mynes* with *menes*. The theme is the power of Venus as limited by God, and it is presented in astrological terms of heavenly positions in which she is in more or less favourable aspect with other planetary powers, and so able to decide upon the result of past and future events. Thus she does not direct (*writhe*) events alone, any more than James alone can effect his liberty (**108**. 1–3). She must wait till certain planetary *coursis* (**108**. 6) have been completed, i.e. till affairs have reached a favourable point and the lover has deservedly won the mercy of his mistress.

107. 5. *byndand: bynd* is followed by the contraction for *and*, which suggests that the scribe found *and* in his MS. The contraction is fairly common in MS.

108. 2. *by* om. MS. 5. *aduertence* 'attention', or 'support', so (Your case does not properly receive my attention (or 'support') till . . .' 7. *iwone* MS is rare but possible; however, the spelling at least is corrupt, as the rhyme shows, and the scribe tends to supply a participial prefix when he does not recognize sounded final *e* in noun or adverb (see 'Language' 32 and notes to **113**. 4, **116**. 6). Some Anglicisms must be attributed to the Scots scribe.

109. 4. *hir hie birth:* for the royal poet this is the language of convention; she is his *souirane* **181**. 7 and, of course, superior in 'origin' or 'kind', which is one of the meanings of *birth* (cf. Chaucer's *Boethius* III, Metre VI). 7: a hand probably not the scribe's has supplied *foule on* above *doken* (see note to **115**. 6–7).

110. 2: probably suggested by old January and young May in *The Marchantis Tale* but Lydgate makes the same contrast in his *Temple* 184–5. At the time of his marriage James was almost thirty years old, his bride doubtless considerably younger. *vnlike to: like vnto* MS. 4: the *tabartis* not *of one array* ('arrangement') are here the short sleeveless surcoats of heralds or knights, differenced in arms, so appropriately applied to the very different reputations of the birds; in *The Cuckoo And The Nightingale* they are respectively the foe and friend of love. *bothe maid of array* MS: *one* before *array* is plainly necessary to the sense and it seems likely that *bothe* is a scribe's insertion in an MS. that wanted *one*. 6. *fischis eye:* perhaps the same as 'fish-eye-stone', a mineral with pearly lustre found in glassy prisms, etc., though *OED* gives no early examples of the term. 7. *prese:* above *er* in *perese* MS is the corrective sign for *r*.

111. 5. *that: than* MS. *goddesse: goddes* as in MS. would be expected by the scribe after the plural verb but *goddesse* is a better rhyme and the construction is possible.

113. 3. *Gud Hope:* see note to **106.** 4: 'friend of you all, to keep you from grieving'. *alleris:* has superfluous Scots genitival *-is. letë: let* MS. The scribe seems to retain, or even insert, final *-en* but sometimes to omit sounded final *-e* as a less familiar ending.

115. 3. *stand in my disdeyne:* 'persist in scorning me'. 6. *at thaire large:* 'freely', 'as they please'. 6–7: perhaps the same hand wrote marginal *Cantus* **34,** corrected **109.** 7, re-wrote *breken* here in *l.* 6 and above *noh eft* in *l.* 7 wrote *l none,* thus supplying the emendation in this text. 7. *gevis charge:* 'takes heed'.

116–8. The tears of Venus, attributed to her for the Spring showers that are sometimes frequent during the sun's stay in her zodiacal House, Taurus, from mid-April to mid-May, are mentioned in astronomical accounts (*The Complaynt of Scotlande,* ed. Murray, p. 54, 'al thing that the erd creatis is confortit be it, be raison of the fresche deu that descendis fra it') as well as in poetical ones. Chaucer's *Lenvoy* explains recent rain by Venus's tears for his friend Scogan's want of constancy in loving.

116. 6. *fastë bete: fast ybete* MS has probably *y-* inserted because the scribe did not sound final *e* in *faste.* The infinitives *ysee, ywrite* occur for this reason in his copy of Chaucer's *Legend, ll.* 238, 2357.

117. 1. *othir quhile,* 'at other times'; there was no need for Skeat to accept Brown's emendation, *anothir quhile.* 6. *ryght:* om. MS, is Wischmann's plausible suggestion; cp. **104.** 7, **178.** 7, **188.** 7.

118. 4. *Styntith . . . murnyth* plur.: see 'Language' para. 35.2.

119. Venus pursues her argument, the season is at its best when love is duly worshipped (see note to **116–8**). 4. *to renewe* MS. 5. *Thaire: That* MS. The emendation is due to my conviction that *as ay is dewe* belongs with the next line: 'who, as is always proper most commonly receives his worship at that time'. 6. *than: ay* MS as repeated is peculiarly awkward; MS *has ay* has been affected by *as ay* just above.

120. 2. *ʒe aught and maist weye* MS.: Skeat amends to *aughten maist,* suggesting that the scribe substituted *and* for Midland *-en,* which he did not understand, but elsewhere the scribe writes *-en* into his copy only too freely and Skeat's change leaves a defective line; *maist* has been repeated from *l.* 1. For my correction, *aught and mosten,* see 'Language' para. 35.2. Wischmann and Lawson would read *most obeye* but cp. Hay's *Law of Armes,* STS, p. 147, 'na soverane to quhame thai wey, i.e. 'no king to whom they give heed'. 3. *to sleuth is forget* MS: *all* is well supplied by Skeat. Mackenzie and Simon oddly give *sleuth* its very rare verbal function, 'delay', and deprive *effectis* of its verb, the Scots pl. *is,* substituting *and.* 5. *bidden: bid* MS.

121. The charge of modern neglect of love's observances, its songs, pastimes, the lover's due attentions to his mistress, is conventional. The author of *The Quare of Jelusy*, who seems to have read the *Quair*, makes the same sad comparison with 'the tyme was of our elderis old' 254. 5. cf. *Anelida and Arcite* 250, 'And your awaytinge and your besinesse'.

122. 1–4: in astrology the conjunction of Venus with Saturn is unfavourable. Gower says, 'Bot whan sche takth hir conseil with Satorne/Ther is no grace' (*Confessio Amantis* VIII. 2275–6). Alexander Neckam's identification of Saturn with divine wisdom may also be remembered. 2. *alliance*: 'allies', the other powerful planets.

123. The goddess speaks both of an earthly and a heavenly bliss. Her law of love is the same Christian one that Minerva will expound. 4: the *confort* to be multiplied may echo the marriage service and its injunction to have children (compare the close of Spenser's *Epithalamion*); the reference is clearly to the Christian heaven

124. 3. *hie presence*: is Skeat's suitable emendation of *hir presentle* MS.

125. 5. *sad renowne*, 'sober glory': *said renewe* MS. 'sober renewal' does not make sense; *renewe* (? from the verb at **122.** 6) is not in *OED* as a noun at this time. C. E. Bain's proposal, *remue*, 'change' (*N & Q*, 1961, pp. 168–9) does not fit the context. I have omitted *i*, the Scots sign of a long vowel, from *said* because confusing and probably scribal, cp. *sad* in rhyme **96.** 2.

126. 3. *has* om. MS; compare the almost identical line, **158.** 7.

127. 4–5: 'And thy request, which is to seek and beg from me some comfort for thy suffering'. Simon's French translation gives the correct sense. Other editors wrongly understand, 'thy request that I should seek and beg some comfort', etc.

128. 2. *hertë: hert* MS. 4. *anothir: an* om. MS.

129. 3. *On: Of* MS. but cp. *l.* 6. 6. *thy lufe on vertew: on lufe thy vertew* MS. My emendation is plainly required in view of *ll.* 2, 3 and **144.** 2. 7. *Vertu:* God or the will of God, here thought of with respect to marriage.

130. 5. *corner-stone*: the ultimate source is *Psalm* 118. 22, 'The stone which the builders refused is become the head stone of the corner'. The passage is cited several times in The New Testament, where it is applied to Christ, e.g. I *Peter*, 2.6, 'Behold I lay in Sion a chief corner-stone, elect, precious: and he that believeth on him shall not be confounded.'

131. 1. *werk*: 'building'. 2. *pace*: Skeat's derivation from OF *pas*, rendered as 'step' or 'stage' in building, may be correct but a more obvious sense is 'weight', in which case we have a Scots spelling of ME *pes* (OF *peise*); see 'Language' 12. In Thomas of Usk's *Testament of Love* (ed. Skeat, p. 72, *ll.* 89–9, 105) Divine Love says of her power to defend 'in adversite' that a straight piller based on sure ground 'may lenger in greet burthen endure'. 5. *defend:* 'keep off'. 6. *thou* om. MS.

132. 5–7: 'and (if thy word is) uttered with discretion in the right place, hour, manner and method, whenever mercy shall accept thy service'. See following note.

133. 1–4: *the wisë man* in this case is Solomon and James cites a version of *Ecclesiastes* ch. 3; cp. *Dicta Salomonis* (publd. with *Ratis Raving*, STS, pp. 181–2, *ll.* 166–76), 'al thing has a tyme in this warld . . . tyme of spekinge, tyme of scilens, tyme of luf'. 2. *wil abit* MS. See 'Language' 35.2. 6–7. *fortunyt: junyt.* Skeat inserts *ay be* 6, *vnto* 7, being unwilling to accept rhyming stress on *-yt*, but see note to **145.**

134–5. The theme is fairly common but see specially *The Testament of Love* (p. 54, *l.* 36—p. 55, *l.* 55) on the seducers of 'these sely women': 'Anon as filled is your lust . . . with traysoune anon ye thinke hem begyle . . . [such men] shewen outward al goodnesse till he has his wil performed. Lo! the bird is begyled with the mery voice of the foulers whistel. When a woman is fast closed in your nette', etc.

134. 2. *bot* om. MS. 7: above *ypocrisye* in MS is the meaningless insertion *heid*, which Skeat prints as *hid* on the analogy of **136.** 4, but neither sense nor metre requires this: *vmbre* can be dissyllabic.

135. 5. *lokin: lok In* MS.

136. 3. *hid:* om. MS, seems required for natural stress on the first syllable of *lambis*, its omission would be eased by its recurrence in *l.* 4.

137. 6. *ar: and* MS.

138. 1–2: if marriage is seriously intended. 3. *than* om. MS. *Bot gif, l.* 1, as 'unless' would require *nought*, but *ll.* 4–5 indicate 'But if'.

139. 4. *I lufe that floure* MS is unexceptionable. Skeat ignores the correspondence of *floure* to *hir, l.* 5, alters to *flouris* 3 sing. and tacitly prints *In lufe.*

140. 3. *me assure:* 'pledge myself'. 5. *Nald I bene he: Wald I be he* MS. *Nald* is Skeat's logical emendation; it seems unlikely that James relied on an understood negative, or stress on *nor* in *l.* 7. I take *bene* from **139.** 5.

141. 3. *faute:* is Skeat's excellent correction of *faynt* MS.; it refers to *desire l.* 6. 7. *bot:* 'except', 'without'.

142. 4–5. *trew withoutin fantise . . . sall I neuer vp rise* MS. Skeat and others would read *trewly without . . . sall neuer be I sall vp rise.* My suggestion in the text is at least more economical of change; *withoutin* is normal for the poet and here needs *ony*; *trew* is less to be expected than *trewly*, which has probably been anticipated from the next line. 7. *putten in balance:* 'put in danger', cf. *Anelida and Arcite* 344.

143. 3. *I: it* MS. 6. *wold* om. MS.

144. 4. *hennesforth: hensforth* MS. See 'Language' 36. 5. *excesse:* is a variant spelling of *axcesse,* 'anguish', from OF *accez.* 6. *has:* the subject is *hert. hir,* om. MS, refers to Fortune.

145. Skeat would like to assign the rhyming stress on *-yng* to scribal interference, but for the specially Northern readiness to rhyme on normally unstressed final syllables see Sander chs. 40, 41 and here sts. **57, 89, 133, 139.** 5. *Apperit is* MS, hitherto accepted, is nonsense. In *Afferand is* (OF *afferir*), 'is pertaining', the verb is common in Scots and confusion of *f* with *p* is easy and frequent; alternatively *Afferis withoutin ony.* 6. *hir:* Fortune.

146. 1. *it* om. MS. 3. *hevin:* the celestial sphere, particularly the zodiac. 4. *wrething:* 'vexation' (reflecting *distresse* **144,** *wo* **145**), and not Skeat's difficult 'turning about', which is due to his mistaking the verb for *wrythen.* 5. *Quhare in the warld:* 'Where you are, in Fortune's world'. There is no need to substitute *Thar in* as Skeat does. 6-7: 'the combination of different heavenly influences is said to determine events'.

147. By the contrary view man has free will and his lot is not determined by the stars at his birth; events happen commonly (*in commune*) by human purpose and it is the result of such purposed events that some call 'Fortune'.

148-9. The power of chance over us is in proportion to our foreknowledge and understanding; thus God alone (*onely* **148.** 5 qualifies *god* and not *cause*) is unaffected by Fortune. James's human imperfection leaves him still dependent on her aid.

148. 2. *fallë: fall* MS. 5. *that: it* MS. *onëly:* Sheat and Craigie would make this a dissyllable and sound syllabic *e* in previous *firste* but natural stress is on *on-*; James inserts a metrical *e,* perhaps influenced by Scots 'anerly'.

149. 6-7: the more you are under (her) control and have to do (*commune*) with her, etc.

150. 5. *haue* om. MS.

151. 3. *quod he* MS. 4. *as ony lyne:* the usual description of a beam of light, e.g. Lydgate's Troy Book 636, 'Descended ben ry3t as any lyne'. 5. *court: contree* MS but see *court* **125.** 7. Fortune is active only on earth, in the world of men.

152. the *lusty plane* is no mere decorative digression; it is the earthly paradise described by so many theologians and poets. John of Ireland (*The Meroure of Wisdom,* vol. 1, STS, pp. 76-8) discourses on its abundant life and fruitfulness, its 'water of baptism' and 'regimen of ressoune'. The author of *The Court of Sapience* writes of its 'ryuer of quyet' and Dante walks by this river in meditation before meeting Beatrice (*Purgatorio,* xxviii). In *The Parlement of Foules* it signifies the creative goodness of God, as also here. The catalogue of creatures was, in such poetry at least, a novel illustration of this theme, for the few trees and native animals of Chaucer's descriptions are hardly comparable.

153. 3. *in a rout can:* is cancelled and rewritten in MS. **4.** *So prattily:* 'In such a lively way'. **5–6:** cp. the *Parlement* 189, 'With finnes rede and scales silverbrighte'. **7.** *As gesserant:* 'like the small linked plates in a light suit of armour'.

154. 1–2: 'And down by this same river-side I found a high-way run continuously', lit. 'I found there to be always in like manner a high-way'. **2.** *Ane hye way fand I like to bene* MS. Skeat and Lawson make *hye* dissyllabic and insert *thar* after *way*; Mackenzie and Simon let the defective line stand. I take *euer ylike* from **70. 2**; that *euer* (and with it following *y*-) should be omitted is understandable because of *ryuer* written above and *euery* in the line below. **5.** *That full of fruyte delitable were to sene* MS is plainly corrupt. In *delitable* stress as at **192** should be on *de-*; *full of* has been repeated from the line above, *that* transferred to the beginning of the line. **6–7:** the catalogue of animals may have been first suggested by the half-dozen named in the *Parlement* 193–6 but has been extended from bestiary sources such as *Physiologus*, Alexander Neckam's *De Naturis Rerum*, the *De Proprietatibus Rerum* of Bartholomæus Anglicus. **6.** *cummys: come* MS. The present tense is more natural; *cummys* is preferable to normally dissyllabic *cummyth* **158. 2**.

155. 2. *The pantere*, 'panther', is like the *smaragdyne*, 'emerald', since both were considered exceptionally beautiful, both symbolized eternal life (in *Physiologus* the panther represents Christ), and both were said to be many-coloured. Mackenzie notes that in the Vulgate *Revelations* iv. 3 the rainbow about God's throne is *similis visione smaragdinæ*. **4.** *druggare*, 'drudging': on such adjectives in *-are* see 'Language' 33.3 **5.** *werely:* 'warlike' because of the quills. **6–7:** the lynx's vision could pierce walls; the unicorn was said to be attracted to virgins and its horn to clear poison (*voidis venym*) from water (*Der Physiologus*, transl. Otto Seel, 1960, p. 21).

156. 1. *his* om. MS. *hant*, not *haunt* as commonly read. **2.** *fery:* 'active' hence 'fierce', see 'Language' 19.1. The tiger was reputed the swiftest and fiercest of animals and therefore often symbolizes the ever busy and menacing devil. With *ll.* 2–3 cp. Henryson's *Parliament Of Fourfuttet Beistis* 883–4, 'the Tiger full of Tirannie/ The Elephant and eik the Dromedarie'. **3.** *standar:* the elephant was said to have no joints in its legs so that it gave birth and slept in a standing position. **4.** *the wedowis inemye:* refers to the fox of *The Nonne Preestes Tale.* **5.** *the elk for alblastrye:* Skeat cites E. Phipson's *Animal Lore*, p. 122, for the use of the elk's skin in covering shields. **6.** *the holsum grey for hortis:* according to Jamieson's Dictionary grease from the *grey*, i.e. badger, was mixed in plasters put on wounds. *hortis* (OF *hurter*), 'hurts', is a spelling in the Scots *Legend of St. Laurence* 357.

157. 1. *The bugill:* the wild ox or buffalo. **2.** *foynȝee* (OF *fuine*): on this common Scots spelling see 'Language' 16.1, 29. **3.** *tippit as the jete:* 'with tail tipped black as jet' (cp. Fortune's mantle **162**).   **5.** *nought says ho:* lit. 'does not say "Stop!" ', i.e. never ceases. MS. has *say*.   **6.** *The lesty beuer:* the 'wonderful craft' of the beaver in building its home is praised in *Bartholomæus de Proprietatibus Rerum* XVIII, cap. 29, and its abnormally clever method of escaping from the hunter, by biting off the medicinal genitals which he seeks, in *Physiologus*, ch. 23. The ferocity and greed of the bear, that 'eateth all things', is also in *Bartholomæus*, XVIII, cap. 112. On the *a-* spelling in *bare: hare* see 'Language', para. 12; it seems unlikely, in view of *bore* **156. 6**, that 'bore' (OE *bār*) was understood by the scribe.   **7.** *chamelot* (OF *camelot*): the material 'camlet' was originally made of camel's hair.

158. 1–2: cp. Henryson's beast fable cited in my note to **156. 2**, *ll.* 877–8: 'I sall reheirs ane part of euerilk kynd/Als fer as now occurris to my mynd'.   **3.** *furth*, 'out of', 'away from'; suggested *forouth*, 'before' (Skeat), and *furth to* (Lawson) will not do since the king is already in the range and now leaves it.

159. 6—160.2. In the alliterative *Morte Arthure* the king dreams that he sees Fortune's wheel and kings 'clauerande one heghe' 3324, and the goddess Fortune dressed 'In a surcott of sylke selkouthly hewede' 3252.

159. 2. *and a* om. MS. A tower is meant, but most likely Fortune is pictured simply as in an illuminated MS., within an open semi-circular retreat, thus facing the poet.   **3.** *eftsone I haue spide* MS.: James may have written *aspide* but trisyllabic *eftsones* as at **42. 2** suffices to regularize the line.   **4.** *hufing:* 'tarrying', the most common meaning, not 'hovering above the ground' as has been suggested. Fortune is always represented as of great height so that, standing or sitting, she overlooks the large wheel (the world of men) that she turns.   **6.** *there* om. MS.

160. 2. *vnto: to* MS.   **3.** *Thus quhilum* replaces *Quhilum thus* MS; stress is usually on the first syll. of *quhilum* and for the position of *Thus* cp. **96. 7.** *hir turn asyde*, 'seek privacy'; *hir* om. MS.   **4.** *of glewis:* om. MS., is convincingly supplied by Skeat but the ordinary sense, 'joys', here the joys of loving seen as depending on Fortune, is preferable to his peculiar gloss, 'tricks', 'destinies'.

161. 1. *ermyn* MS is trisyllabic so spelled *eremyn* in text to indicate this.   **2.** *the self*, 'the same'.   **6.** *As: And* MS is probably copied from the line above; it can mean 'if' but 'as if' is the sense required, since nothing can be affirmed of Fortune except that she is changeable. *for* om. MS.   **7.** *was* om. MS.

162. 1. *the quhele eke sawe I there: eke* om. MS is suggested by **163. 6**; this is a degree more likely than Skeat's proposed sounding of unetymological *e* in *quhele* (OE *hwēol*).   **2.** *als*, 'as' om. MS. The pit of death, or hell, is not known to me elsewhere in such descriptions.

163–5. In illustrations the wheel is almost always upright; it is supposed to turn violently, jerkily, to a topmost point from which the climber is thrown. He grasps a spoke at the outer rim or has a seat thereon.

163. 3. *strong* with the senses 'violent', 'perilous', is common and fits here. Skeat's alteration to *strangë*, 'wonderful', is not required. 4. *vp* om. MS.

164. 2. *oure-straught:* lit. 'stretched over', i.e. crowded. *it was* om. MS. Omission of *was* recurs in MS and is here made easy by *was* being directly above in *l.* 1. 6. *fallyng:* past part. (see 'Language' 25.4). *so* om. MS.

165. 1. *yslungin: slungin* MS. The prefix *y-* as in *ythrungin l.* 3 supplies the wanted syll.; compare the rhyming parts. in st. **170.** 3. *thame* om. MS. 5. *newë: new* MS. 6. *sought* om. MS.

166. 1. *presence: presene* MS.

167. 2. *lyis* is dissyllabic. 3. *It:* has cancelled *Ar* before it in MS. 5. *endlang and ouerthwert:* lit. 'length-wise and across', i.e. 'altogether', referring back to *all l.* 4.

168. 2. *bringë: bring* MS. 3. *bot that:* '(I pray) only that', and not 'unless', as translated by Skeat. 7. *my game . . . to mate:* 'my chess-play in which I am about to be check-mated'; cp. Deschamps, *Rémède de Fortune* 1191, on the goddess, 'Qu' en veinquant dit: Eschac et mat', and Sir Gilbert Hay's *Alexander*, STS, II. 1590, 'Quha playis nocht weill may sone be mait'.

169. 5. *stale*, 'stale-mate', from OF *estal*, 'a fixed position'. 6. *werdis wele* MS may be correct but *warldis wele* is the common phrase.

170. 1–3 *callit: stallit* MS. The prefix *y-* is needed before *callit* (see note to **165.**1.) and so likely before *stallit.* 2. *wantis* is dissyllabic. *the* pron.: *thy hert* MS. The scribe has anticipated the same two words in the next line. Other editors retain *thy hert* or try to restore natural stress by omitting *that* and reading *herte*, which is normally monosyllabic. 5–7: described as the despair of commentators, these lines make good sense when read and emended with their source firmly in view: 'Though your beginning has been retrograde, by perverse opposite (power) fiercely whirled, now you will turn and look upon the mark'. James remembers the tale of Constance, 292–305: her marriage voyage was doomed in its beginning by Primum Mobile, that 'cruel firmament' that 'hurlest' the planets back from their natural eastward direction, so that 'cruel Mars' then happened to be in a retrograde ascendant (see the notes in Skeat's and Robinson's editions). In astrology such an ascendant signified 'Retardation of the thing propounded, or matter in hand or hoped' (*Dariotus Redivivus*, London, 1653, p. 48.). The king's voyage too began in March, when the sun was in *Aries*, where Mars is said to be 'exalted', and in the sign's first 'face' where he is specially powerful, a circumstance thought unpropitious to marriage. Only now does the retrograde movement then given to his life's course cease. See also the comment on Lydgate's *Pilgrimage* as a source in the Introduction. 6. *whirlit aspert: quhare till aspert* MS. Previous editors suppose Fortune to speak of the king's enemies as *opposyt* to him, i.e. opposed to his climbing on her wheel, and to say that she will cast them in the 'dirt' (*dert*). Skeat renders MS 'where-unto expert', though admitting that this gives awkward sense, and Wischmann supposes that the said enemies are to be 'astonished' (OF *esperdre*). The source and meaning cited above, however, indicate a verb corresponding to Chaucer's 'hurlest', and this is provided by *quhirlit* as applied to Fortune's wheel **189**. 7, of which *quhare till* is a possible corruption; *till*, prep., is suspect since only found here in the poem. *aspert*, adv., is explained in *OED* as a mixture of OF *aspert, apert*, 'bold' or 'open', with *espert*; it has also probably been affected by *asper* (OF *aspre*), 'rough', 'fierce'. 7. *thou: thai* MS is the chief cause of editorial confusion. *luke vpon: luke on* MS. *dert:* for the sense 'mark', 'prize', see Skeat's useful note to the Wife of Bath's Prologue 75, 'the dart is set up of virginitee'.

171. 4–6: the time in the king's day of life is said to be an hour and something more past *prime*, i.e. it is past 10 a.m., and if the *hole* is the Psalmist's span of 70 years (LXXX. 10) this should mean that James has not reached his thirtieth year. In 1423, the year of the marriage negotiations, he was 29 years old.

172. 1. *this tofore*: 'this sight before you', less probably 'these (people) before you'. 2. *Fro that: That fro* MS. 'From the time that' makes better sense since the subject seems to be the wheel; in Chaucer's *Truth* 9 Fortune's wheel also 'turneth as a ball'. 5. 'Thus, as it pleases me, up or down to drive it'. *call* (ON *kalla*) with the meaning 'drive' is peculiarly Northern and Scots. Editors have allowed *fall* MS, repeated from *l.* 4, to stand. It can be retained, however, only if 'go' is understood before *vp* and *doune* alone is felt to qualify the rhyme-verb; this seems an unnatural reading. 6. *by the ere me toke*: 'struck me a blow on the ear'. The king's good fortune has begun but unexpected roughness is expected of the changeful goddess.

173. Simon, p. 244, needlessly suspects here the neo-Platonic heresy of pre-existence. There is only, however, a conjunction of symbols, nest and 'unnatural' west (see note to **170**), to image the soul's distance from its source and objective, God. See *Troilus* IV. st. 44, 'O wery goost that errest to and fro ... O soule lurking in thy wo unneste', alongside Lydgate's *Pilgrimage* 12375–84, where man's soul is compared to a sphere that suffers retrograde motion but still turns, 'Tyll he come to hys restyng place/Wych is in god, yiff he wel go,/ His ownë place wych he kam fro'. Sacrobosco's *De Sphaera*, I. cap. 2, similarly likens the planetary movement from east to west and back to east to man's intelligence, which proceeds 'a creatore per creaturas in creatorem'. Troilus's spirit would flee to his beloved, the king's *also* to its Creator. 6. *waking: walking* MS has Scots intrusive, unpronounced *l* (see 'Language' 27), omitted here to facilitate understanding.

174. 1. *Touert: Couert* MS; the caps. T, C, are written much alike. 3. *sueuyng* MS is an alternative Scots form of *sueuenyng*, the latter here required by the metre. 6. *I* om. Ms.

175. 3. *right* om. MS. 4, 5: transposed in MS but marked *a, b* for correction.

177–8. The dove traditionally symbolizes faithful married love, also, as often in the Bible, the grace of God. Noah's leaf-bearing dove is one instance of the latter meaning. In the *Pilgrimage* the white dove of Grace Dieu brings 'a lytel bylle' of counsel to the Pilgrim (19726) when he is thrown from Fortune's wheel and despairs; in the *Quair* a scroll is plainly meant though not specified. On this passage see Introduction, p. 72.

177. 7. *kalendis:* 'the beginning' (see note to **34.** 2.).

178. 1. Here the second scribe begins. *fairë: fair* MS. 2. *red jorofflis:* 'gilly-flowers', 'pinks'. James's capture was in March; the gillyflower was sown in March (*Le Ménagier de Paris*, ed. Eileen Power, p. 197), one popular species being variously known as *Hesperis matronalis* after the Roman *matronalia* cele-brated on the first of March, 'the queen's flower', and 'Cherisaunce' as signi-fying affection (Alice M. Coates, *Flowers and their Histories*, 1968, p. 47). 3–6: see note to sts. **177–8.** The bird bears an illuminated scroll having a fair pattern (*branche*) of gillyflowers, where is written in gold on every margin (or adjoining space), in bright and lovely patterns of letters, circle-wise (*In compas fair*), a clear meaning. 7. *apon: on* MS.

179. 6. *present:* is the past participle.

180. 3. *hert full of: of* om. MS. Skeat's *hertëful* may be correct but there are only two likely cases of sounded final *e* with *hert* (**48.** 4, **128.** 2) and stress may well be on *full*.

181. 1–3: *The quhich, l.* 1, and *That, l.* 2, both refer to the lover's mistress, the *souirane* in *l.* 7: 'The same person truly, afterwards, day by day, who had before mastered all my senses, henceforth caused my pains to go away'. Skeat and Simon make the two relatives refer to the love-token, ignoring the sug-gestion of *tofore, l.* 2. that the state of mind described had existed before the token's arrival. Lawson only confounds further by making *That, l.* 2, qualify *paynis, l.* 3. Mackenzie, as so often, is discreetly silent. With *l.* 2 compare **41.** 2–3, 'my wittis all/Were so ouercome', etc. 3. *From hennesferth:* as in **69, 144** but *Quhich hensferth* MS. 6. *larges:* 'freedom', from both prison and the lover's despair.

182. 2. *evyn:* sb., 'cause'. Lawson cites Sir Gilbert Hay's *Buke of The Law of Armys*, STS, p. 80, 'thai first lordis conquest, and held the landis apon lyttill evin and small title of rycht'. *Wald* is altered to *Nald* by Skeat, who prefers to read *Quho* as the interrog. rather than indef. pron. *o thank:* 'one thanksgiving'. *vi or vii* MS.

183. 4: divine love's *goldin cheyne* linking all things is praised in Boethius, Book II, Metre 8; the phrase is used of Venus in *The Temple of Glass* 1106. 5. *thinkis: this* MS. 7. *sufficiance* 'complete', a variant of *sufficiante.*

184–5. Compare the prayer for 'Loves servaunts', *Troilus* I. sts. 4–7.

184. 6–7: *his first ese* . . . *hir and resoune*: repeat the theme of *Desire* . . . *in Cristin wise* **142.** 1–2.

185. 2. *The dance of lufe*: a recurring phrase in poetry, e.g. *loves daunce, Troilus* II. 1106. 3: 'early and unready to begin'. 4–5: are transposed without correction in MS. 6. *cummyng*: past part.

186. 3. *the rose*: as in *Le Roman de la Rose* symbolizes the beloved.

187. 2–3. *my sore/ Of my rancoure and woful chance* MS. Skeat, followed by other editors, supplies *all my* after *and* but *rancoure*, 'hatred' or 'ill will' towards others, has nowhere been a theme of the captive, whose complaint has been general, against Fortune. The poet refers to st. **10**, *ll.* 3–4, 'In tender ȝouth how sche was first my fo,/And eft my frende'. Accordingly I insert *foos*, gen. sing., before *rancoure*. *my l.* 2 seems awkward and has probably strayed from its place before *wofull*. 5. *floure: flouris* MS. *ȝou* om. MS but see **182.** 7.

188. 3. *halë: halely* MS, but dissyllabic *hale* is otherwise regular for the adverb. 6. *laud: land* MS.

189. 1. *blisfull*: om. MS., Lawson's suggestion, is brought in from **192.** 4 as agreeing with the heavy play on *bliss* — here and in **192, 193.** 2. *glitteren*: at first reading *glateren* because *tt* is written as if *ct* (as in *attendit* **187**); *ict* is identical with *at* in this scribe's hand. 6. *exiltree: exilkee* MS (axle-key) is unknown to me. 7. *quhele: quhile* MS.

190. 1. *fair and lufe befall* MS, but compare *faire in lufe befill* **80.** 6: for the personal meanings of the gillyflower see note to **178.** 2.

191. 1. *fairë: fair* MS. 3. *sanctis marciall*: the saints whose feast-days were in March; for other references to March see notes to **20–1, 170.** 5–7, **178.** 2. 5. *suete*: om. MS. is supplied by me from **67.** 2, which is echoed here. 6. *me: one* MS.

192. 6. *veray faith*: 'true faith'. 7. *ȝit* om. MS.

193. 2. *lufis ȝok*: a phrase in *The Cuckoo And The Nightingale* 140 where, as here, it refers to marriage. 3. *guerdoun dere: dere* is supplied by me. 6–7: it is the married lover who speaks here.

194–5. The conventional *Excusatio*, which sometimes as with *Troilus* V. 1786–96, the *Tyme, Space and Dait* at the close of Douglas's *Eneados*, and here, expresses a practical concern that the reader should not mispronounce and so mismetre the lines.

194. 2: 'causing ignorance and poverty of eloquence to be known'.

195. 1. *cum in the presence*: Skeat retains *cummyst* MS. and rejects *the* MS, in favour of the too general *in presence*, 'in company', but for *the presence* see **126.** 1, **192.** 1. *crukit eloquens* is a phrase in *The Court of Love* st. 6. 5. *bot geve: geve* MS for more usual *gif* is not necessarily a scribal slip.

196. 'And thus by the grace (*magnificence*) of God, whose seat is highest in the heavens (i.e. in the Empyrean, above Primum Mobile), to which He has committed all direction, ends the unhappy part of their influence. We thank Him who has written the whole course of our life, as one might have read it many a year before (in the stars that are) high in the heavenly sphere'. The reference is to a horoscope at nativity. James echoes *The Tale of the Man of Lawe* 190–6: the fate of the marriage proposed for Constance might have been read by astrologers 'in thilke large book/Which that men clepe the heven'. The same tale ends with a prayer to 'Jesu Crist that of his might may sende/Joye after wo', which has been the king's experience. The poet's deterministic language has to be reconciled with Minerva's Boethian assertion of free will and effective reason and his own final celebration of God's rewarding grace. 1. *fotall* MS. 5. *we thank: we think* MS. *lyf*, om. MS, is convincingly supplied by Skeat; the corresponding word in Chaucer is 'deeth'. 7: the poem's first line is relevantly repeated; see note thereto.

197. 1. *Vnto the impnis: Vnto inpms* MS. On the spelling see 'Language' 28.3. Editors have objected to a poem being recommended to other poems but we should understand, 'I recommend my hymn (to love and God) to the company of the (similar) hymns of my masters', etc.; cp. *ympnis* **33.**3. 2: the influence of 'moral Gower', as Chaucer calls him in *Troilus*, has been didactic rather than poetical, but see notes to **55, 122.**

Glossary

a, *num. adj.*, one 64; o, *num. adj.*, one 162, 182
abaisit, *past part.*, abashed 41
abate, *sb.*, shock 40
abit, *3 pres. sing.*, abides, awaits 133
abufe, *prep.*, above 188
adoune, *adv.*, down 53
aduert, *vb.*, turn, direct 25
aduertence, *sb.*, charge 108
afferand, *pres. part.*, pertaining 145
agane, ageyne, *prep.*, against 29, 91; *adv.*, again 103, 162
airly, *adv.*, early 23
alblastrye, *sb.*, archery 156
aleyes, *sb. pl.*, alleys 32
alight, *pret. pl.*, alighted 61
allace, *interj.*, alas 57
alleris, *pron., gen. pl.*: зoure alleris, of you all 113
alluterly, *adv.*, entirely 129
als, *conj.*, as 109, 151
alyte, *adv.*, a little 2
amaille, *sb.*, enamel 48
amaisit, *past part.*, dazed 73
amang, *prep.*, among 16, 28; *adv.*, at times 33, 66, 81
amongis, *prep.*, among 91
amorettis, *sb. pl.*, love-knots (signifying truth in love) 47
ane, *pron.*, one 76; *adj.*, a 28, 31; one, *num. adj.*, one 161
anewis, *sb. pl.*, rings (links of a circlet or garland) 160
anker, *sb.*, anchor 100
anone, *adv.*, anon 16
aport, *sb.*, bearing 50, 177
appesare, *sb.*, appeaser 99
ar, *3 pres. pl.*, are 85
araisit, *past part.*, raised 75
argewe, *vb.*, argue with 27
array, *sb.*, dress 46, 121; 110 (see note)
artow, art thou 58, 173
aspert, *adv.*, roughly, fiercely 170 (see note)
aspye, *vb.*, spy 31

astert, *vb.*, escape 44; *pret.* sing. started 40

astonait, *past part.*, astonished 162; astonate 98

atonis, *adv.*, at once 68

atoure, *prep.*, over 81

auaile, *vb.*, avail 139

auance, *vb.*, improve, better 50, 186; promote 79

auenture, *sb.*, fortune 10, 100; chance 22; lot 26

aught, *2 pres. pl.*, ought 120

auise, *sb.*, advice 114

avise, *vb.*, tell; on avise = tell of, mention 97

awerk = to work 4

awin, *adj.*, own 12, 182; owin 43

aworth, *adv.*, worthily 6

axis, *sb.*, anguish 67; excesse 144

ay, *adv.*, always 11

balance, *sb.*, danger, doubt 111, 142

balas, *sb.*, *pl.*, rubies (see note) 46

band, *sb.*, bondage 40

bandoune, *sb.*, thraldom 25

bare, *sb.*, bear 157

be, *prep.*, by 22, 170; be this day = as I live 60

be, *past part.*, been 175

becummyn, *past part.*, become 121

bedis, *sb.*, *pl.*, prayers 62

befill, *pret. sing.*, befell 80

begilit, *past part.*, beguiled 90

begouth, *pret.*, *sing.*, began 13, 16, 98

behald, *vb.*, behold 162; behalding, *pres. part.*, 159

belangith, *3 pres. sing.*, belongs 111

beme, *sb.*, ray of light; bemes, *pl.*, 72

bene, *vb.*, be 15; bene, *pres. pl.*, are 69

benigne, *adj.*, benign, gracious 39, 125; benignely, *adv.* 104

bere, *vb.*, bear 131; bore, *past part.*, borne 181

bereft, *past part.*, stolen, ravished 55

beschadit, *pret.*, *pl.*, shadowed 32

beseche, *vb.*, beseech 113; beseke 176; beseching, *pres. part.*, 184

beste, *sb.*, beast 158; bestis, *pl.*, 154

besy, *adj.*, busy 64; besynesse, *sb.*, activity 155

bet, *adv.*, better 101

bete, *vb.*, beat 116; beting, *vbl. sb.*, 122

beuer, *sb.*, beaver 157

beugh, *sb.*, bough 35; bewis, *pl.*, 32, 191

bid, *vb.*, bid 122; bydis, *3 pres. sing.*, bids, calls upon 65; bidden, *past part.*, requested 120

billis, *sb. pl.*, written complaints 82

birn, *vb.*, burn 168; birnyng, *pres. part.*, 48

blamischere, *sb.*, blemisher 140

blawe, *vb.*, blow 60

blisse, *sb.*, bliss 181; blisfull, *adj.*, blissful 192; blissit, *past part.*, blessed 189

blude, *sb.*, blood 40; bludy, *adj. as adv.*, painfully 55

boke, *sb.*, book 2; buke 8, 13; *pl.* bokis 19, bukis 78

bore, *See* bere

borowe, *sb.*, surety, protection 23

bot, *conj.*, unless 69, but 83, except 91; bot that = only that 168; bot geve = unless 195

bote, *sb.*, boat, 17

boundin, *past part.*, fastened, forced 61

branche, *sb.*, pattern 178 (see note)

brede, *sb.*, breadth 21

breken, *pres.*, *pl.*, break 115

brethir, *sb. pl.*, brothers 184

brid, *sb.*, bird 135; bridis, *pl.*, birds 65

bugill, *sb.*, wild ox 157

buke. *See* boke

but, *prep.*, without 8

bute, *sb.*, help 69

butles, *adv.*, unavailingly 70

cace, *sb.*, event 143; case 16

calde, *adj.*, cold 69

calk, *sb.*, chalk 177

call, *vb.*, drive 172 (see note)

cam. *See* cum

can, *vb.*, be able to, know how to 14, 141; knows 113, has charge of 106; *pret. sing. with infin.*, can . . . confort = comforted 4; coude, *pret. sing.*, knew 2; couth, *pret. sing.*, knew 16, was able to 196

cas, *sb.*, quiver 94

case. *See* cace

casualtee, *sb.*, event, cause 22

chamelot, *sb.*, camlet 157

chancis, *sb.*, *pl.*, fortunes 78

charge, *sb.*, charge 120; gevis charge = gives heed 115

chere, *sb.*, cheerfulness 36; mak . . . chere = entertain 54

chiere, *sb.*, chair 94

chose, *sb.*, choice 147

clepe, *vb.*, call 18; clepen 3 *pres. pl.* 149; cleping, *pres. part.*, 147; clepit, *past part.*, 3

clere, *adj.*, bright 1

cleuering, *pres. part.*, clambering 159; cleuerith, *pres. sing.*, 9

clippit, *past part.*, embraced 75

clymbare, *adj.*, climbing 156

clymbe, *vb.*, climb, 164

come. *See* cum

commune, *vb.*, deal 145; in commune = commonly 147

compace, *vb.*, encompass 141

compacience, *sb.*, compassion 118, 150

compas, *sb.*, compas, round extent 96, 159, 178

compilit, *past part.*, compiled, made 3

compiloure, *sb.*, author 3

comprisit, *pret. sing.*, included, selected 28

condyt, *sb.*, guide 113

confort, *sb.*, comfort 15, 74

connyng, *sb.*, skill 18

consecrat, *past part.*, consecrated 33

consequent, *sb.*, result 189

conserue, *vb.*, keep 112

contree, *sb.*, country 22

contynew, *vb.*, continue 105

conuoye, *vb.*, convoy 19, protect 101

conyng, *sb.*, rabbit 157

copill, *sb.*, couplet, set of verses 33

coplit, *past part.*, coupled 93

corage, *sb.*, heart 38, courage 164; curage 80

couate, *vb.*, covet 142

counsele, *sb.*, counsel 3; counsailis, *pl.*, 85

counterfeten, *vb.*, pretend 36, 135

cowardy, *sb.*, cowardice 89

cremesye, *sb.*, 'cramoisi', crimson cloth 109

cristin, *adj.*, Christian 142

croce, *sb.*, cross 13 (see note)

croppin, *past part.*, crept 182

cruell, *adj.*, severe 20

crukit, *adj.*, lame, halting 195

cukkow, *sb.*, cuckoo 110

cum, *vb.*, come 14; cummyth, *pres. sing.*, 36; cummyng, *vbl. sb.*, 126; *pret. sing.*,
cam 2, 173, come 29; *past part.*, cum 90, cummyn 40

curall, *adj.*, coral 153

cure, *sb.*, charge 22, cares 84, cure 95; *vb.*, cure 167

cuttis, *sb.*, *pl.*, lots 145

darre, *vb.*, dare 140

dayesye, *sb.*, daisy 109

declare, *vb.*, expound 7.

decretit, *past part.*, decreed 179

dede, *sb.*, deed 55

dede, *adj.*, dead 58

dedely, *adj.*, deadly, death-like 26, 169

dedeyne, *vb.*, deign 168

dee, *vb.*, die 57; deye 103; deis, *3 pres. sing.*, 52

defade, *vb.*, spoil, wear out 170

defaute, *sb.*, deficiency 194

defend, *vb.*, ward off 131

deficultee, *sb.*, difficulty 18

degoutit, *past part.*, spotted 161

degysit, *past part*, dressed 81

deis. *See* dee

depeyntit, *past part.*, painted 96

dere, *adj.*, dear 55, 193; *adv.*, dearly 36

dert, *sb.*, target 170 (see note)

descryving, *pres. part.*, describing 4; discriue, *vb.*, describe 16

determyt, *past part.*, determined 13

deuise, *vb.*, tell 12; deuisit, *past part.*, designed 28

digne, *adj.*, worthy 125

dirknesse, *sb.*, darkness 71

discerne, *vb.*, give judgment 107

disport, *sb.*, pleasure 134

ditee, *sb.*, song 62

do, *vb.*, do, perform 52; cause 44; done = do 162; doon = perform 97; dois, *2 pres. sing.*, 166; doith, dooth, *3 pres. sing.*, causes 44; did away = caused to go away 181; doon, *past part.*, done 38

doken, *sb.*, nettle 109

doubilnesse, *sb.*, complexity 19, deceitfulness 136

doune, *adv.*, down 8; dounward, *adv.*, downwards 81

dout, *sb.*, doubt 71

draware, *sb.*, and *adj.*, drawer 157

drawe, *past part.*, drawn 82, drewe, *pret. sing.*, 42

drede, *sb.*, dread, fear, 52; *vb.*, 14, 49

dressit, *pret. sing.*, prepared 175

dromydare, *sb.*, dromidary 156

druggare, *sb. and adj.*, drudger 155

dryve, *past part.*, driven 92

durst, *pret. sing.*, dare 128

eche, *pron.*, each one 79; eche, *adj.*, each 8

effect, *sb.*, purpose, result 13; substance, gist 141; effectis, *pl.*, influences 107

eft, *adv.*, afterwards 10

efter, *prep.*, after 3, 64; by 147

eftsones, *adv.*, very soon 42, 159

eke, *adv.*, also 27, 59

ellis, *adv.*, else 59

emeraut, *sb.*, emerald 46

empire, *sb.*, empire 76

enbroudin, *past part.*, decked 152

endlang, *prep.*, along 152; endlong 81; *adv.*, lengthwise 167
eneuch, *adv.*, enough 47
enprise, *sb.*, enterprise 20
ensample, *sb.*, example 172
entent, *sb.*, mind 13; will 56
ere, *sb.*, ear 152
eremyn, *sb.*, ermine 161
ernestly, *adv.*, vigorously 172
estate, *sb.*, high estate 3, rank 8
esy, *adj.*, easy 193
euerich, *pron.*, everyone 27; euerichone, *pron.*, each one 64
euour, *adj.*, ivory 155
evyn, *sb.*, cause 182
excesse. *See* axis
exiltree, *sb.*, axle-tree 189
eyen, *sb.*, *pl.*, eyes 8, 41; eyne 35
facture, *sb.*, shape 50, 66
fader, *sb.*, father 122
faille, *vb.*, lack 26; without faille = truly 48
falowe, *sb.*, fellow 23
fand. *See* fynd
fantasye, *sb.*, fancy 11, 37
fast, *adv.*, firmly 17, close 31, strongly 116
fatoure, *sb.*, deceiver 135
faucht, *pret. plur.*, fought 85
faute, *sb.*, fault 141
fay, *sb.*, faith: in fay = truly 59
feble, *adj.*, feeble 17; febily, *adv.*, 98
feere, *sb.*, fear 71
felyng, *vbl. sb.*, knowledge, possession 57
fere, *sb.*, mate 155
fereforth, *adv.*, onwards 25
ferre, *adv.*, far 22, 45
fery, *adj.*, very active 156
fest, *vb.*, feast 61
fete, *sb. pl.*, feet 159
feynen, *pres. pl.*, feign 136; feynis *3 pres. sing.* 134; feynyt, *past part.*, 36
flawe, *pret. sing.*, flew 61
flee, *vb.*, fly 14
flikering, *pres. part.*, flickering 173
flourit, *ppl. adj.*, ornate, eloquent 4
flourith, *pres. sing.*, flourishes 133, 193
flude, *sb.*, flood, water 20
folk, *sb.*, people 28, attendants 27
fond, *vb.*, ask for 127

fond. *See* fynd.

fone, *sb. pl.*, foes 71; foos, *gen. sing.*, 187

for, *prep.*, because of 2, 8; for quhy = because 4

forby, *adv.*, by, past 31

forehede, *sb.*, forehead, face 106

foreknawin, *ppl. adj.*, prescient 148; foreknawing, *vbl. sb.*, prescience 149

forfaut, *past part.*, forfeited 141

forget, *past part.*, forgotten 120

forgeue, *vb.*, forgive 102

forjugit, *past part.*, condemned 3

forlyin, *past part.*, tired with lying 11

forpleynit, *past part.*, tired with lamenting 73

fors, *sb.*, force 24

forsuke, *pret. pl.*, forsook 89

fortirit, *past part.*, tired out 30

fortunate, *adj.*, of fortune 168

fortunyt, *past part.*, fortuned 133

forwakit, *past part.*, weary with waking 111

forwalowit, *past part.*, tired with tossing about 11

forwepit, *past part.*, tired with weeping 73

foting, *sb.*, footing 9, 163

foynȝee, *sb.*, marten 157

fremyt, *adj.*, unfriendly, unlucky 24

fret, *pret.*, *pl.*, adorned 35

fretwise, *adv.*, for adornment 46

fricht, *past part.*, frightened 162

froward, *adj.*, 'fromward', perverse 170

fruyte, *sb.*, fruit 14; instruction 7

fude, *sb.*, food 30

fundin. *See* fynd

furiouse, *adj.*, extreme 176

furth, *adv.*, out 67, 75; forth 23; furth, *prep.*, out of 158

furthward, *adv.*, onwards 17

furthwithall, *adv.*, forthwith 13

fynd, *vb.*, find 158; fand, *pret. sing.*, 77; fond, *pret. sing.*, 96; fundin, *past part.*, found 169

fyne, *adj.*, fine 48

fynnis, *sb.*, pl. fins 153

fyre, *sb.*, fire 1, 46

gan, *pret. sing. or aux.*, began 8, 10, 30; gynneth, *pres. sing.*, begins 17; gynnen, *pres. plur.*, 119

gat, *pret. sing.*, got 10

gayte, *sb.*, goat 156

gerafloure, *sb.*, gillyflower, pink 190

gesserant, *sb.*, light mail-armour 153

geve, *vb.*, give 108, 128; gyve 92; gevis, *pres. sing.*, 115; gevin, *past part.*, 92
geve. *See* gif
gif, *conj.*, if 28, 38; bot gif = unless 132, bot geve = unless 195
gilt, *sb.*, guilt 137; *vb.*, *past part.*, been guilty of 26, 38
girt, *past part.*, girded 49
glewis, *sb. pl.*, joys 160
glitteren, *pres. pl.*, glitter 189; glitterit, *pret. sing.*, 153
goddys, *sb.*, *gen. sing.*, god's 21
gone, *pres. pl.*, go 38
gouernoure, *sb.*, ruler 65
gouirnance, *sb.*, direction 196
gree, *sb.*, degree, rank 83; greis, *sb. pl.*, degrees 21
gref. *sb.*, grief 127
grey, *sb.*, badger 156
ground, *sb.*, base 130; *vb.*, base 131
gruche, *pres. pl.*, repine, protest 91
grundyn, *past part.*, sharpened 94
gude, *adj.*, good 30, 126; in gude tym = early 185; *adv.*, well 139
gudeliar, *adj. compar.*, better 49
gudelihed, *sb.*, beauty 49
guerdoun, *sb.*, reward 193
gyde, *sb.*, guide 126; *vb.*, guide 15
gye, *vb.*, guide 15, 19
gynneth, gynnen. *See* gan
hable, *adj.*, liable 14; powerful 99
hable, *vb.*, make capable of 39
hailith, *pres. sing.*, draws 70
hailsing, *pres. part.*, greeting 166
haire, *sb.*, hair 46
haire, *sb.*, hare 156
hald, *vb.*, hold 60; halden, *pres. plur.*, maintain 147; haldin, *past part.*, held 90
hale, *adv.*, wholly 58, 101
halflyng, *adv.*, half 49, 89
hang. *See* hingen
hant, *sb.*, haunt 156
hap, *sb.*, good fortune 133
happin, *pres. pl.*, happen 147; hapint, *pret. sing.*, befell 187; happinnit, *pret. pl.*, happened 86
harmys, *sb. pl.*, harms, hurts 69
hart. *See* herte
has, *2 pres. sing.*, hast 54, 169; hastow = hast thou 57; has, *3 pres. pl.*, have 107, 186
hede, *sb.*, head 8, 42
hede, *sb.*, heed 81, 83

hedit, *past part.*, 95

heigh, *adj.*, high, 1, 20; heye 66; hich 196; hie 109, 120; hyare, *compar.*, *higher* 131; hiest *superl.*, 196

hele, *sb.*, health, well-being, 74, 191

helit, *past part.*, hidden, 194

hennesfurth, *adv.*, henceforth 69; hennesforth 144; hennesferth 181

hent, *past part.*, *or pret.*, seized 180

herbere, *sb.*, arbour 31

here, *vb.*, hear 4; herith, *pres. sing.*, hears 70; herd, *pret. sing.*, 11, 162; *past part.*, 127

herkner, *sb. as adj.*, quick of hearing 156

hert, *sb.*, hart 157

herte, *sb.*, heart 40; hart = heart 114; hertis, *gen. sing.*, 168

hertly, *adj.*, sincere 121; *adv.*, 144.

hestis, *sb. pl.*, behests 112

hete, *sb.*, heat 21

heved, *pret. sing.*, lifted 1

hevin, *sb.*, heaven 63; hevynnis, *gen. sing.*, 1

hewis, *sb. pl.*, hues, colours 160

heye. *See* heigh

hich. *See* heigh

hicht, *sb.*, height 172

hider, *adv.*, hither 166

hingen, *pres. pl.*, hang 88; hyng, *pres. pl.*, 89; hang, *pret. sing.*, 48; hong, *pret. sing.*, 160; *pret. pl.*, 81

hippit, *pret. pl.*, hopped 35

hir, *pron.*, her 42; *gen.* 46

ho, *interj.*, stop!: says ho = ceases 157

hole, *sb.*, whole 171; *adj.*, 18

holsum, *adj.*, wholesome, curative 156

hong. *See* hingen

hony, *sb. as adj.*, honey 117

hore, *adj.*, grey 80, 83

hortis, *sb. pl.*, hurts 156

hote, *adj.*, hot 76

hudis, *sb. pl.*, hoods 81

hufing, *pres. part.*, tarrying 159

huke, *sb.*, frock 49

humily, *adv.*, humbly 106, 176

humylnesse, *sb.*, humility 126

hye, *sb.*, haste: in hye = hurriedly 30, 75

hye, *adj.*; *see* heigh

hye, *vb.*, hasten 15, 164.5

hyndrit, *past part.*, hindered 137

iblent, *past part.*, blinded 74

ifallyng, *past part.*, fallen 45
ilaid, *past part.*, laid 120
ilk, ilke, *adj.*, same 163, 154
ilokin, *past part.*, locked 69
impnis, *sb. pl.*, hymns 196; ympnis 33
incidence, *sb.*, tarrying 7
indegest, *adj.*, unready 14
inemye, *sb.*, enemy 156
infortune, *sb.*, misfortune 5, 14
infortunate, *past part.*, ill-starred 24
inmytee, *sb.*, enmity 87
jangill, *vb.*, talk, chatter 38
jenepere, *sb.*, juniper 32
jete, *sb.*, jet 157
jonettis, *sb. pl.*, the great St John's wort (see note)
jorofflis, *sb. pl.*, gillyflowers, pinks 178
kalendis, *sb. pl.*, calends, beginning 34, 177
kepe, *vb.*, keep 141
kest, *pret. sing.*, cast 35, 40
kid, *past part.*, shown 137
knaw, *vb.*, know 101; knawing, *vbl. sb.*, 148
kneis, *sb. pl.*, knees 98, 166
kneling, *pres. part.*, kneeling 72
knytt, *vb.*, knit 194; knet, *past part.*, knit 31
lak, *sb.*, lack 15, 18
lakkit, *pret. sing.*, lacked 16; lakkith, *1 pres. sing.*, lack 27
lang, *adj.*, long, 73, 81; langer, *adv.*, longer 10, 84
langis, *pres. sing.*, belongs 106, 107; langith = belongs to, fits 114
lap, *pret. pl.*, leapt 153
large, *adj.*, at large = free 38
larges, largesse, *sb.*, freedom 181, 183; largesse = kindness 50
lat, *pres. sing.*, let 7, 78; lete, *pret. sing.*, 125; latting, *vbl. sb.*, See lete, letting
lauch, *vb.*, laugh 179
lawe, *adj.*, low 103; *adv.*, 90
lede, *sb.*, lead 153
lede, *vb.*, lead 130
lef, *sb.*, leaf; *pl.*, leuis 60, levis 95
lemyng, *pres. part.*, shining 46
lere, *vb.*, learn 171
lest, *sb.*, pleasure 5, 57
lest, *vb.*; *see* list
lestnyt, *pret. sing.*, listened 11
lesty, *adj.*, skilful 157
lete, *vb.*, prevent 113

leue, *sb.*, leave 124; leve 151
list, *sb.*, border 178
list, *pres. sing.*, is pleased 34; lest 9; list, *pres. pl.*, are pleased 115; lest, *pret. sing.*, was pleased 25
loke, *vb.*, look 5; luke 30; loke = refer 174; lukit, *pret. sing.*, 191; lukit, *past part.*, taken care 25
lore, *sb.*, learning 111; knowledge 181
loueris, *sb. pl.*, lovers 78; lufaris 96
louse, *adj.*, loose 49; *vb.*, free 43
lowe, *sb.*, fire 48
luf, *sb.*, love 36; luffis, *gen. sing.*, 183
lufare, *sb. as adj.*, lover 155
lufe, *vb.*, love 139; lufis, *3 pres. sing.*, 44
luke. See loke
lust, *sb.*, joy 65
lusty, *adj.*, joyous 121, 152
lye, *vb.*, lie 11; lyis, *3 pres. sing.*, lies 167; lyith 101
lyf, *sb.*, life 68, 121; person 12, 32; on lyve = alive 84; lyvis, *gen. sing.*, person's 28
lyne, *sb.*, thread 25; line 151; lynis, *pl.*, lines 197
lyoune, *sb.*, lion 155
lyve, *vb.*, live 52; lyven, *pres. pl.*, 186
mache, *sb.*, match 109
maid. See mak
maist, *2 pres. sing.*, 57
maist, *adv.*, most 182
maistrit, *past part.*, mastered 181
maistry, *sb.*, mastery 37, 59; force 92
mak, *vb.*, make 44; maid, *pret. sing.*, made 13; *2 pret. sing.*, 105; *past part.*, 31
make, *sb.*, mate, companion 58; makis, *pl.*, 35
maken, *vb.*, make 39; maked, *past part.*, made, 110
manace, *sb.*, menace 41
maner, *sb.*, kind (of) 152
mantill, *sb.*, mantle 160
marcial, *adj.*, of March 191
margarettis, *sb.*, *pl.*, daisies or marguerites 47
martrik, *sb.*, marten 157
martris, *sb.*, *pl.*, martyrs 79
mate, *vb.*, checkmate 168
matyns, *sb.*, *pl.*, matins 11
maugre, *prep.*, despite 24
mene, *sb.*, means 183; menes, *pl.*, means 111; menys 192
mene, *vb.*, mean 16, 174; menen, *pres. pl.*, 137
mesure, *sb.*, moderation 50
met, *pret. sing.*, dreamed 73
mete, *adj.*, becoming 97

GLOSSARY

mich, *adj. and adv.*, many an 150; much 51, 129. *See* moche
mirth, *sb.*, joy 61
mo, *adv.*, more 111
moche, *adv.*, much 84, 192. *See* mich
mone, *sb.*, moon 110
monethis, *sb.*, *pl.*, months 165
mony, *adj.*, many 2, 78
monyfald, *adj.*, manifold 131; monyfold 95
moon, *sb.*, moan 45
mornis, *sb.*, *pl.*, mornings 29
morow, *sb.*, morning 20, 23
most, *vb.*, must 15; mosten, *2 pret. plur.*, must 120; mot, *pres. subj.*, may 71, 190
mydday, *sb.*, 21. *See* note
mydnyght, *sb.* 1. *See* note
myn, *possess. adj.*, my 8
mynd, *sb.*, remembrance 2, 11
mynes, *possess. pron.*, mine's 107
mynt, *vb.*, aim 105
na, *adv.*, not 67
nakit, *adj.*, naked 194; nakitnesse, *sb.*, 109
nald, *pret. sing.*, would not 140
nas, *pret. sing.*, there was not 75
nat, *adv.*, not 10
natiuitee, *sb.*, horoscope at birth 147
nay, *adv.*, not 89
ne, *neg.*, not 162
nedith: quhat nedith = why does it need 36
notis, *sb. pl.*, notes 62
nought, *adv.*, not 10
nouthir, *adv.*, neither 139
now, *adv.*, now: as now = at this time 158
nowmer, *sb.*, number 19, 22
nyce, *adj.*, foolish 155; nycely, *adv.*, 12
nye, *prep.*, near 77
nyl, *pres. sing.*, *neg.*, will not 142
nyne, *adj.*, nine 25
o, *ad .*, one 162, 182
onely, *adv.*, only 42, 132
ones, *adv.*, once 57
ony, *adj.*, any 162
opyn, *vb.*, open 142; opnyt, *pret. sing.*, 77
or, *adv.*, before 5, 180
othir, *adj. sing.*, other 158; *pl.*, 28; *pron.*, others 87, 91; otheris, *gen. pl.*, 108
othir quhile, at other times 117
ouer, *prep.*, over, above 143, in addition to 61

ouerset, *past part.*, upset 73

ouerthrawe, *past part.*, overthrown 163

ouerthwert, *prep.*, across 82, 167

ought, *pron.*, anything 99, something 139

oure, *pron.*, our 37, 122

ourehayle, *vb.*, review 10; ourehailing, *pres. part.*, 158

oure-straught, *past part.*, stretched across 164

owin. *See* awin

pacience, *sb.*, patience 194

pacient, *adj.*, patient 126; paciently, *adv.*, 106

pall, *vb.*, weaken, become faint 18

pane, payne. *See* peine

pantere, *sb.*, panther 155

pape-jay, *sb.*, parrot 110

partit, *past part.*, variegated 46

partye, *sb.*, part 16; prize 48 (see note)

penance, *sb.*, suffering 6, 26

pepe, *interj.* (imitative of a bird cry), 57

percyng, *pres. part.*, piercing 103; with piercing eyes 155

perfyte, *adj.*, perfect 125, 188

peyne, *sb.*, pain 26, 68; pane 188, payne 129

philomene, *sb.*, nightingale 62, 110

plane, *adj.*, plain 36; pleyne 116

playntis, *sb. pl.*, complaints 92

plesandly, *adv.*, pleasantly 178

pleye, *vb.*, complain, lodge pleas 86

pleyne, *vb.*, complain 90

pleyne, *vb.*, play 40

plumys, *sb. pl.*, plumes, feathers 47

plumyt, *past part.*, feathered 94

poleyt, *adj.*, polished, eloquent 4

porpapyne, *sb.*, porcupine 155

port, *sb.*, gate 77

pouert, *sb.*, poverty 3; pouertee 194

poure, *vb.*, pore, muse 72

prattily, *adv.*, vigorously 153

prese, *vb.*, prize 110

present, *past part.*, presented 179

prise, *sb.*, esteem, praise, 188

processe, *sb.*, narration 126, process 192

prolixitee, *sb.*, prolixity 18

proyne, *vb.*, preen 64

prye, *vb.*, gaze 72

purchace, *vb.*, obtain 59

pure, *adj.*, poor 101

purpose, *sb.*, 29, 158; in purpose = with purpose 5
puruait, *past part.*, provided 23
purueyance, *sb.*, providence 130
pykit, *past part.*, adorned 7
pyne, *sb.*, pain 3, 28, 175
quham, *pron.*, whom 177, 196
quhare, *adv.*, where 17; quhare as = where 26, 40
quharefore, *conj.*, wherefore 2, 133
quhareto, *conj.*, why, to what end 68
quhat, *pron.*, what 26, 60; *adv.*, how 37
quhich, *dem. adj.*, which 40; the quhich, *pron.*, which 120; for quhich, wherefore 2, 5
quhele, *sb.*, wheel 9, 163
quhen, *adv.*, when 9, 16
quhethir, *conj.*, whether 24
quhile, *sb.*, while, time 2, 35
quhilk, *pron.*, which 180; quhilkis, *pl.*, 62
quhill, *conj.*, till 108
quhilom, *adv.*, once, at one time 3; quhilum, formerly 20, 88
quhirlit, *past part.*, whirled 170, 189; quhirlyng, *vbl. sb.*, whirling 165
quhite, *adj.*, white 48
quho, *pron.*, who 57; quhois, *gen.*, whose 56; the quhois 79
quhy, *adv.*, why 81; *sb.*, reason 93
quikin, *vb.*, give life to, *or* speed 181
quit, *past part.*, rewarded 128
quitis, *3 pres. sing.*, quits, gives up 6 (see note); quite = free 195
quod, *pret. sing.*, said 168
quoke, *pret. sing.*, quaked 162
rage, *sb.*, madness 15
railit, *past part.*, railed, fenced 31
rancoure, *sb.*, ill will 117, 187
rase, *pret. sing.*, rose 11
ravin, *adj.*, ravenous 157
rawe, *sb.*, row 154; on rawe = in a row 90
recouer, *sb.*, recovery 5; recure 10
rede, *adj.*, red 46
rede, *vb.*, read 2
redy, *adj.*, convenient 128
rele, *vb.*, reel 9
relesche, *sb.*, relief 150, 176; relesch, *vb.*, relieve 184
remanant, *sb.*, rest 137, remainder 171
remede, *sb.*, remedy 138
remyt, *sb.*, pardon 195
renowne, *sb.*, glory 125
repaire, *sb.*, repair, attendance 77

report, *sb.*, narrative 4
requere, *vb.*, pray 195; requerith, *pres. sing.*, requires 111
ressaue, *vb.*, receive 123; ressauen, *pres. pl.*, 145; ressauit, *past part.*, 52
rethorike, *sb.*, rhetoric 197; rethorikly, *adv.*, poetically 7.
retrete, *sb.*, retreat 96
rew, *vb.*, take pity 63, 101
reyne, *sb.*, rain 116
riall, *adj.*, royal 125, 157
richesse, *sb.*, riches (of mind) 50
ro, *sb.*, roe 157
rody, *adj.*, ruddy, bright 1
rokkis, *sb. pl.*, rocks 15, 18
rong. *See* ryng
ronne. *See* rynnis
rought, *pret. sing.*, cared, had pity 27
rout, *sb.*, company, shoal 153
rowm, *adj.*, spacious 77
rude, *sb.*, rood, cross, 139
ryf, *adj.*, rife 121
ryght, *adj.*, straight, direct 75; *adv.*, entirely 33, exactly 54, straight 124
ryng, *vb.*, ring 11; rong, *pret. pl.*, rang 33
rynnis, *pres. sing.*, runs 171; ronne, *past part.*, run 55, 108
rynsid, *pret. sing.*, rinsed, steeped 1
rype, *adj.*, ripe, mature 114; rypenesse, *sb.*, ripeness 16
sad, *adj.*, grave 96, 125
saing, sais. *See* seye
sall, *1 pres. sing.*, shall 122; schall 12; *2 pres. sing.*, 128, 170; suld, *pret. sing.*, should 15
salute, *pret. sing.*, greeted 98
sanct, *sb.*, saint 23, 62; sanctis, *pl.*, 191
sang, *sb.*, song 64; songis, *pl.*, 62, 121
satt. *See* sittis
sauf, *adj.*, safe 143, 165
saulis, *sb. pl.*, souls, 123, 186, 197
sauen, *vb.*, save 103
sawe. *See* se
scalis, *sb. pl.*, scales 153
scarse, *adv.*, hardly 31
schall. *See* sall
schame, *sb.*, shame 89
schap, *sb.*, shape 47
schape, *vb.*, make, contrive 69; schapith, *imperat.*, provide 102; schupe, *pret. sing.*, arranged 24; schapin, *past part.*, shaped 38
sche, *pron.*, she 10, 60
schene, *adj.*, bright 95

schet, *pret. sing.*, shut 8

schewe, *vb.*, show 106, 114; schewing, *pres. part.*, 3

schill, *adj.*, shrill 66

schip, *sb.*, ship 15

schire, *adj.*, glittering 76

schone, *pret. sing.*, shone 74

schouris, *sb. pl.*, showers 20

schuldris, *sb. pl.*, shoulders 160

scole, *sb.*, lore, learning 7

se, *vb.*, see 163; sene 67, 143; seyne 8, 120; seis, *2 pres. sing.*, 54, 83; se, *1 pres. pl.*, 78; sawe, *pret. sing.*, 40; *pret. pl.*, 125; sye, *pret. sing.*, 159

see, *sb.*, sea 22, 27

seide. *See* seye

seildyn, *adv.*, seldom 9

sek-cloth, *sb.*, sackcloth 109

seke, *vb.*, seek 18; seken 99

seke, *adj.*, sick 58

seknesse, *sb.*, sickness 111

sely, *adj.*, feeble, helpless 14, 134, 169; unready 185

semyt, *pret. sing.*, seemed 89

sen, *conj.*, since 26, 38

sen, *vb.*, *see* send

send, *pret. sing.*, sent 25; sen, *imperat.*, grant, would that 57

sentence, *sb.*, subject 7

seruandis, *sb. pl.*, servants 86

serue, *vb.*, serve 38; seruen 102

seruis, *sb.*, service, 119; seruise 117

set, *vb.*, direct 38, 142; setten, *vb.*, fasten 37, direct 134; sett, *past part.*, set, placed 188

sex, *adj.*, six 182

seye, *vb.*, say 120; say 123; seyne 78; sais, *3 pres. sing.*, says 77; seide, *pret. sing.*, said 104

sike, *vb.*, sigh 44

sittis, *3 pres. sing.*, sits 54; sat, *pret. sing.*, 54; satt, *pret. pl.*, 197.

slawe, *adj.*, slow 155

sleuth, *sb.*, sloth 120; delay 144

slokin, *vb.*, slake 69, extinguish 168

sloppare, *adj.*, slippery 163

sluggart, *sb.*, sluggard 58

smaragdyne *sb.*, emerald 155

smert, *sb.*, smart 25

smert, *vb.*, smart, hurt 8, 101; smertis, *pres. sing.*, hurts 141

smyte, *vb.*, smite 105; smytis, *pres. sing.*, 95; smyt, *past part.*, smit 58

snawe, *sb.*, snow 67

sodayn, *adj.*, sudden 40; sodaynlye, *adv.*, 11; sudaynly 41

solempt, *adj.*, solemn 79
somer, *sb.*, summer 34
sone, *sb.*, son 106
sone, *adv.*, soon, forthwith 75
sonne, *sb.*, sun 110
sothe, *adj.*, true 9, 91. *See* suth
souirane, *sb.*, sovereign 181
soune, *sb.*, sound 13
soyte, *sb.*, suit 64
space, *sb.*, time 78, 104
spede, *vb.*, speed, succeed 70; speid 186
spekis, *pres. sing.*, speaks 12
spere, *sb.*, sphere 76
sperk, *sb.*, spark 48
sprede, *vb.*, spread 117; spred, *pret. sing.*, spread 21; sprad, *pret. pl.*, 21; spred,
    past part., 179
springis, *3 pres. pl.*, bloom 119
spurne, *vb.*, stumble, fail 186
squerell, *sb.*, squirrel 155
stage, *sb.*, rank, station 9, 79
stale, *sb.*, checkmate 169
stallit, *past part.*, fixed 170
standar, *sb. as adj.*, standing 156
standis, *2 pres. sing.*, 15; *3 pres. sing.*, 108; stant, *3 pres. sing.*, 15, 167; stude,
    pret. sing., stood 41, 80
stele, *sb.*, steel 95
stellifyit, *past part.*, made a star 52
stent. *See* stynt
stere, *sb.*, rudder, direction 130
stere, *vb.*, steer 17
stereles, *adj.*, rudderless 15, 16
sterre, *sb.*, star; sterres, *pl.*, 1
steruen, *vb.*, die 102; starf, *pret. sing.*, died 139
stond, *vb.*, stand 88, 143
stound, *sb.*, while 53, time 118
stranger, *adv.*, more severely 68; strangest = most severe 149; strong = hard 163
straught, *adj.*, straight 151; *adv.*, 126; streight, *adv.*, 23
strayte, *adj.*, close 25
streight. *See* straught
stremes, *sb. pl.*, rays 103
strowit, *past part.*, strewn 65
studye, *vb.*, consider 42
stynten, *1 pres. sing.*, cease 117; styntith, *3 pres. pl.*, 118; stynt, *pret. sing.*, ceased
    53; stent, *pret. sing. and pl.*, 5, 35
suete, *adj.*, sweet 20, 41; suetly, *adv.*, 103

sueuenying, *vbl. sb.*, dreaming 174

sufficiance, *adj.*, sufficient, complete 183

suffisance, *sb.*, sufficiency, happiness 6, 16

suffise, *vb.*, last 140

suich, *adj.*, such 11, 37

suld. *See* sall

sum, *pron.*, some 9, 90; *adj.*, a 13

suoun, *past. part.*, in a swoon 73

supplye, *sb.*, help 15, 112

surcote, *sb.*, upper garment 160

suth, *sb.*, truth 137. *See* sothe

sye. *See* se

syne, *adv.*, later 192

syng, *vb.*, sing; song, *pret. sing.*, sang 80

tabartis, *sb. pl.*, tabards 110

tak, *vb.*, take 83; toke, *pret. sing. and pl.*, took 2, 61, 84; tuke, 13, 81; take, *past part.*, taken 90

takenyng, *vbl. sb.*, token 176; tokenyng 119

takin, *sb.*, token 118

tald, *pret. sing.*, told 23

tender, *adj.*, young 65

thaire, *pron.*, their 83

tham, thame, *pron.*, them 5, 78

than, *adv.*, then 4

thidderwart, *adv.*, thither 185

thilke, *pron.*, that, that same 5, 119

thinkis, *pres. pl.*, think 183

thir, *pron.*, these 10, those 56

tho, *pron.*, those 39, 88

tho, *adv.*, then 12; as tho = at that time 2

thought, *sb.*, 30; thoughtis, *pl.*, 10; thought, *pret. sing.*, 12; me thought = it seemed to me 11

thraldom, *sb.*, bondage 183

thrall, *sb. as adj.*, imprisoned 38

thrawe, *sb.*, while, time 35, 45, 67

thre, *adj.*, three 22

threwe. *See* throwe

thrid, *adj.*, third 95

thrist, *sb.*, thirst 69

throu, *prep.*, through 63; throw 51

throwe, *vb.*, throw, drive 17; threwe, *pret. sing.*, threw 51

tippit, *past part.*, tipped 157

tissew, *sb.*, under garment 49

to, *prep.*, for 116, 120; to suich delyte = such a delight 49

tofore, *prep.*, before 103; *adv.*, 1

toforowe, *adv.*, before 23, 49, 105
togider, *adv.*, together 64, 124
toke. *See* tak
tokenyng. *See* takenyng
tolter, *adj.*, unstable 9; *adv.*, jerkily 164
tong, *sb.*, tongue, language 7
touert. *See* toward
toure, *sb.*, tower 40; touris, *gen. sing.*, 31
toward, *prep.*, concerning 46; touert = to 174
towardis, *prep.*, towards 104
to-wrye, *vb.*, twist, turn 164
traist, *vb.*, trust 130; trusten 137
translate, *vb.*, transform 8
trauaile, *vb.*, travel 16, labour 70; trauaille, *sb.*, trouble 14
trauerse, *sb.*, screen 90; trevesse 82
tretisse, *sb.*, book 194
trety, *sb.*, book 18
trevesse. *See* trauerse
tueyne, *adj.*, two 42
tuke. *See* tak
turment, *sb.*, torment 19, 67; *vb.*, 68
turture, *sb.*, turtle dove 177
twistis, *sb. pl.*, twigs, branches 33, 119
twyne, *vb.*, spin 25
tyde, *sb.*, time 160
vale, *vb.*, go down 172
venym, *sb.*, venom 155
vere, *sb.*, Spring 20
verray, *adj.*, true 5; *adv.*, very 169
vertew, *sb.*, virtue 6, 129; power 74, 99; vertu = vigour 20
veyne, *adj.*, vain 38, 70
vgly, *adj.*, ugly 162
viage, *sb.*, journey 15
virking. *See* wirking
vmbre, *sb.*, shade 134
vncouth, *adj.*, unknown, strange 63, 66; vncouthly, *adv.*, strangely 9
vnderstond, *past part.*, understood 127
vnknawin, *pres. part.*, not knowing 45
vnkyndenes, *sb.*, 87; vnkyndenesse 116
vnnethis, *adv.*, hardly 98
vnquestionate, *ppl. adj.*, unquestioned 125
vnreconsilit, *ppl. adj.*, unreconciled 90
vnrypit, *ppl. adj.*, unripened 14
vnsekernesse, *sb.*, insecurity, danger 15
vnsekir, *adj.*, unstable 6

voce, *sb.*, voice 74, 83

voidis, *pres. sing.*, empties, clears 155

vpward, *adv.*, upwards 76, northward 20

vre, *sb.*, luck 10

vschere, *sb.*, usher, door-keeper 97

vtrid, *past part.*, uttered (see note) 132

wag, *vb.*, stir 60

waile, waille, *vb.*, lament 14, 69, 122

wald, *pret. sing.*, would, 11, 37; *2 pret. sing.*, 167; wold 24, 26

wan, *pret. sing.*, won 5; wonne, *past part.*, 35, 108

wandis, *sb.*, *plur.*, rods 31

wanting, *vbl. sb.*, loss 86

wantis, *2 pres. sing.*, art without, lackest 15, 169

wantounly, *adv.*, playfully 48

war. *See* were

ware, *adj.*, wary, alert 164

warld, *sb.*, world 26; mankind 122, 137; multitude 82; warldis, *gen. sing.*, 3, 15

warldly, *adj.*, worldly 44, 51

wate: wote, *1 pres. sing.*, know 43; wate, *2 pres. sing.*, 129; wostow, *interrog.*, 59; wate, *3 pres. sing.*, knows 60; wote 44; wist, *1 pret. sing.*, knew 76; *2 pret. sing.*, 14

wawis, *sb. pl.*, waves 16, 24

wayis: oure wayis = on our way 23; hir wayis = on her way 179

wayke, *adj.*, weak 14, 149

wayte, *vb.*, await 17

wede, *sb.*, garment 81

wedowis, *gen. sing.*, widow's 156

wele, *sb.*, well-being, happiness 39; warldis wele = worldly good fortune 169

wele, *adv.*, well 14, 53

weltering, *pres. part.*, rolling 24, 163

werdes, *sb. pl.*, weirds, lots 9; werdis, *gen. sing.*, 169 MS (see note)

were, *pret. pl.*, 32; weren, *1 pret. pl.*, 24; were, *imperf. subj.*, 22, 53; war 182; were = would be 143

werely, *adj.*, warlike, armed 155

werit, *pret. sing.*, wore 160

wers, *adv.*, worse 95

wete, *adj.*, wet 55

wery, *adj.*, weary 11

weye, *sb.*, way 86

weye, *vb.*, give heed 120

wight, *sb.*, person 9, 28

will, *pres. sing.*, wills 106; *1 pres. sing.*, will, decree 113

wilsum, *adj.*, wandering 19

wirken, *vb.*, work on, torture 68

wirking, *vbl. sb.*, working 146; virking 188

wist. *See* wate.

wite, *vb.*, blame; to wyte = to be blamed 90
withoutin, *prep.*, without 62, 93
wittis, *sb. pl.*, senses 18, 181; wits, faculties 134
wold. *See* wald
wonne. *See* wan
worschip, *sb.*, honour 136, 142
worschippe, *imperat. pl.*, worship 34
wortis, *sb. pl.*, herbs 156
wostow, wot. *See* wate
wrangit, *past part.*, wronged 92
wrest, *past part.*, troubled, tormented 10
wrething *vbl. sb.*, vexation 146
wring, *vb.*, lament 57
writ, *pres. sing.*, writes 133; writt, *past part.*, 106
writh, *vb.*, direct 107
wrokin, *past part.*, wreaked, inflicted 69
wrought, *past part.*, made 77
wrye: on wrye = bent 73
wyle, *sb.*, wile, trick 2
wynd, *sb.*, wind 17
wynd, *vb.*, hoist 18
wyre, *sb.*, wire 1
wyte. *See* wite
ȝa, *adv.*, yes 68
ȝalow, *adj.*, yellow 95
ȝate, *sb.*, gate 125
ȝe, *pron.*, ye 11, 63
ȝelde, *vb.*, yield 52
ȝeris, *sb. pl.*, years 22
ȝit, *conj.*, yet 28
ȝok, *sb.*, yoke 193
ȝond, *adv.*, yonder 57, 83
ȝone, *adj.*, yon, those 83, 88
ȝong, *adj.*, young 7, 40
ȝoure alleris = of you all 113
ybought, *past part.*, bought 36
ycallit, *past part.*, called 170
ylike, *adv.*, alike, in the same way, 70, 154
ymaginacioune, *sb.*, imagination 12
ymagynit, *past part.*, imagined 13
ympnis. *See* impnis
ypocrisye, *sb.*, hypocrisy 134
yslungin, *past part.*, cast 165
ystallit, *past part.*, fixed 170
ythrungin, *past part.*, thrust 165